THE BIBLE BOOK BY BOOK AND PERIOD BY PERIOD

A MANUAL FOR THE STUDY OF THE BIBLE

JOSIAH BLAKE TIDWELL

SSEL

CONTENTS

THE BIBLE BOOK BY BOOK

Preface to First Edition.	9
Preface to Second Edition.	12

SOME INTRODUCTORY STUDIES.

Why We Believe The Bible.	15
The Names of God.	20
The Sacred Officers and Sacred Occasions.	23
Sacred Institutions of Worship and Seven Great Covenants.	27
The Division of the Scriptures.	31
The Dispensations.	34
Ages and Periods of Biblical History.	37
Some General Matters and Biblical Characters.	41

THE BIBLE BOOK BY BOOK.

1. Genesis.	47
2. Exodus.	51
3. Leviticus.	54
4. Numbers.	58
5. Deuteronomy.	61
6. Joshua.	64
7. Judges and Ruth.	67

8. First and Second Samuel.	71
9. First and Second Kings.	74
10. First and Second Chronicles.	77
11. Ezra, Nehemiah and Ester.	80
12. Job.	85
13. Psalms and Proverbs.	89
14. Ecclesiastes and the Song of Solomon.	95
15. Isaiah.	100
16. Jeremiah and Lamentations.	106
17. Ezekiel and Daniel.	111
18. Hosea and Joel.	117
19. Amos and Obadiah.	122
20. Jonah and Micah.	126
21. Nahum and Habakkuk.	130
22. Zephaniah and Haggai.	134
23. Zechariah and Malachi.	138
24. Matthew.	142
25. Mark.	150
26. Luke.	156
27. John.	164
28. Acts.	172
29. Romans.	176
30. First and Second Corinthians.	182
31. Galatians and Ephesians.	188
32. Philippians and Colossians.	195
33. First and Second Thessalonians.	201
34. First and Second Timothy.	205
35. Titus and Philemon.	209
36. Hebrews and James.	213
37. First and Second Peter.	219

38. First, Second and Third John and Jude.	223
39. Revelation.	229

THE BIBLE PERIOD BY PERIOD

Author's Preface.	237
1. From The Creation to The Fall.	239
2. From the Fall to the Flood.	245
3. From the Flood to Abraham.	252
4. From Abraham to Egypt.	261
5. From Egypt to Sinai.	274
6. From Sinai to Kadesh.	283
7. From Kadesh to the Death of Moses.	289
8. Joshua's Conquest.	297
9. The Judges.	306
10. The Reign of Saul.	312
11. The Reign of David.	317
12. Solomon's Reign.	324
13. The Divided Kingdom.	330
14. The Kingdom of Judah.	338
15. The Captivity of Judah.	345
16. The Restoration.	352
17. From Malachi to The Birth of Christ.	360
18. From the Birth to The Ascension of Jesus.	365
19. From the Ascension to The Church at Antioch.	381

20. From Antioch to The Destruction of
Jerusalem.   387
21. Destruction of The Temple to The
Death of The Apostle John.   396

THE BIBLE BOOK
BY BOOK

PREFACE TO FIRST EDITION.

The aim of this book is to furnish students of the Bible with an outline which will enable them to gain a certain familiarity with its contents. While it is intended especially for students in academies, preparatory schools and colleges, the needs of classes conducted by Women's Societies, Young People's Organizations, Sunday School Normal Classes, Y. M. C. A. and Y. W. C. A. and advanced classes of the Sunday Schools have been constantly in mind. Its publication has been encouraged not only by the hope of supplying the needs mentioned but by expressions that have followed public lectures upon certain books, indicating a desire on the part of Christians in general for a book that would, in a brief compass, give them some insight into the purpose, occasion and general setting of each of the books of the Bible.

The work has been done with a conviction that the students of American schools should become as well acquainted with the sources of our religion as they are required to do with the religions of ancient heathen nations, and all the more so, since the most of our people regard it as the true and only religion, and still more so, since "it is made the basis of our civilization and is implied and involved in our whole national life." It is believed by the Author that a knowledge of the simple facts of the history, geography and chronology of the Bible is essential to a liberal education and that to be familiar with the prophecies, poetry, and ethics of the scripture is as essential to the educated man of today as was a "knowledge of Greek history in the time of Pericles or of English history in the reign of Henry the VIII." And, in order that such knowledge may be gained, effort has been made to put into the book only a minimum of matter calculated to take the student away from the Bible itself to a discussion about it and to put into it a maximum of such matter as will require him to study the scripture at first hand.

Having intended, first of all to meet the needs of those whose advantages for scripture study have been limited, the information has been put in tabular form, giving only such facts as have been carefully gathered from reliable sources, with but little attempt to show how the conclusions were reached. It is expected that the facts given may be mastered and that an interest may be created which will lead to further study upon the subjects treated. And to this end some of the studies have been made sufficiently complicated for college work and instruction for such work given in suggestions for teachers, leaders and classes. Besides the studies of the books there have been introduced some matters of general interest which have been found helpful as drills for academy pupils, and which will be found interesting and helpful to all classes of students.

The general plan is the outgrowth of the experience of a few years of teaching, but the material presented lays little claim to originality. It has been gathered from many sources and may in some cases seem almost like plagiarism, but due acknowledgment is here made for all suggestions coming from any source whatsoever, including Dr. George W. Baines, who read all the material except that on the New Testament.

Let it be said also, that in preparing these studies the Author has proceeded upon the basis of a belief in the Bible as the Word of God, a true source of comfort for every condition of heart and a safe guide to all faith and conduct whether of individuals or of nations. It is hoped therefore that those who may study the topics presented will approach the scripture with an open heart, that it may have full power to make them feel the need of God, that they may make its provisions real in their experience and that it may bring to them new and changed lives.

If the pastors shall deem it valuable as a book of reference for themselves and to their members who are desirous of pursuing Bible study, or if it shall be found serviceable to any or all of those mentioned in paragraph one of this Preface, the Author will be amply rewarded for the effort made.

J. B. TIDWELL.
Waco, Texas, August, 1914.

PREFACE TO SECOND EDITION.

In sending forth this second edition of The Bible Book by Book it has seemed wise to make some changes in it. The descriptive matter has been put in paragraph instead of tabular form; the analyses have been made shorter and less complex; the lessons based on the Old Testament books have been omitted or incorporated in the topics of study which have been increased, It is believed that the make-up of the book is better and more attractive.

The author feels a deep gratitude that the first edition has been so soon sold. He indulges the hope that it has been found helpful and sends out this edition with a prayer that it may prove more valuable than did the former.

J.B. Tidwell

SOME INTRODUCTORY STUDIES.

WHY WE BELIEVE THE BIBLE.

There are two lines of proof of the reliability of the scriptures, the external and the internal. These different kinds of evidences may be put down, without separation, somewhat as follows:

1. The Formation and Unity of the Bible. There are sixty-six books written by nearly forty men, who lived at various times, and yet these books agree in making a perfect whole. These writers were of different classes and occupations. They possessed different degrees of training and lived in widely different places and ages of the world. The perfect agreement of their writings could not, therefore, be the result of any collusion between them. The only conclusion that can explain such unity is that one great and infinite mind dictated the scripture.

2. The Preservation of the Bible. That the Bible is a divine book is proven in that it has survived the wreck of empires and kingdoms and the destruction of costly and carefully gathered libraries and that, too, when there was no special human effort to save

it. At times all the constituted powers of earth were arrayed against it, but it has made its way against the tide of fierce opposition and persecution.

3. Its Historical Accuracy. The names of towns, cities, battles, kings, empires and great events, widely apart in time and place, are given without a blunder. The ruins of cities of Assyria, Egypt and Babylon have been unearthed and tablets found that prove the accuracy of the Bible narrative. These tablets corroborate the stories of the creation and fall of man, of the flood, the tower of Babel, the bondage in Egypt, the captivity, and many other things. This accuracy gives us confidence in the reality of the book.

4. Its Scientific Accuracy. At the time of the writing of the Bible. there were all sorts of crude and superstitious stories about the earth and all its creatures and processes. It was humanly impossible for a book to have been written that would stand the teat of scientific research, and yet at every point it has proven true to the facts of nature. Its teachings areas to the creation of all animal life is proven in science, in that not a single new species has come into existence within the history of man and his research or experiment. David said the sun traveled in a circuit (Ps. 19:6), and science has proven his statement. Job said the wind had weight (Job 28:25) and science has finally verified it. That the earth is suspended In space with no visible support is declared by Job, who said that "God hangeth the earth upon nothing", Job 26:7. Besides these and other specific teachings of science which correspond to Bible utterances, the whole general teachings of the scripture is sustained by our investigations. Many theories have been advanced that contradicted the Bible (at one time a French Institution of Science claimed that there were eighty

hostile theories), but not a single such theory has stood. Wherever a teaching of science contradicting the Bible has ever been advanced, it has been proven false, while the Bible was found to correspond to the facts.

5. Its Prophetic Accuracy. At least sixteen prophets prophesied concerning future events. They told of the coming destruction of cities and empires, calling them by name. They told of new kingdoms. They told of the coming of Christ, his nativity, the place of his birth, and the result of his life and death and made no mistake.

Christ himself showed how their old prophecies were fulfilled in Him. He told the destruction of Jerusalem and the nature of his Kingdom and work, all of which has been shown to be true. No other but a Divine book could have foretold the future in detail.

6. The Richness and Universality of Its Teachings. Its contents are fresh and new to every age and people. Its teachings furnish the highest standards for right human government and for personal purity of character. Its virtues are superior to all others. Every generation finds new and wonderful treasures in it, and while hundreds of thousands of books have been written about it, one feels that it is still a mine, the riches of whose literary excellence, moral beauty and lofty thought have scarcely been touched.

7. The Fairness and Candor of Its Writers. In portraying its heroes, the Bible does not attempt any gloss. Their faults are neither covered up nor condoned, but condemned. This is unlike all other books.

8. Its Solution of Man's Difficulties. What is the origin of the world? What is the origin of man? How came sin in the world? Will there be punishment of sin that will satisfy the unfairness and inequalities of

life? Is there redemption for weak and helpless man? Is there a future life? These are some of the questions that have troubled man in all ages. The Bible alone answers them in a simple yet adequate way. It alone gives us the knowledge of the way to secure happiness. Its remedies alone furnish a certain balm for bruised human hearts.

9. Its Miracles. The Bible, which records how God sent his son and others on special missions, also tells how He attested their work by signs or miracles. These miracles were performed in the presence of creditable witnesses and should, therefore, be believed. Moreover, they are so different from the superhuman deeds of ancient mythology as to stamp them as divine and true and at the same time to discredit all the false.

Bible miracles are never for mere exploitation or for personal profit to the one who performs the miracle. They are for the good of others. The blind and deaf and lame are healed. The sick and dead are raised. Lepers are cured and sins forgiven. Moreover, those who perform the miracle claim no power of their own, but attribute it all to God and only perform the miracle that God may be exalted.

10. Its Spiritual Character. It is evident that man alone could not have conceived the lofty ideas of the scripture. All his experience proves that he can not produce anything so far beyond himself. These high truths therefore, have come from a greater than man.

11. Its Fruit. No other book will do for man what the Bible does. The spread of its truths makes man better. Wherever the Bible goes civilization and enlightenment follow. This is so, no matter what the former condition of the people. Where everything

else fails, the Bible succeeds in lifting men out of ignorance and shame.

12. Its Own Claims to Divine Origin. (1) It clearly claims to be the the word of God. (a) All scripture is given by inspiration Of God. 2 Tim. 3:16. (b) God spake unto the fathers by the prophets, Heb. 1:1. (c) Holy men of God spake as they were moved by the Holy Ghost. 2 Peter 1:21. (d) He spake by the mouth of his holy prophets, Luke 1:70. (e) Which the Holy Ghost by the mouth of David spake. Acts 1:16. (f) God showed by the mouth of all his prophets. Acts 3:18. (g) By the revelation of Jesus Christ, Gal. 1:12. (h) Not as the word of men, but as it is in truth the word of God, 1 Thes. 2:13. (2) It claims to be a good book and to be given for man's good. Both of these claims have been amply justified. But it could not be a good book and claim what is not true. This it would do if it ware not the Word of God.

THE NAMES OF GOD.

Several names are used for God, each having its own significance, and every Bible reader should in some general way know the meaning of each name. We cannot always distinguish the exact meaning, but the following, while not all, will be of use in reading the English translation.

1. God. This comes from one word and two of its compound or forms and will mean accordingly: (1) The Strong one used 225 times in the Old Testament; (2) The Strong one as an object of worship; (3) The Strong one who is faithful and, therefore, to be trusted and obeyed. This last is a plural term and is used 2300 times in the Old Testament. It is the name used when God said. "Let us make man" and "God created man in his own image," etc., Gen. 1:26-27. It was by this name that God the Trinity covenanted for the good of man before man was created.

2. LORD. Small capitals in the old version and translated Jehovah in the in the revised translation. It means: (1) The self-existing one who reveals himself;

(2) God as Redeemer. It was under this name that he sought man after the fall and clothed him with skins. Gen. 3:9-17; (3) God who makesand keeps his covenants. It is used more than 100 times in connection with the covenants, as in Jer. 31:31-34 where he promises a new covenant.

3. Lord. Small letters except the L and always denotes God as Master in his relation to us as servants. There are two kinds of servants- hired and bought servants, the latter being always superior and more beloved. The servant is expected to obey and is guaranteed protection and support for his service.

4. Almighty God. This means a Strong-breasted one, the Pourer or Shredder forth of spiritual and temporal blessings. It refers to God: (1) As a nourisher, strength-giver, satisfier and a strong one who gives; (2) As the giver of fruitfulness which comes through nourishment. He was to make Abraham fruitful, Gen. 17:1-8; (3) As Giver of chastening. This he does in the way of pruning that there may be more fruit.

5. The Most High or Most High God. This means: (1) The Possessor of heaven and earth, who as owner distributes the earth among the nations; (2) The one who, as possessor, has dominion and authority over both, Dan. 4:18, 37; Ps. 91:9-13.

6. Everlasting God, This represents him as: (1) The God of the mystery of the ages and, therefore, (2) The God of secrets; (3) The God of everlasting existence whose understanding is past finding out, Is. 40:28.

7. LORD (Jehovah) God, This name is used: (1) Of the relation of Deity to man, (a) as Creator, creating and controlling his destiny, especially of his earthly relations, (b) as having moral authority over

him, (c) as redeemer; (2) Of his relation to Israel, whose destiny he made and controlled.

8. Lord (Jehovah) of Hosts. This refer: Usually to the host of heaven, especially of angels; (2) To all the divine or heavenly power available for the people of God; (3) The special name of deity used to comfort Israel in time of division and defeat or failure, Is. 1:9, 8:11-14.

Note. Drill on the use of these names and find some scripture passage illustrating the use of each.

THE SACRED OFFICERS AND SACRED OCCASIONS.

The Sacred Officers.

The following facts about the officers of the Bible should be familiar to all Bible students.

1. The Priests. They represent the people to God. The head of the household was the first priest. Gen. 8:20. Later the first born or oldest son became priests of the chosen people, Ex. 28:1. They served in the tabernacle and later in the temple where they conducted religious services, offered sacrifices for public and private sins and were teachers and magistrates of the law.

2. The Prophets. These speak for God to the people. They received revelations from God and made them known to men. They were selected according to God's own will to impart his spiritual gifts (1 Cor. 12:11) and extended down through those who wrote prophetic books to Malachi. They were philosophers, teachers, preachers and guides to the people's piety

and worship. Abraham was the first to be called a prophet (Gen. 20:7) and Aaron next (Ex. 7:1).

3. The Scribes. The word means a writer and Seraiah is the first one mentioned, 2 Sam. 8;17. As writers they soon became transcribers, then interpreters and teachers or expounders. They became known as lawyers and were accorded high standing and dignity. In the time of the kings they were supported by the state as a learned, organized and highly influential body of men. In Christ's time they were among the most influential members of the Sanhedrin.

4. The Apostles. These formed the beginning of Christ's church. They were separate from the old order and were, therefore, under no obligation to any caste. Nor were they tied to the old administration of divine things. The word means a messenger or one sent. They were, therefore, to be with him and to be sent forth to preach. Twelve were chosen, and when Judas, one of them, betrayed him, Matthias was chosen in his place (Acts 1:15-26). Paul was appointed in a special way (Acts 9:1-43) and perhaps others. Barnabas was called an apostle (Acts 14:14).

These men led the new movements (Acts 5:12-13) and devoted themselves especially to ministerial gifts (Acts 8:14-18). They had first authority in the church (Acts 9:27; 15:2; 1 Cor. 9:1; 12:28; 2 Cor. 10:8; 12:12; Gal. 1:17; 2:8-9).

5. Ministers or Preachers-They are: (1) Those who minister to or aid another in service, but as free attendants, not as slaves; (2) They became the teachers and hence our term ministers (Acts 13:2; Rom. 15:16); (3) Today they are preachers and teachers of the word and minister to the spiritual needs of God's people and of others.

Note. Read all the scriptures here referred to and invite others to be given by the class. Then drill on these facts until they are familiar.

The Sacred Occasions.

1. The Sabbath. For the meaning and use of the term see Lev. 25:4; Math. 28:1; Lu. 24:1; Acts 25:7. The first mention is Gen. 2:2-3 and the first mention of the weekly Sabbath is Ex. 16:22-30. It is suggested in the division of weeks. Gen. 8:10-12; 29:27-28, and Israel was directed to keep it, Ex. 20:8-11.

2. The New Moons. They were special feasts on the first day of the month (Num. 10:10) and were celebrated by sacrifices (Num. 28:11-15). Among the ten tribes it was regarded as a time suitable to go to the prophets for instruction, 2 K. 4:23. 3. The Annual Feasts. There were several of these. (1) *The Passover*, April 14 (Ex. 12:1-51), commemorating the exodus from Egypt and the saving of the first born. (2) *Pentecost*, June 6 (Ex. 34:22; Lev. 23:15-16; Deut. 16:9-10; Num. 28:26-31), commemorating the giving of the Law.

(3) *The Feast of Trumpets*, October 1 (Lev. 23:23-25; Num. 29:1-6), the beginning of the civil year. (4) *The Day of Atonement*, October 10 (Lev. 16: 1-34; 23:27-32), atonement made for the sins of the people. (5) *The Feast of Tabernacles*, October 15, lasting a week (Lev. 23:34-43; Ex. 23:16; 34:22; Deut. 16:13-15), commemorating the life in the wilderness. (6) *The Feast of Dedication*, December 25 (1 Kings 8:2; 1 Chron. 5:3), commemorating the dedication of the temple. (7) *The Feast of Purim*, March 14 and 15 (Esth. 9:20-32), commemorating the deliverance through Esther.

4. The Sabbatical Year. The land of Israel should rest every seven years as the people rested every seven days. No seeds must be sown or vineyards pruned. All that grew was public property and the poor could take it at will. All debts must then be forgiven except to foreigners (Ex. 23:10-11; Lev. 25:2-7; Deut. 15:1-11).

5. The Year of Jubilee. Every fiftieth year was known as Jubilee, Lev. 25:8-55. It began on the tenth day of the seventh month and during it the soil was unfilled just as on the Sabbatical year. All alienated land went back to the original owner and the Hebrew bondmen became free if they desired.

6. The Lord's Day. It is the first day of the week and commemorates the resurrection of Jesus and the finished work of redemption as the Sabbath commemorated the finished work of creation.

Note. Find other scripture references to each of these occasions and become familiar with the name, date and import of each.

SACRED INSTITUTIONS OF WORSHIP AND SEVEN GREAT COVENANTS.

The Sacred Institutions of Worship.

1. The Alter. Make a careful study finding: (1) The first mention of it. (2) The different persons who are recorded as erecting altars, Gen. 1-Ex. 20. (3) The materials of construction, Ex. 20:24-25. (4) The purpose for which they were erected, including that of Joshua, Josh. 22:10, 22-29.

2. The Tabernacle, Ex. chs. 25-29. Study: (1) The instructions to build it, including the offerings and articles to be given. (2) Its furniture. (3) Its erection. (4) Its purpose, Ex. 29;42-45; Heb. Chs. 9-10. (5) Its history, when first set up, how long used, etc.

3. The Temple. (1) *Solomon's Temple*. Study David's desire to build and his preparation for it. 2 Sam. 7:1-2; 2 Chron. 28, 29; its material, erection and dedication, 1 Kings 5-8; 2 Chron. 2:6; its destruction by Nebuchadnezzar's general, 587 B. C. (2) *Zerubbabel Temple*. Study the decree of Cyrus, return of the Jews, rebuilding and dedication, Ezra Chs. 1-6; its destruc-

tion by Pompey 63 B. C. and by Herod the Great 37 B. C. (3) *Herod's Temple*. It was begun 20 or 21 B. C., John 2:20; Matt. 24:1-2; Matt. 13:1-2; Lu. 21:56, and destroyed under Titus, A. D. 70.

4. The Synagogue. Greek work meaning an assemblage. There were synagogues wherever there were faithful Jews, about 1500 in Palestine and perhaps 480 in Jerusalem. The officers were (1) Ruler. Lu. 8:49; 13:14; Mk 5:15, etc; (2) Elders, Lu. 7:3; Mk. 5:22, etc; (3) Minister, Lu. 4:20. The service was one of prayer and reading and expounding the scriptures. It was through the worship at the synagogue that the apostles everywhere had opportunity to teach Christianity.

5. The Church. The word means an assemblage and is most commonly used of a local congregation of Christian workers. It is sometimes called the church of Christ, Church of God, Saints, etc. Churches were established in cities and in homes. It is not proper to call all the Christians of a particular denomination a church. Nor can we call all of any denomination in a given territory a church. It would be wrong to say the Baptist church of the south. In the New Testament we can get a rather clear idea of it as an institution by a study of a few principal churches and leaders of the Christian movement after the ascension of Christ.

The Seven Great Covenants.

There are two kinds of covenants. (1) Declarative or unconditional, example, Gen. 9-11, "I will." (2) Mutual or conditional, example, "If thou wilt." All scripture is a development of or is summed up in seven covenants.

1. The Adamic Covenant, Gen. 3:14-19. Outline the elements of the covenant, showing the persons affected and the results or conditions involved.

2. The Noahic Covenant, Gen. 8:20-9:27. Outline the elements of the covenant, and the results affected.

3. The Abrahamic Covenant. Gen. 12:1-3; Acts 7:3. other details, Gen. 13:14-17; 15:1-18; 17:1-8. Outline, giving the elements, blessings proposed, temporal and spiritual or eternal. This is sometimes called several covenants but it seems best to consider it one that is enlarged upon from time to time.

4. The Mosaic Covenant, Ex. 19-30. Given in two parts: (1) *Law of Duty* (10 commandments), (2) *Law of Mercy*, Priesthood and Sacrifices Lev. 4:27:31; Heb. 9:1-7. (3) To whom given, Ex. 19:3 and to all, Rom. 2,12; 3:19, etc. (4) Its purpose: (a) Negative, Rom. 3:19-20, Gal. 2:16-21. etc; (b) Positive, Rom. 3:19, 7:7-13. (5) Christ's relation to the Mosaic Covenant: (a) was under it, Gal. 4;4; Matt. 3:13, etc; (b) Kept it, Jno. 8:46; 15:10; (c) Bore its curse for sinners, Gal. 3:10-13; 4:45; 2 Cor. 5:21, etc; (d) Took the place of and ended the Priesthood and sacrifices, Heb. 9:11-15; 10:1-12, etc; (e) New covenant provided for believers in Christ, Rom.8:1; Gal. 3:13-17.

5. The Deuteronomic Covenant, Deut. 30:1-9. Outline its elements, giving things promised and prophesied.

6. The Davidic Covenant, 2 Sam. 7:5-19. (1) Elements of the covenant and summary in the Old Testament. (2) In the New Testament.

7. The New Covenant. (1) Formed, Heb. 8:6-13. (2) In prophecy. Jer. 31:31-34. (3) It is founded on the sacrifice of Christ. Matt. 26: 27-28; 1 Cor. 11:25; Heb. 9:11-12. (4) It is primarily for Israel, but Chris-

tians are partakers, Heb. 10:11-22; Eph. 2:11-20. (5) Jews are yet to be brought into it, Ezek. 20:34-37; Jer. 23:5-6; Rom. 11:25-27.

Note. Try to see how all of these covenants met in Christ.

THE DIVISION OF THE SCRIPTURES.

In language and contents, the Bible is divided into two main divisions.

1. The Old Testament, 39 Books. 2. The New Testament, 27 Books. Total. 66 Books.

The Jews were accustomed to divide the Old Testament into three main parts, as follows:

1. The Law-the first five books, Genesis to Deuteronomy, otherwise called the Pentateuch and books of Moses.

2. The Prophets. These are divided into the "former prophets" or historical books and the "later prophets," or books, which we commonly call the prophetic books.

3. The Writings, which was made to include; (1) Poetical books-Psalms, Proverbs and Job; (2) Five Rolls-Song of Solomon, Ruth, Esther, Lamentations and Ecclesiastes; (3) Other Books: Daniel, Ezra, Nehemiah and I and II Chronicles.

The Bible itself divides the Old Testament into the three following divisions:

1. The Law, which includes the first five books of the Bible, also called the books of Moses.

2. The Prophets, which includes the next twelve books, commonly called historical books and the seventeen books we know as the prophetic books.

3. The Psalms, including the five poetical books.

The Books of the Bible

The books of the Old and New Testaments may each be divided into three or five groups as follows:

First Into three groups.

1. History.
(1) Old Testament-Genesis-Esther (17 books).
(2) New Testament-Matthew-Acts (5 books).
2. Doctrine.
(1) Old Testament-Job-Song of Solomon (5 books).
(2) New Testament-Romans-Jude (21 books).
3. Prophecy.
(1) Old Testament-Isaiah-Malachi (17 books).
(2) New Testament-Revelation (1 book).

Second, into five groups.

1. Old Testament.
(1) Pentateuch-Genesis-Deuteronomy (5 books).
(2) Historical Books-Joshua-Esther (12 books).
(3) Poetical Books-Job-Song of Solomon (5 books).
(4) Major Prophets-Isaiah-Daniel (5 books).
(5) Minor Prophets-Hosea-Malachi (12 books).

2. New Testament.
(1) Gospels-Matthew-John (4 books).
(2) Acts-Acts (1 book).
(3) Pauline Epistles-Romans-Hebrews (14 books).
(4) General Epistles-James-Jude (7 books).
(5) Revelation-Revelation (1 book).

Direction For Study. (1) Drill on the Scripture divisions, Jewish divisions and the three and five groups of each Testament. (2) Drill on the number of chapters in each book and on the abbreviation of each. (3) Drill on books having the same number of chapters, as all those having one chapter, two chapters, etc.

THE DISPENSATIONS.

A dispensation is a period of time during which God deals in a particular way with man in the matter of sin and responsibility. The whole Bible may be divided into either three or seven dispensations.

Three Dispensations.

1. *The Patriarchal Dispensation.* From creation to the giving of the Law, Gen. 1-Ex. 19 and Job.

2. *The Mosaic Dispensation.* From the giving of the Law to the birth of Christ, Ex. 20-Mal. 4.

3. *The Christian Dispensation.* From the birth of Christ to his second coming, Matt.-Rev.

Seven Dispensations.

In each of these, man is put in a given state or condition, has a responsibility in it, fails to meet the responsibility, and suffers consequent Judgment.

1. *The Dispensation of Innocence.* From creation to the expulsion from the garden, Gen. 1-3. In this period. Adam and Eve were under obligations to keep their innocence by abstaining from the fruit of the tree of knowledge of good and evil. Their failure has

been the most destructive and for reaching of all man's failures.

2. *The Dispensation of Conscience.* From the fall to the flood, Gen. 4-9. Man had a natural conscience, or knew good from evil, and was under obligation to do good and not evil. The time covered B. C. 4004-2348=1636 years for 1 and 2.

3. *The Dispensation of Human Governments.* From the flood to the call of Abraham, Gen. 10-12. God gave the eight persons saved from the flood power to govern the renewed earth. The time covered, B. C. 2348-1921.= 427 years.

4. *The Dispensation of Promise.* From Abraham to the giving of the law. Gen. 12-Ex.19. God promised Abraham land, natural seed, spiritual seed and other conditional promises. For the sake of study, this dispensation is divided into two sections. (1) Abraham and the chosen people, Gen. 12:50. (2) Moses and the Exodus, Ex. 1-19. The time covered, B. C. 1921-1491=430 years.

5. The Dispensation of the Law. From Sinai to Calvary or from Exodus to the cross, Ex. 20-John 21. The history of Israel in the wilderness and their lapses into idolatry and their other sins while in Canaan, their captivity by Babylon and final dispersion are evidences of their failure in this dispensation. All of the Old Testament was written during this period. The time covered, B. C. 1491-A. D. 34=1525 years.

6. The Dispensation of Grace. From Calvary to the second coming of Christ, Act 8-Rev. Grace is God giving instead of requiring righteousness. It is unmerited favor. During this dispensation, perfect and eternal salvation is fully offered to both Jews and Gentiles upon the condition of faith. It will end with

the destruction of the wicked. The time covered is not known.

7. The Dispensation of the Kingdom. The Millennium (1000).

Directions for Study. (1) Drill the class on the names of dispensations, the portion of scripture included and the period of time covered. (2) Have each student to select for himself some prominent person or historical event found in each dispensation with which he will familiarize himself.

AGES AND PERIODS OF BIBLICAL HISTORY.

Bible history is commonly divided into the following ages or periods according to the purpose to be served or the minuteness of the study to be taken.

Seven Ages.

1. The Adamic Age. Gen. 1-8-From the creation to the flood.

2. The Noachian Age, Gen. 9-11-From the flood to the call of Abraham.

3. The Abrahamic Age, Gen. 12-Ex. 19-From the call of Abraham to the giving of the law.

4. The Mosaic Age, Ex. 20-1 Sam. 31-From the giving of the Law to the reign of David.

5. The Davidic Age. 2 Sam. 1-2 Kings 25-From David's ascension to the throne to the restoration.

6. The Ezraitic Age. Ezra-Mal.-From the restoration to the birth of Christ.

7. The Christian Age. Matt-Rev.-From the birth to the second coming of Christ.

Fifteen Historical Periods.

1. *The Ante-diluvian Period,* From the creation to the flood. Gen. 1-6. The time covered, B. C. 4004 minus 2348 equal 1656 years.

2. *The Post-diluvian Period.* From the flood to the call of Abraham. Gen. 7-11. Time covered, B. C. 2348 minus 1921 equal 427 years.

3. *The Patriarchial Period.* From the call of Abraham to the descent into Egypt. Gen. 12-50. Time covered. B. C. 1921 minus 1706 equal 215 years.

4. *The Period Of Bondage.* From the descent into Egypt to the Exodus Ex. 1-12. Time covered B. C. 1706 minus 1491 equal 215 years.

5. *The Period of Wilderness Wandering.* From the exodus to the entrance into Canaan. Ex. 2-Deut. 34. Time covered, B. C. 1491 minus 1451 equal 40 years.

6. *The Period of the Conquest of Canaan.* From the entrance of Canaan to the time of the Judges, Job. 1-Judge 2. Time covered, B. C. 1451 minus 1400 equal 51 years.

7. *The Period of the Judges.* From the beginning of the Judges to the beginning of the Kingdom. Judg. 3-Sam 8. Time covered, B. C, 1400 minus 1095 equal 305 years.

8. *The Period of the Kingdom of Israel.* From the beginning to the division of the Kingdom, 1 Sam.9; King 11; 1 Chron. 10;2 Chron. 9. Time covered B. C. 1095 minus 975 equal 120 years.

9. *The Period of the Two Kingdoms.* From the division of the kingdom to the fall of Israel, 1 Kings 12; 2 Kings 18; 2 Chron. 10-29. Time covered, B. C. 975 minus 722 equal 253 years.

10. *The Period of the Kingdom of Judah.* From the fall of Israel to the fall of Judah, 2 Kings 21-25; 2 Chron. 33-36. Time covered, B. C. 722 minus 587 equal 135 years.

11. *The Period of Babylonian Captivity*. From the fall of Judah to the restoration to Jerusalem. 2 Kings, Is., Jer, Eze., Dan. Time covered, B. C. 587 minus 537 equal 50 years.

12. *The Period of the Restoration*. From the return to Jerusalem to the end of the Old Testament, Ezra, Neh., Esth., Hag., Zech. Time covered, B. C. 537 minus 445 equal 92 years.

13. >*The Period Between the Testaments*. From the end of the Old Testament to the Birth of Christ-no scripture. Time covered, B. C. 445 minus 4 equal 441 years.

14. *The Period of the Life of Christ*. From the birth of Jesus to the ascension. Matt.-John. Time covered, B. C. 4 minus A. D. 30 equal 34 years.

15. *The Period of the Church after the Ascension*. From the ascension to the second coming, Acts-Rev. Time covered A. D. 34 to the end of the age.

Twenty-one Shorter Periods.

1. From the Creation to the Fall, Gen. 1-3.
2. From the Fall to the Flood. Gen. 4-8.
3. From the Flood to Abraham, Gen. 9-11.
4. From Abraham to Egypt. Gen. 12-50.
5. From Egypt to Sinai. Ex. 1-19.
6. From Sinai to Kadesh, Ex. 20-Num. 14.
7. From Kadesh to the death of Moses, Num. 14-Dt. 34.
8. Joshua's Conquest, Josh. 9. The Judges, Jud. 1-1 Sam. 7.
10. Saul's Reign. 1 Sam. 8-end.
11. David's Reign, 2 Sam.
12. Solomon's Reign. 1 K. 1-11.
13. The Divided Kingdom 1 K. 12-2 K. 17.
14. From the captivity of Israel to the captivity of

Judah. 2 K. 18- 25. 15. From the captivity of Judah to the Restoration, Dan. and Eze.

16. From the Restoration to Malachi, Ezra, Neh., and Esther.

17. From Malachi to the Birth of Christ, no scripture.

18. From the Birth of Christ to the ascension, Matt-John. 19. From the Ascension to the Church at Antioch, Acts 1-12.

20. From Antioch to the Destruction of Jerusalem, Acts 13-28.

21. From the Destruction of Jerusalem to the close of the New Testament. John and Rev.

Note 1. The author's "Bible Period by Period" is based upon these twenty-one periods and will furnish material for a study of the whole story of the Bible.

Note 2. To the scripture given for each period should be added corresponding scripture such as sections in Chron. corresponding to that of Kings.

Directions for Study. (1) Drill separately on the ages, fifteen periods with the scripture and period covered by each until the class is thoroughly familiar with them. Require the students to select some event or character found in each age and period and drill on them until they know something found in each.

SOME GENERAL MATTERS AND BIBLICAL CHARACTERS.

Some General Matters.

Any intelligent reading of the Bible requires a knowledge of some general matters. This chapter looks to the study of some of the most important of them.

Sacred Mountains and Hills.

(1) Ararat, Gen. 8:4. (2) Lebanon. 1 K. 5:6; Josh, 13:5-6. (3) Hor, Num. 34:7-8. (4) Hermon, Dt. 4:48; S. of S. 4:8. (5) Gilead, Gen. 31:25; Dt. 32:49. (7) Tabor, Josh. 19:22; Jud. 4:6. (8) Carmel, Is. 32:9; 1 K. 18-19. (9) Moriah, 2 Chron. 3:1-10. Zion, 2 Sam. 5:7-9; Ps, 87:2, 5. (11) Sinai, Ex. 19:1, 11 etc. (12) Horeb, Ex. 3:1; 1 K. 19:8 etc. (13) Calvary Mt. 27:45. (14) Olivet or Olives, Zech. 14:4: Mk. 13:3.

The Jewish Months.

Hebrew Names Roman Names.
1. Nisan or Ahib March and April
2. Iyar or Ziv April and May.
3. Sivan May and June.

4. Tammuz June and July.
5. Ab July and August.
6. Elul August and September.
7. Tisri or Eharium September and October.
8. Marchesvan October and November.
9. Casleu or Chisleu November and December.
10. Tebeth December and January.
11. Shebat January and February.
12. Adar February and March.

Politico-Religious Parties.

1. The Parties. (1) The Galileans. (2) Samaritans. (3) Proselytes. (4) Hellenists. (5) Herodians. (6) Publicans.

2. The Religious Classes. (1) Scribes. (2) Pharisees. (3) Sadducees. (4) Zealots. (5) Essenes.

Note. By reference to some good Bible dictionary become familiar with the history and importance of all the topics of the chapter.

Some Biblical Characters.

Twenty Principal Men

(1) Adams, Gen. 1-3. (2) Noah, Gen. 5-9. (3) Abraham, Gen. 12-25. (4) Jacob, Gen. 25-50. (5) Moses, Ex-Dt. (6) Joshua, Josh. (7) Gideon, Jud. 6-8. (8) Samuel, 1 Sam. 1-25. (9) David, 2 Sam. and 1 Chron. 11-29. (10) Solomon, 1 K. 1-11, 2 K. 2. (11) Hezekiah, 2 K. 18-20. (12) Josiah, 2 K. 22-23. (13) Daniel, Dan. 1-12. (14) Ezra, Ezr. 7-10; Neh. 8. (15) John the Baptist, Mt. Lu. Jno. (16) Peter, Four Gospels and Acts. (17) Paul, Acts 9-28 and the Epistles. (18) John, the Gospels and Revelation.

Some Prophets.

First Group. Tell something of the character and work of each of the following: (1) Enoch, Jude 14; (2) Noah, 2 Pet. 2:5; Gen. 6:25-27; (3) Samuel, 1 Sam. 9:9; 1 Chron. 29:29; (4) Nathan, 2 Sam. 7:2-4;12:2-7;

(5) Gad, 1 Sam. 22:5; 2 Sam. 24:11; (6) Ahijah, 1 K. 14:2; (7) Elijah, 1 K. 17-19; 1 Sam. 1-2; (8) Elisha, 2 K. 3-8; (9) Jonah, the book; (10) Malachi, the book; (11) Agabus, Acts 21:10; (12) Daughters of Philip, Acts 21:9.

Second Group. Sam. - King. What prophet prophesied to each of the following kings and what message did he bring: (1) Saul. 1 Sam. 15:17. (2) David, 2 Sam. 7:2-3; 12:2-7. (3) Solomon, (4) Rehoboam, 1 K. 12:22; (5) Asa. (6) Ahab, 1 K. 17:1 ff. (7) Jeroboam. (8) Joash, 2 K. 13:14. (9) Jeroboam II, 1 K. 11:29 ff. (10) Ahaz. Is. 7:1-3. (11) Hezekiah, Is. 19:2. (12) Josiah and his sons, 2 K. 22:14.

Third Group. Which prophet prophesied against the following nations and what was the nature of their prophecy: (1) Syria, Is. 17:3; Jer. 49:23; Amos. 1:3; Zech. 9:2; (2) Ninevah, Jonah, 1;1. Nahum 2:8 etc; (3) Babylon, Is. 13:1; Jer. 25:12; (4) Moab, Is. 15:1 Jer. 25:21; Jer. 47; Eze. 25:8; Amos 2:1. (5) Ammon, Jer. 49:6; Eze. 21:28; Amos 1:13; (6) Philistia, Is. 14:29. Zech. 9:6; Jer. 47:1. 4 Eze. 25:15; (7) Egypt. Is. 19:1; Jer. 44:28; Eze. 29; (8) Tyre of Phoenicia.

Some Women.

First Group. In what connection and in what books of the Bible are the following women considered? (1) Eve, Gen. 2:20; 4:1. (2) Sarah, Gen.11, 29; 17:15. (3) Hagar, Gen. 16:1. (4) Rebekah, Gen. 24:15. (5) Keturah, Gen. 25:1. (6) Rachel, Gen. 29: 16ff. (7) Leah, Gen. 29:16ff. (8) Dinah, Gen. 30:21; 34:11. (9) Adah, Gen. 36:2. (10) Asenath, Gen. 41:45. (11) Shiphrah and Puah, Ex. 1:15. (12) Jehochebed, Ex. 6:20. (13) Miriam. Ex. 2:4; 15:20; Num. 12:1 etc. (14) Zipporah, Ex. 2:21; 4:23; 18:20. (15) Rahab. Josh, 2:1-21. Heb. 11:31; Mt. 1:5. (16) Deborah. Jud. 4:4. (17) Ruth, Ruth 1:4. (18) Hannah, 1 Sam. chs. 1-2.

(19) Bathshebah, 2 Sam. 11:3. (20) Abishag, 1 K. 1:3. (21) Jezebel, 1 K. 21:5. (22) Vashti, Esth. 1:19. (23) Esther, Esth. 2:7. (24) Mary. Mt. 1:18; Lu. 1:27. (25) Elizabeth. Lu. 1:5. (26) Martha. Jno. 12:2. (27) Sapphira, Acts 5:1. (28) Tabitha, Dorcas, Acts 9:36. (29) Lydia Acts. 16:14.

Second Group. In what connection are the following mentioned; (1) The witch of Endor, 1 Sara. 28:7. (2) The women of Tekoa. 2 Sam. 14. (3) The queen of Sheba, 1 King 17:9. 10 (Elijah). (5) The woman of Shunem, 2 King 4:8 (Elisha). (6) The Samaritan woman. Jho. Ch. 4. (7) The Syrophenician woman, Matt. 15:21-28. (8) Peter's mother in-law. Matt. 8: 14-17. (9) The widow of Nain, Lu. 7:11. (10) The daughter of Jairus, Matt. 9:23-26.

Third Group. Who is the mother of: (I) Seth. Gen. 5:3. (2) Isaac, Gen. 21:1 ff. (3) Ishmael, Gen. 16:16. (4) Jacob, Gen. 25:20ff (5) Judah. Gen. 29:35. (6) Joseph, (7) Ephraim. Gen. 41:52. (8) Moses, Ex. 6:20. (9) Samuel. 1 Sam. 1:20. (10) Joab. I Chron. 2:16. (11) Absalom, 2 Sam. 3:3. (12) Solomon, 2 Sam. 12:24. (13) Rehoboam, I King 14:21-22. (14) John the Baptist, Lu. 1:57.

THE BIBLE BOOK BY BOOK.

1
GENESIS.

The Name means beginning, origin, or creation. The leading thought, therefore, is creation and we should study it with a view to finding out everything, the beginning of which is recorded in it. Certainly we have the record of: (1) The beginning of the world which God created. (2) The beginning of man as the creature of God. (3) The beginning of sin, which entered the world through the disobedience of man. (4) The beginning of redemption, seen alike in the promises and types of the book and in the chosen family. (5) The beginning of condemnation, seen in the destruction and punishment of individuals, cities and the world.

The Purpose. The chief purpose of the book is to write a religious history, showing how, after man had fallen into sin, God began to give him a religion and to unfold to him a plan of salvation. In doing this God is revealed as Creator, Preserver, Law-Giver, Judge and Merciful Sovereign.

The Importance of Genesis to Science. While

the book does not attempt to explain many matters which are left to investigation, it does set out several facts which indicate the general plan of the universe and furnish a basis for scientific research. Among the more important things indicated are that: (1) There was a beginning of things. (2) Things did not come by chance. (3) There is a Creator who continues to take interest in and control the universe. (4) There was orderly progress in creation from the less and more simple to the greater and more complex. (5) Everything else was brought into existence for man who is the crowning work of creation.

The Religious Importance of the Book. The germ of all truth which is unfolded in the scripture is found in Genesis and to know well this book is to know God's plan for the blessing of man. Above all we learn about the nature and work of God.

Analysis.

Note. In an ordinary academy class I would not tax the students with the memory of more than the general divisions indicated by the Roman notation, I, etc. But, in this, and all other outlines, drill the class till these divisions, with the scripture included, are known perfectly. I would also try to fix some event mentioned in each section.

I. Creation, Chs. 1-2.
1. Creation in general, Ch. 1.
2. Creation of man in particular, Ch. 2.
II. Fall. Ch. 3.
1. Temptation, 1-5.
2. Fall, 6-8.
3. Lord's appearance, 9-13.

4. Curse, 14-21. 5. Exclusion from the garden, 22-24.

III. Flood, Chs. 4-9.
1. Growth of sin through Cain, 4:1-24.
2. Genealogy of Noah, 4: 25-5 end.
3. Building of the Ark, Ch. 6.
4. Occupying the Ark, Ch. 7.
5. Departure from the Ark, Ch. 8.
6. Covenant with Noah, Ch. 9.

IV. Nations, 10:1-11:9.
1. Basis of Nations, Noah's sons, Ch. 10. How?
2. Occasion of forming the nations, 11:1-9. Why?

V. Abraham, 11:10-25:18.
1. Genealogy of Abram from Shem, 11:10 end.
2. Call and promise, Ch. 12.
3. Abraham and Lot, Chs. 13-14.
4. Covenant, 15: 1-18: 15.
5. Destruction of Sodom and Gomorrah, 18:16-19 end.
6. Lives at Gerar, Ch. 20.
7. Birth of Isaac, Ch. 21.
8. Sacrifice of Isaac, Ch. 22.
9. Death of Sarah, Ch. 23.
10. Marriage of Isaac, Ch. 24.
11. Death of Abraham and Ishmael, 25:1-18.

VI. Isaac. 26:19-36 end.
1. His two sons, 25:19 end.
2. Divine covenant. Ch. 26.
3. Jacob's deception, Ch. 27.
4. Jacob's flight into Haran, Ch. 28.
5. Jacob's marriage and prosperity, Chs. 20-30.
6. Jacob's return to Canaan. Chs, 31-35.
7. Generations of Esau, Ch. 36.

VII. Jacob, including Joseph, Chs. 37-50.
1. Jacob and Joseph, Chs. 37-45.

2. Sojourn in Egypt, Chs. 46-48.

3. Death of Jacob and Joseph, Chs. 49-50.

For Study and Discussion. (1) All that we may learn from this book concerning the nature and work of God. (2) The different things the origin of which this book tells: (a) Inanimate things, (b) Plant life, (c) Animal life, (d) Human life, (e) Devices for comfort and safety, (f) Sin and its varied effects, (g) Various trades and manners of life, (h) Redemption, (i) Condemnation. (3) Worship as it appears in Genesis, its form and development. (4) The principal men of the book and the elements of weakness and strength in the character of each. The teacher may make a list and assign them for study to different pupils. (5) List the disappointments, family troubles and sorrows of Jacob, and study them in the light of his early deception and fraud. (6) The over-ruling divine providence seen in the career of Joseph, with the present day lessons from the incidents of his life. (7) The fundamental value of faith in the life and destiny of men. (8) The Messianic promises, types and symbols of the entire book. List and classify them.

2
EXODUS.

Name. The name Exodus means a going out or departure.

Subject The subject and key-word of the book is redemption (3:7, 8; 12:13 etc.), particularly that half of redemption indicated by deliverance from an evil plight. It records the redemption of the chosen people out of Egyptian bondage, which becomes a type of all redemption in that it was accomplished (1) wholly through the power of God, (2) by a means of a deliverer (3) under the cover of blood.

Purpose. At this point Old Testament history changes from that of the family, given in individual biographies and family records, to that of the nation, chosen for the divine purposes. The divine will is no longer revealed to a few leaders but to the whole people. It begins with the cruel bondage of Israel in Egypt, traces the remarkable events of their delivery and ends with a complete establishment of the dispensation of the Law. The aim seems to be to give an account of the first stage in the fulfillment of the promises made by God to the Patriarchs with reference to the place and growth of the Israelites.

Contents. Two distinct sections are usually given by students: the historical, included in chapters 1-19 and the legislative, comprising chapters 20-40. The first section records: the need of deliverance; the birth, training and call of the deliverer; the contest with Pharaoh; the deliverance and march through the wilderness to Sinai. The second gives the consecration of the nation and the covenant upon which it was to become a nation. The laws were such as to cover all the needs of a primitive people, both moral, ceremonial and civic with directions for the establishment of the Priesthood and Sanctuary.

Exodus and Science, Scientific research has gone far toward establishing the truthfulness of the Exodus record, but has brought to light nothing that in any way discounts it. It has shown who the Pharaoh of the oppression and Exodus was (Rameses. II, the Pharaoh of the oppression and Merenpth II, the Pharaoh of the Exodus.) and has discovered Succoth. It has shown that writing was used long before the Exodus and has discovered documents written before that period. It has thus confirmed the condition of things narrated in the Bible.

Analysis.

I. Israel in Egypt, 1:1-12:36.
1. The bondage, Ch. 1.
2. The deliverer, Chs. 2-4.
3. The contest with Pharaoh, 5:1-12:38.
II. Israel Journeying to Sinai, 12:37-18: end.
1. The exodus and passover, 12:37-13:16.

2. Journeying through Succoth to the Red Sea, 13:17-15:21.

3. From the Red Sea to Sinai, 15:22-18 end.

III. Israel at Sinai, Chs, 10-40.

1. The people prepared, Ch. 19.

2. The moral law, Ch. 20.

3. The civil law, 21:1-23:18.

4. Covenant between Jehovah and Israel, 23:20-24 end.

5. Directions for building the tabernacle, Chs. 25-31.

6. The covenant broken and renewed, Chs. 32-34.

7. The erection and dedication of the Tabernacle, 35-40.

For Study and Discussion. (1) The preparation of Israel and Moses for the deliverance. (2) The conception of God found in Exodus: (a) As to his relation to nature, (b) As to his relation to his enemies, (c) As to his relation to his people, (d) As to his nature and purposes. (3) The conception of man found in Exodus. (a) The need and value of worship to him, (b) His duty to obey God. (4) The plagues. (5) The divisions of the decalogue: (a) Those touching our relation to God. (b) Those touching our relation to men. (6) The different conferences between Jehovah and Moses, including Moses' prayer. (7) The current evils against which the civil laws were enacted and similar conditions of today. (8) The character of the different persons mentioned in the book: (a) Pharaoh, (b) Moses, (c) Aaron, (d) Jethro, (e) Magicians. (8) Amalek, etc. (9) The Messianic teachings of the book-here study (a) the sacrifices, (b) the material, colors, etc., of the Tabernacle, (c) the smitten rock, (d) Moses and his family.

3
LEVITICUS.

Name. By the rabbis, it was called "The Law of the Priest" and "The Law of Offerings," but from the time of the Vulgate it has been called Leviticus, because it deals with the services of the sanctuary as administered by the Levites.

Connection with Former Books. In Genesis, man is left outside of the Garden and the remedy for his ruin is seen in the promised seed. In Exodus, man is not only outside of Eden, but is in bondage to an evil enemy and his escape from his bondage is shown to be in the blood of the lamb, which is shown to be sufficient to satisfy man's need and God's justice. In Leviticus there is given the place of sacrifice, as an atonement for sin, and it is shown that God accepted the sacrifice of the victim instead of the death of the sinner. It is a continuation of Exodus, containing the Sinaitic legislation from the time of the completion of the Tabernacle.

Contents. Except the brief historical sections found in chapters 8-10 and 24:10-14, it contains a system of laws, which may be divided into (1) Civil, (2) Sanitary, (3) Ceremonial, (4) Moral and (5) Religious laws, emphasis being placed on moral and religious duties.

Purpose. (1) To show that God is holy and man is sinful. (2) To show how God can maintain his holiness and expose the sinfulness of man. (3) To show how a sinful people may approach a Holy God. (4) To provide a manual of law and worship for Israel. (5) To make Israel a holy nation.

Key-Word. The key-word then is Holiness, which is found 87 times in the book, while in contrast with it, the words sin and uncleanliness (in various forms) occur 194 times, showing the need of cleansing. On the other hand, blood, as a means of cleansing, occurs 89 times. The key verse is, I think, 19:2, though some prefer 10:10 as the best verse.

The Sacrifices, or Offerings. They may be divided in several ways, among which the most instructive is as follows: (1) *National Sacrifices*, which include (a) Serial, such as daily, weekly, and monthly offerings, (b) Festal, as the Passover, Cycle of Months, etc., (c) for the service of the Holy Place, as holy oil, precious incense, twelve loaves, etc. (2) *Official Sacrifices*, which include (a) those for the priests, (b) those for princes and rulers, and (c) those for the holy women, Ex. 38:8; 1 Sam. 2:22. (3) *Personal Sacrifices*, including (a) the blood offering-peace offering, sin offering and trespass offering, (b) the bloodless offerings-the meat, or meal, offering.

Besides this general division, the offerings are divided into two kinds, as follows: (1) *Sweet-savor Offerings*. These are atoning in nature and show that Jesus is acceptable to God because he not only does no sin, but does all good, upon which the sinner is presented to God in all the acceptableness of Christ. These offerings are (a) the burnt offering, in which Christ willingly offers himself without spot to God for our sins, (b) the meal offering, in which Christ's perfect humanity, tested and tried, becomes the bread of His people, (c) the peace offering representing Christ as our peace, giving us communion with God, and thanks. (2) *Non-Sweet-Savor Offerings*. These are perfect offerings, overlaid with human guilt. They are (a) the sin offering, which is expiatory, substitutional and efficacious, referring more to sins against God, with little consideration of injury to man, (b) the trespass offering, which refers particularly to sins against man, which are also sins against God.

Analysis.

I. Law of Sacrifices, Chs. 1-7.
1. Burnt offering, Ch. 1.
2. Meal offering, Ch. 2.
3. Peace offering, Ch. 3.
4. Sin offering, Ch. 4.
5. Trespass (or guilt) offering, 5:1-6:7.
6. Instructions to priests concerning the offerings, 6:8-7 end.

II. Law of Purity. Chs. 11-22.
1. Pure food, animals to be eaten, Ch. II.
2. Pure body and house, rules for cleansing, Chs. 12-13.
3. Pure nation, offering for sin on the day of atonement, Chs. 16-17.
4. Marriages, Ch. 18.
5. Pure morals, Chs. 19-20.
6. Pure priests, Chs. 21-22.

IV. Law of Feasts, Chs. 23-25.

1. Sacred feasts, Ch. 23.
2. Parenthesis, or interpolation, lamps of the Tabernacle, shew-bread, the blasphemer, Ch. 24.
3. Sacred years, Ch. 25.
V. Special Laws, Chs, 26-27.
1. Blessing and cursing, Ch. 26.
2. Vows and tithes, Ch. 27.

For Study and Discussion. (1) Make a list of the several offerings and become familiar with what is offered, how it is offered, the result to be attained in each case. (2) The laws (a) for the consecration and purity of the priests (Chs. 8-10 and 21-22), (b) governing marriages (Ch. 18), (c) concerning clean animals and what may be used for food (Ch, 11), (d) governing vows and tithes (Ch. 37). (3) The sacrifice of the two goats and two birds, (a) the details of what is done with each goat and each bird, (b) the lessons or truths typified by each goat and bird. (4) The name, occasion, purpose, time and manner of observing each of the feasts. (5) Redemption as seen in Leviticus, (a) the place of the priest, (b) of substitution, (c) of imputation, (d) of sacrifice and blood in redemption. (5) The nature of sin as seen in Leviticus, (a) its effect on man's nature, (b) its effect on his relation to God.

4
NUMBERS.

Name. It is named from the two enumerations of the people, at Sinai, Ch. 1. and at Moab, Ch. 26.

Connection with Former Books. Genesis tells of Creation, Exodus of redemption, Leviticus of worship and fellowship, and Numbers of service and work. In Leviticus Israel is assigned a lesson and in Numbers she is getting that lesson. In this book as in Exodus and Leviticus Moses is the central figure.

Central Thought. Service which involves journeying, which in turn implies walk as a secondary thought. All the types of the books bear upon this two-fold idea of service and walk.

Key-Phrase. "All that are able to go forth to war" occurs fourteen times in the first chapter. There was fighting ahead and all who could fight must muster in.

The History Covered is a period of a little more than thirty-eight years (Num. 1:1; Deut. 1:3) and is a record (1) of how Israel marched to the border of Canaan, (2) wandered thirty-eight years in the wilderness while the old nation died and a new nation was trained in obedience to God, (3) then returned to the border of the promised land.

Analysis.

I. The Preparation at Sinai, 1:1-10:10.

1. The number and arrangement of the tribes, Chs. 1-2.
2. The choice and assignment of the Levites, Chs. 3-4.
3. Laws for the purity of the camp, Chs. 5-6.
4. Laws concerning the offerings for worship, Chs. 7-8.
5. Laws concerning the passover and cloud, 9:1-14.
6. Signals for marching and assembling 9:15-10:10.

II. The Journey to Moab, 10:11-22:1.

1. From Sinai to Kadesh, 10:11-14 end.
2. From Kadesh to Kadesh (the wilderness wanderings), 19:1-20:21.
3. From Kadesh to Moab, 20:22-22:1.

III. The Sojourn at Moab, 22:2-36 end.

1. Balak and Balaam, 22:2-25 end.
2. The sum of the people, Ch. 26.
3. Joshua. Moses' successor, Ch. 27.
4. Feasts and offerings, Chs. 28-30.
5. Triumph over Midian, Ch. 31.
6. Two and half tribes given land east of Jordan, Ch. 32.
7. Wilderness journeys enumerated, Ch. 33.
8. Divisions of Canaan and the cities of Refuge, Chs. 34-36.

For Study and Discussion. (1) Make a list of the

different times when God came to the relief of Israel, by providing guidance, protection, food, etc. and from them study God's wonderful resources in caring for his people. (2) Make a list of the different times and occasions when Israel or any individual sinned or rebelled against God or His leaders, and study the result in each case. (3) Make a list of the miracles of the book and give the facts about each. Show which were miracles of judgment and which were miracles of mercy. (4) The story of the spies and the results of the mistake made as seen in all the future history of Israel. (5) The story of Balak and Balaam. (6) God's punishment of disobedient and sinful nations. (7) Doubt as a source of complaint and discontent. (8) The types of Christ and Christian experience: (a) The Nazarite; (b) Aaron's Budding Rod, 17:8; Heb 9:4; (c) The Blue Ribband, 15:38; (d) The Red Heifer, 19:2; (e) The Brazen Serpent, 21:9; (f) The cities of refuge, 35:13.

5
DEUTERONOMY.

Name. The name comes from the Greek word which means a second or repeated law. It contains the last words of Moses which were likely delivered during the last seven days of his life. It is not a mere repetition of the law, but rather an application of the law in view of the new conditions Israel would meet in Canaan, and because of their former disobedience.

Purpose. To lead Israel to obedience and to warn them against disobedience. The spirit and aim of the law is explained in such a way as to present both encouragement and warning.

Contents. It consists of three addresses of Moses, given on the plains of Moab at the close of the wilderness wanderings of Israel, in which he gives large sections of the law formerly given, together with additions necessary to meet the new conditions. There is also the appointment of Joshua as Moses' successor and the farewell song of blessing of Moses and the record of his death.

Style. The style is warmer and more oratorical than that of former books. Its tone is more spiritual and ethical and its appeal is "to know God," "love God" and "obey God."

Occasion and Necessity of the Book. (1) A crisis had come in the life of Israel. The life of the people was to be changed from that of wandering in the wilderness to that of residence in cities and villages and from dependence upon heavenly manna to the cultivation of the fields. Peace and righteousness would depend upon a strict observance of the laws. (2) A new religion of Canaan against which they must be put on guard. The most seductive forms of idolatry would be met everywhere and there would be great danger of yielding to it.

The Key-Word. "Thou shalt," so often repeated as, "thou shall," and "shalt not." The key-verses are 11:26-28.

Analysis.

I. Review of the Journeys, Chs. 1-4.

1. Place of their camp, 1:1-5.
2. Their history since leaving Egypt, 1:6-3 end.
3. Exhortation to obedience, 4:1-40.
4. Three cities of refuge on this side of Jordan. 4:41-49.

II. Review of the Law, Chs. 3-26.

1. Historical and hortatory section, Chs. 5-11.
2. Laws of religion. 12:1-16:17.
3. Laws of political life. 16:18-20 end.
4. Laws of society and domestic relations, Chs. 21-26.

III. Future of Israel Foretold, Chs. 27-30.

1. Memorial tablets of stone. Ch. 27.

2. Blessing and cursing, Ch. 28.

3. Renewed covenant and Israel's future foretold. Chs. 29-30.

IV. Moses' Last Days, Chs. 31-34.

1. Charge to Joshua, Ch. 31.

2. Song of Moses, Ch. 32.

3. Blessing of Moses, Ch. 33.

4. Death of Moses, Ch. 34.

For Study and Discussion. (1) Make a list of the principal their past history of which Moses reminds Israel in Chapters 1-4, and find where in the previous books each incident is recorded. (2) From Chapter 11 make a list of reasons for obedience, the rewards of obedience and the importance of the study of God's law. (3) The laws of blessing and cursing (Ch. 28), make a list of the curses, the sin and the penalty, the blessings, indicating the blessing and that for which it is promised. (4) Make a list of the different countries or peoples concerning whom Israel was given commandment or warning. (5) Moses' farewell blessing on the several tribes (Ch. 33). Make a list of what shall come to each tribe. (6) The names, location and purpose of the cities of refuge and the lessons for today to be drawn from them and their use. (7) The inflexibility of God's law.

6
JOSHUA.

Historical Books of the Old Testament. The twelve books, including those from Joshua to Esther, are called historical. They narrate the history of Israel from the entrance of Canaan to the return from captivity, which is divided into three periods or epochs. (1) *The Independent Tribes*. This consists of the work of the conquest of Canaan and of the experiences of the Judges and is recorded in Joshua, Judges and Ruth. (2) *The kingdom of Israel*. (a) Its rise, 1 Sam. (b) Its glory, 2 Sam., 1 K. 1-11, 1 Chron. 11-29, 2 Chron. 1-9. (c) *Its division and fall*, 1 K. 12-22, 2 K. 1-25; 2 Chron. 10-36. (3) *The Return from Captivity*, Ezr. Neh. and Est.

Name. Taken from Joshua, the leading character, who may be described as a man of faith, courage, enthusiasm, fidelity to duty, and leadership.

Connection with Former Books. Joshua completes the story of the deliverance begun in Exodus. If Israel had not sinned in believing the evil spies and turning back into the wilderness, we would not have had the last twenty-one chapters of Numbers and the book of Deuteronomy. Joshua then would have followed the fifteenth chapter of Numbers, thus completing the story of God leading Israel out of Egypt into Canaan.

The Key-Word is redemption with the emphasis put upon possession while redemption in Exodus put the stress upon deliverance. The two make full redemption which requires being "brought out" and "brought in."

Purpose of the Book. (1) To show how Israel was settled in Canaan according to the promise of God. (2) To show how, by the destruction of the Canaanites, God punishes a people for their sins. (3) To show that God's people are finally heirs of earth and that the wicked shall be finally dispossessed.

Some Typical and Spiritual Matters. (1) The conflict with Canaan. In the wilderness the conflict was with Amalek who was an illustration of the never ending conflict of the flesh or of the "new man" and the "old man." In Canaan the conflict is typical of our struggle against principalities and powers and spiritual hosts in heavenly places, Eph. 6:10-18. (2) Crossing the Jordan is an illustration of our death to sin and resurrection with Christ. (3) The scarlet line illustrates our safety under Christ and his sacrifice. (4) The downfall of Jericho. This illustrates the spiritual victories we win in secret and by ways that seem foolish to men. (5) Joshua. Joshua is a type of Christ in that he leads his followers to victory over their enemies; in that he is their advocate in time of defeat and in the way he leads them into a permanent home.

Analysis.

I. Conquest of Canaan, Chs. 1-12.
1. The preparation, Chs. 1-2.
2. Crossing the Jordan, Chs. 3-4.
3. Conquest of Jericho, Chs. 5-6.
4. Conquest of the South, Chs. 7-10.
5. Conquest of the North, Ch. 11.
6. Summary, Ch. 12.

II. Division of Lands, Chs. 13-22.
1. Territory of the different tribes, Chs. 13-19.
2. Cities of Refuge, Ch. 20.
3. Cities of the Levites, Ch. 21.
4. Return of the Eastern Tribes, Ch. 22.

III. Joshua's Last Counsel, and Death. Chs. 23-24.
1. Exhortation to fidelity, Ch. 23.
2. Farewell address and death, Ch. 24.

For Study and Discussion. (1) The cooperation of the two and one-half tribes in the conquest of Canaan. (2) Make a list of the different battles and indicate any in which Israel was defeated. (3) The portion of the country allotted to each of the tribes of Israel. (4) The story of the sins of Achan. Its results and his discovery and punishment. (5) The story of the Gibeonites, their stratagem and consequent embarrassment of Joshua. (6) Make a list of incidents or occurrences that show a miraculous element running through the narrative. (7) The story of Rabab, the harlot. (8) The names of the several tribes of Canaan and the history of each. (9) The place of prayer and worship in the narrative. Give instances. (10) Evidences found in the book that God hates sin.

7
JUDGES AND RUTH.

Judges.

The Name. The name is taken from the Judges whose deeds it records.

The Character of the Book. The book is fragmentary and unchronological in its arrangement. The events recorded are largely local and tribal instead of national, but are of great value as showing the condition and character of the people.

The Condition of the Nation. Israel was unorganized and somewhat unsettled. They lacked moral energy and the spirit of obedience to Jehovah and were constantly falling into idolatry and then suffering at the hands of heathen nations. This condition is summed up in the oft repeated words: "The children of Israel again did evil in the eyes of the Lord" and "the Lord sold them into the hand of the oppressor."

The Contents. Judges records the conflict of the nation with the Canaanite people and with itself; the condition of the country, people and times and the faithfulness, righteousness and mercy of God. It gives an account of "Seven apostasies, seven servitudes to the seven heathen nations and seven deliverances." It furnishes an explanation of these "ups and downs" and is not merely a record of historical events but an interpretation of those events.

The Work of the Judges. The Judges were raised up as occasion required and were tribesmen upon whom God laid the burden of apostate and oppressed Israel. They exercised judicial functions and led the armies of Israel against their enemies. They, therefore, asserted the nation's principles and upheld the cause of Jehovah. As deliverers they were all types of Christ.

The Key-word is Confusion and the key-verse is "every man did that which was right in his own eyes" 17:6, which would certainly bring about a state of confusion.

Analysis.

I. From the Conquest to the Judges, 1:1-3:6.
II. The Judges and their Work. 3:7-16 end.
1. Against Mesopotamia, 3:7-12.
2. Against Moab, 3:13-30.
3. Against Philistia, 3:31.
4. Against the Canaanites, Chs. 4-5.
5. Against the Midianites, Chs. 6-10.
6. Against the Amorites, Chs. 11-12.
7. Against the Philistines, Chs, 13-16.
III. The Idolatry of Micah, Chs. 17-18.
IV. The Crime of Gibea, Chs. 19-21.

For Study and Discussion. (1) Learn the names of the Judges in order with the time each served, or the period of rest after his work had been accomplished. (2) The enemy each judge had to combat and what work was accomplished by each judge. (3) What elements of strength and of weakness are to be found in the character of each judge. (4) From the story of Gideon and Sampson, point out New Testament truths. (5) From the story of Jephthah and Deborah gather lessons for practical life today. (6) Religious apostasy as a cause of national decay. (7) Political folly and social immorality as a sign of national decay. (8) The method of divine deliverance.

Ruth.

This book together with the Judges treats the life of Israel from the rule of death of Joshua to the rule of Eli.

Name. From the principal character.

Contents. It is properly a continuation of Judges, showing the life of the times in its greatest simplicity. It is also especially important because it shows the lineage of David through the whole history of Israel and thereby is a link in the genealogy of Christ.

Typical Matters. (1) Ruth is a type of Christ's Gentile bride and her experience is similar to that of any devout Christian. (2) Boaz the rich Bethlehemite accepting this strange woman in an illustration of the redemptive work of Jesus.

The Key-words are love and faith.

Analysis.

I. The Sojourn at Moab, 1:1-5.
II. The Return to Jerusalem, 1:6-22.
III. Ruth and Boaz, Chs. 2-4.

1. Gleaning the fields of Boaz, Ch. 2.
2. Ruth married to Boaz, Chs. 3-4.
   A. A bold act, Ch. 3.
   B. Redemption of Naomi's inheritance, 4:1-12.
   C. Becomes wife of Boaz, 4:13-17.
   D. Genealogy of David, 4:18-22.

Some one has said that Ch. 1 is Ruth deciding, Ch. 2 is Ruth serving, Ch. 3 is Ruth resting, Ch. 4 is Ruth rewarded.

For Study and Discussion. (1) Each of the characters of the book. (2) The whole story of Ruth in comparison with the stories of Judges (Chs. 17-21) to get a view of the best and worst in their social conditions. (3) The value of a trusting soul (Ruth).

8
FIRST AND SECOND SAMUEL.

Name. The name is taken from the history of the life of Samuel recorded in the early part of the book. It means "asked of God." The two were formerly one book and called the "First Book of Kings," the two books of Kings being one book and called Second Kings. Samuel and Kings form a continuous story, and give us a record of the rise, glory and fall of the Jewish Monarchy.

First Samuel.

Contents. This book begins with the story of Eli. the aged priest, judge and leader of the people. It records the birth and childhood of Samuel, who later becomes priest and prophet of the people. It tells of Saul's elevation to the throne and of his final downfall. Along with this is also given the growing power of David, who is to succeed Saul as king.

The Prophets. Samuel was not only both judge and priest and prophet, but as prophet he performed conspicuous services in several directions. Probably the most notable of all his work was the establishment of schools of prophets, which greatly dignified the work of the prophets. After this time, the prophet and not the priest was the medium of communication between God and his people.

Saul. As king, Saul began well and under favorable circumstances. He gave himself to military exploits and neglected the finer spiritual matters and soon made a complete break with Samuel, who represented the religious-national class-and thereby lost the support of the best elements of the nation. He then became morose and melancholy and insanely jealous in conduct and could not, therefore, understand the higher religious experiences that were necessary as a representative of Jehovah on the throne of Israel.

Analysis.

I. Career of Samuel, Chs. 1-7.
1. His birth and call, Chs. 1-3.
2. His conflict with the Philistines, Chs. 4-7.
II. Career of Saul to his rejection, Chs. 8-15.
1. Chosen as King, Chs. 8-10.
2. Wars with Philistines, Chs. 11-14.
3. He is rejected, Chs. 15.
III. Career of Saul after his rejection, Chs. 16-31.
1. While David is at his court, Chs. 16-20.
2. While David is a refugee in Judah, Chs. 21-26.
3. While David is a refugee in Philistia, Chs. 27-31.

For Study and Discussion. (1) The story of Eli and his sons. (2) The birth and call of Samuel. (3) The anointing of Saul. (4) The anointing of David. (5) The evils of jealousy as seen in Saul. (6) The importance of respect for existing forms of government-see David's attitude toward Saul. (7) How a man's attitude toward God and his servants can make or mar his destiny. (8) Examples of how God uses both good and bad carrying forward his purposes.

Second Samuel.

In this book, there is given the story of the career of David while king of Israel. He was the strongest king Israel ever had and was characterized as a fine executive, a skillful soldier and of a deeply religious disposition. He was not without his faults, but in spite of them developed a great empire.

Analysis.

I. His Reign Over Judah a Hebren, Chs. 1-4.
II. His reign Over All Israel, Chs. 5-10.
III. His Great Sin and Its Results, Chs. 11-20.
IV. An Appendix, Chs. 21-34.

For Study and Discussion. (1) How David became king. (2) His victories in war. (3) His great sin and some of its consequences. (4) His kindness toward his enemies (see also his attitude toward Saul recorded in First Samuel). (5) The kindness of God as illustrated by the story of David's kindness to Mephibosheth, Ch. 9. (6) David's psalm of praise, Chs. 22-23. (7) The different occasions when David showed a penitent spirit (8) The great pestilence. Ch. 24.

9
FIRST AND SECOND KINGS.

Name. The name is taken from the Kings whose deeds they narrate.

Contents. It takes up the history of Israel where Second Samuel left off and gives the account of the death of David, the reign of Solomon, the Divided Kingdom, and the captivity.

Purpose. The political changes of Israel are given in order to show the religious condition. Everywhere there is a conflict between faith and unbelief, between the worship of Jehovah and the worship of Baal. We see wicked kings who introduce false worship and righteous kings who bring about reforms and try to overthrow false worship. Israel yields to evil and is finally cut off, but Judah repents and is restored to perpetuate the kingdom and to be the medium through which Jesus came.

The Kingdom of Solomon. Solomon began in glory, flourished a while and then ended in disgrace. He sacrificed the most sacred principles of the nation in order to form alliances with other nations. He attempted to concentrate all worship on Mount Moriah, probably hoping that in this way he might control all nations. He finally became a tyrant and robbed the people of their liberty.

The Two Kingdoms. This is a sad story of dissension and war and defeat. Israel or the northern kingdom was always jealous of Judah. It was by far the stronger and possessed a much larger and more fertile land. There were nineteen king, from Jeroboam to Hoshea, whose names and the number of years they reigned should be learned together with the amount of scripture included in the story of each. Judah or the southern kingdom was always a little more faithful to the true worship. There were twenty kings, from Rehoboam to Zedekiah, whose lives with the number of years they reigned and the scripture passages describing each, should be tabulated and learned.

The Captivity. It is made clear that the captivity is because of sin. God having spared them for a long time. (1) Israel was taken captivity by the Assyrian Empire, whose capital was Nineveh. This marks the end of the northern tribes. (2) Judah was captured by the Babylonian Empire, but after a period of seventy years, the people were restored to their own land.

Analysis of First Kings.

I. The Reign of Solomon, Chs. 1-11.
1. His accession, Chs. 1-4.
2. Building the Temple, Chs. 5-8.
3. His greatness and sin, Chs. 9-11.

II. The Revolt and Sin of The Ten Tribes, Chs. 12-16.

III. The Reign of Ahab and the Career of Elijah, Chs. 17-22.

Analysis of Second Kings.

I. The last days of Elijah, Chs. 1-2.
II. The career of Elisha, Chs. 3-8.
III. The dynasty of Jehu, Chs. 9-14.
IV. The fall of Israel, Chs. 15-17.
V. The Kingdom of Judah, Chs. 18-25.

For Study and Discussion (1) Contrast the character of David with that of Solomon. Give the ideal elements and the defects of each. Also compare them as rulers. (2) Contrast the character of Elijah with that of Elisha. Point out the elements of strength and weakness in each. Compare the great moral and religious truth taught by each as well as the great deeds performed by them. (3) Study this as the cradle of liberty. Note Elijah's resistance of tyrants and Ahab in the vineyard of Naboth. Look for other instances. (4) Consider the place of the prophets. Note their activity in the affairs of government. Glance through these books and make a list of all prophets who are named and note the character of their message and the king or nation to whom each spoke. (5) Make a list of the kings of Israel and learn the story of Jeroboam I, Omri, Ahab, Jehu, Jeroboam II and Hoshea. (6) Make a list of the kings of Judah and learn the principal events and the general character of the reign of Rehoboam, Jehoshaphat, Joash, Uzziah, Ahaz, Hezekiah, Manasseh, Josiah and Zedekiah. (7) The fall of Judah. (8) The failure of human governments, (a) the cause, (b) the manifestation and result.

10
FIRST AND SECOND CHRONICLES.

Name. The name Chronicles was given by Jerome. They were the "words of days" and the translators of the Septuagint named them the "things omitted." They were originally one book.

Contents. Beginning with Adam the history of Israel is rewritten down to the return of Judah from captivity.

Relation to Former Books. It covers the same field as all the others. To this time the books have fitted one into another and formed a continuous history. Here we double back and review the whole history, beginning with Adam, and coming down to the edict of Cyrus which permitted the exiled Jews to return to Jerusalem.

Religious Purpose of the Narratives. Several things show these books to have a religious purpose. (1) God's care of his people and his purpose to save them is given special emphasis. (2) The building of the temple is given much prominence. (3) The kings who served God and destroyed idols are given the most conspicuous place. (4) He follows the line of Judah. only mentioning Israel where it seemed necessary. In this way he was following the Messianic line through David. (5) The priestly spirit permeates these books instead of the prophetic elements as in the earlier historical books. The aim, therefore, seems to be to teach rather than to narrate. He seems to teach that virtue and vice, in private or in national affairs, will surely receive their dues-that God must be taken into account in the life of individuals and of nations.

Analysis of First Chronicles.

I. The Genealogies, Chs. 1-9.
II. The Reign of David, Chs. 10-29.
1. Accession and great men, Chs.10-12.
2. Zeal for Jehovah's house, Chs. 13-17.
3. His victories, Chs. 18-20.
4. The numbering of the people, Chs. 21.
5. Provision for the temple, Chs. 22-29.

Analysis of Second Chronicles.

I. The Reign of Solomon, Chs. 1-9.
1. Building of the temple, Cha. 1-4.
2. Dedication of the temple, Chs. 5-7.
3. Solomon's greatness and wealth, Chs. 8-9.
II. Judah After the Revolt of the Ten Tribes, Chs. 10-36.
1. Reign of Rehoboam, Chs. 10-12.
2. Victory of Abijah, Chs. 13.
3. Reign of Asa, Chs. 14-16.
4. Reign of Jehoshaphat, Chs. 21-28.
5. Reign of Hezekiah, Chs. 29-32.
6. Reign of Manasseh and Amon, Ch. 33.

7. Reign of Josiah, Chs. 34-35.

8. The captivity, Ch, 36.

For Study and Discussion. (1) The great men of David. (2) The different victories won by David. (3) The dedication of the temple, especially the prayer. (4) The wealth and follies of Solomon. (5) The scripture and God's house as a means and source of all information, see: (a) Asa's restoration of the altar and its vessels, (b) Jehoshaphat's teaching the people God's law, (c) Joash and God's restored house, (d) The reforms Of Josiah. (6) The reign of Manasseh. (7) The nature of the worship of Judah. (8) The captivity. (9) The value of true religion to a nation. (10) The evil results of idolatry.

11
EZRA, NEHEMIAH AND ESTER.

Ezra and Nehemiah.

Name. Ezra and Nehemiah were formerly counted as one book and contain the account of the restoration of the exiles to Jerusalem and the re-establishment of their worship. They soon came to be called First and Second Ezra. Jerome first called the second book Nehemiah. Wycliffe called them the first and second Esdras and later they were called the books of Esdras otherwise the Nehemiahs. The present names were first given in the Geneva Bible (1560). Ezra is so called from the author and principal character, the name meaning "help". Nehemiah is so called from the principal character, whose name means "Jehovah comforts."

Other Books. Three other books should be read in connection with this study. (1) The book of Esther, which relates to this time and should be read between chapters 6 and 7 of the book of Ezra. (2) The books of Haggai and Zechariah. These two prophets were associated with the first return of Zerubbabel and their words incited the Jews to complete the temple in spite of opposition.

The Return from Captivity. The return consisted of three expeditions led respectively by Zerubbabel. Ezra and Nehemiah. The time covered can not be accurately calculated. It is probably not fewer than ninety years. Some think it may have been as many as one hundred and ten years.

Analysis of Ezra.

I. The Rebuilding of the Temple, Chs. 1-6.
1. The proclamation of Cyrus, 1.
2. Those who returned, 2.
3. The foundation laid, 3.
4. The work hindered, 4.
5. The work finished, 5-6.

II. The Reforms of Ezra, Chs. 7-10.
1. Ezra's Journey, 7-8.
2. The confession of sin, 9.
3. The covenant to keep the law. 10.

For Study and Discussion. (1) The traits of character displayed by Ezra. (2) The reforms of Ezra. (a) What were they? (b) Parallel conditions of today. (3) The adversaries of Judah. (a) Who were they? (b) The nature of their opposition. (4) The decree of Cyrus. (5) The expedition of Zerubbabel and Ezra. (6) Ezra's commission and the king's orders 7:1-26. (7) God's use of friends and enemies in forwarding his purposes.

Analysis of Nehemiah.

I. The Rebuilding of the Wall, Chs. 1-7.

1. Nehemiah permitted to go to Jerusalem, 1-2.
2. The work on the walls and its hindrance, 3-7.

II. The Covenant to Keep the Law, Chs. 8-10.
1. The law read, 8.
2. Confession made, 9.
3. The covenant made, 10.

III. The Walls Dedicated and Nehemiah's Reform, Chs. 11-13.
1. Those who dwelt in the city, 11:1-12:26.
2. The walls dedicated, 12:27-47 end.
3. Evils corrected, Ch. 13.

For Study and Discussion. (1) Point out elements of strength in the character and work of Nehemiah. (2) The greatness and difficulty of Nehemiah's task, (a) the rubbish, (b) the size and length of the wall, (c) the strength of their enemies. (3) The reforms of Nehemiah, (a) religious, (b) moral, (c) political. (4) The public meeting and new festival, 8:1-18. (5) The covenant 9:1-10:39. (6) The repeopling of Jerusalem, Chs. 11-12.

Esther.

Name. This is taken from its principal character, a Jewish maiden became queen of a Persian King.

Purpose. To explain the origin of the feast of Purim work of providence for God's people.

Time. The events narrated are thought to have occurred about 56 years after the first return of Zerubbabel in 536 B. C. The King then would be Xerxes the Great, and the drunken feast may have been preparatory to the invasion of Greece in the third year of his reign. Connection with Other Books. There is no connection between Esther and the other books of the Bible. While it is a story of the time when the Jews were returning to Jerusalem, and very likely should come between the first and second return, and, therefore, between the sixth and seventh chapters of Ezra, the incident stands alone. Without it we would lose much of our knowledge of that period.

The Story. While Esther stands out as the principal character, the whole story turns on the refusal of Mordecai to bow down to Haman, which would have been to show him divine honor. He did not hate Haman but, as a Jew could not worship any other than God. He dared to stand for principle at the risk of his life.

The Name of God. One of the peculiarities of the book is that it nowhere mentions the name of God, or makes any reference to him. This may be because his name was held secret and sacred at that time. However, God's power and His care of His people are everywhere implied in the book.

Analysis.

I. Esther Made Queen, Chs. 1-2.

1. Queen Vashti dethroned. Ch. 1.

2. Esther made queen. Ch. 2.

II. Haman's Plot and its Defeat. Chs. 3-8.

1. Haman plots the destruction of the Jews. Ch. 3.

2. The Jews' mourning and Mordecai's plea to Esther. Ch. 4.

3. Esther banquets Haman and the King, Ch. 5.

4. Mordecai highly honored for former service. Ch. 6.

5. Esther's plea granted and Haman hanged, Ch. 7,

6. The Jews allowed defense and Mordecai advanced, Ch. 8.

III. The Jews' Deliverance, Chs. 9-10.

1. Their enemies slain, 9:1-16.
2. A memorial feast is established. 9:17-32 end.
3. Mordecai made great, Ch. 10.

For Study and Discussion. (1) The character of the king, Vashti, Mordecai, Esther and Haman. (2) Mordecai's plea to Esther. (3) The honor of Mordecai and humiliation of Haman, Ch. 6. (4) The destruction of their enemies. (5) The feast of Purim, 9:17-32. (6) Truth about God seen in this book. (7) Why not name the book Mordecai or Vashti-are they not as heroic as Esther? (8) The race devotion of the Jews, then and now. (9) Persian life as seen in the book.

12
JOB.

Name. Job, from its chief character, or hero, and mean "Persecuted."

Date. Neither the date nor the author can be determined with certainty. I incline to the theory of the Job authorship.

Connection with Other Books. It stands alone, being one of the so- called wisdom books of the Bible. It nowhere alludes to the Mosaic law or the history of Israel.

Literary Characteristics. Chapters one and two and parts of chapter forty-two are prose. All the rest is poetry. The different speakers may have been real speakers, or characters created by one writer to make the story. There is, however, little doubt that the story is founded on historical facts.

The Problems of the Book. This book raises several great questions, that are common to the race, and directly or indirectly discusses them. Among those questions the following are the most important.

(1) Is there any goodness without reward? "Doth Job serve God or naught"? (2) Why do the righteous suffer and why does sin go unpunished? (3) Does God really care for and protect his people who fear him? (4) Is adversity and affliction a sign that the sufferer is wicked? (5) Is God a God of pity and mercy!

The Argument. The argument proceeds as follows: (1) There is a conference between God and Satan and the consequent affliction of Job. (2) The first cycle of discussion with his three friends in which they charge Job with sin and he denies the charge. (3) The second cycle of discussion. In this Job's friends argue that his claim of innocence is a further evidence of his guilt and impending danger. (4) The third cycle. In this cycle Job's friends argue that his afflictions are just the kind that would come to one who yielded to temptations such as those to which he is subject. In each of the three cycles of discussion with his friends, Eliphaz, Bildad and Zophar, each argues with Job except that Zophar remains silent in the third cycle. They speak in the same order each time. (5) Elihu shows how Job accuses God wrongly while vindicating himself and asserts that suffering instructs us in righteousness and prevents us from sinning. (6) God intervenes and in two addresses instructs Job. In the first address, Job is shown the creative power of the Almighty and his own folly in answering God whom animals by instinct fear. In the second address, Job is shown that one should know how to rule the world and correct its evils before one complains at or accuses God. (7) Job prays and is restored.

Purpose. The purpose of the book, then, is to justify the wisdom and goodness of God in matters of human suffering and especially to show that all suffering is not punitive.

Job's temptation. Job's temptation came by stages and consisted largely in a series of losses as follows: (1) His property, (2) His children, (3) His health, (4) His wife's confidence-she would have him curse God and die. (5) His friends who now think him a sinner, (6) The joy of life-he cursed the day of his birth, (7) His confidence in the goodness of God-he said to God, "Why hast thou set me as a mark for thee?" In his reply to Elihu he doubts the justice if not the very existence of God.

Analysis.

I. Job's Wealth and Affliction. Chs. 1-2.
II. The Discussion of Job and His Three Friends. Cha. 3-31.
1. The first cycle, 3-14.
2. The second cycle, Chs. 15-21.
3. The third cycle, Chs. 22-31.
III. The Speech of Elihu, Chs. 32-37.
IV. The Addresses of God, Chs. 38-41.
1. The first address, 38-39.
2. The second address, 40-41.
V. Job's Restoration, Ch. 42.

For Study and Discussion. (1) The personality and malice of Satan. Point out his false accusations against Job and God, also the signs of his power. (2) Concerning man look for evidence of: (a) The folly of self-righteousness, (b) The vileness of the most perfect man in God's sight, (c) The impossibility of man, by wisdom, apart from grace, finding God. (3) Concerning God, gather evidence of his wisdom, perfection and goodness. (4) Job's disappointment in his friends. (5) Elements of truth and falsehood in the theory of Job's friends. (6) Job's despair of the present, his view of Sheol and his view of the future. Does he believe in a future life or think all ends with the grave? (7) Does the book really explain why the righteous are allowed to suffer? (8) Make a list of the striking passages especially worthy of remembering.

13
PSALMS AND PROVERBS.

Psalms.

Name. The Hebrew word means praises or hymns, while the Greek word means psalms. It may well be called the "Hebrew Prayer and Praise Book." The prevailing note is one of praise, though some are sad and plaintive while others are philosophical.

Authors. Of the 150 Psalms, there is no means of determining the authorship of 50. The authors named for others are David, Asaph, the sons of Korah, Herman, Ethan, Moses and Solomon. Of the 100 whose authorship is indicated, David is credited with 73, and in the New Testament he alone is referred to as the author of them. Lu. 20:42.

Relation to the Other Old Testament Books. It has been called the heart of the entire Bible, but its relation to the Old Testament is especially intimate. All divine manifestations are viewed in regard to their bearing on the inner experience. History is interpreted in the light of a passion for truth and righteousness and as showing forth the nearness of our relation to God.

The Subjects of the Psalms. It is very difficult to make any sort of classification of the Psalms and any classification is open to criticism. For this reason many groupings have been suggested. The following, taken from different sources, may be of help. (1) Hymns of praise, 8, 18, 19, 104, 145, 147, etc. (2) National hymns, 105, 106, 114, etc. (3) Temple hymns or hymns for public worship, 15, 24, 87, etc. (4) Hymns relating to trial and calamity, 9, 22, 55, 56, 109, etc. (5) Messianic Psalms, 2, 16, 40, 72, 110, etc. (6) Hymns of general religious character, 89, 90, 91, 121, 127, etc.

The following classification has been given in the hope of suggesting the most prominent religious characteristics of the Psalms. (1) Those that recognize the one infinite, all-wise and omnipotent God. (2) Those that recognize the universality of his love and providence and goodness. (3) Those showing abhorrence of all idols and the rejection of all subordinate deities. (4) Those giving prophetic glimpses of the Divine Son and of his redeeming work on earth. (5) Those showing the terrible nature of sin, the divine hatred of it and judgment of God upon sinners. (6) Those teaching the doctrines of forgiveness, divine mercy, and the duty of repentance. (7) Those emphasizing the beauty of holiness, the importance of faith and the soul's privilege of communion with God.

Analysis.

1. Davidic Psalms. 1-41. These are not only ascribed to him but reflect much of his life and faith.

2. Historical Psalms. 42-72. These are ascribed to several authors, those of the sons of Korah being prominent and are especially full of historical facts.

3. Liturgical or Ritualistic Psalms. 73-89. Most of them are ascribed to Asaph and, besides being specially prescribed for worship, they are strongly historical.

4. Other Pre-Captivity Psalms. 90-106. Ten are anonymous, one is Moses' (Ps. 90) and the rest David's. They reflect much of the pre-captivity sentiment and history.

5. Psalms of the Captivity and Return. 107-150. Matters pertaining to the captivity and return to Jerusalem.

For Study and Discussion. (1) On what occasion were the following Palms probably composed: (a) Psalm 3 (2 Sam. 15). (b) Psalm 24 (2 Sam. 6:12-17). (c) Psalm 56 (1 Sam. 21:10-15). (d) Psalms 75 and 76 (2 Kings 19:32-37). (e) Psalm 109 (1 Sam. 22:9-23). (f) Psalm 74 (2 Kings 25:2-18). (g) Psalm 60 (1 Chron. 18:11-13). (2) What is the subject of Psalms 23, 84, 103,133 and 137? (3) What doctrine of the divine character is taught in each of the following Psalms; 8, 19, 33, 46, 93, 115 and 139?

Proverbs.

Practical Value of the Book of Proverbs. The proverbs emphasize the external religious life. They teach how to practice religion and overcome the daily temptations. They express a belief in God and his rule over the universe and, therefore, seek to make his religion the controlling motive in life and conduct. They breathe a profound religious spirit and a lofty religious conception, but put most stress upon the doing of religion in all the relations of life. Davison says: "For the writers of Proverbs religion means good sense, religion means mastery of affairs, religion means strength and manliness and success, religion means a well furnished intellect employing the best means to accomplish the highest ends." This statement is correct as far as the side of duty emphasized is concerned.

Nature of Proverbs. (1) There is a voice of wisdom which speaks words of wisdom, understanding, knowledge, prudence, subtility, instruction, discretion and the fear of Jehovah, and furnishes us with good advice for every condition of life. (2) There is a voice of folly, which speaks words of folly, simplicity, stupidity, ignorance, brutishness and villainy, and lifts her voice wherever wisdom speaks. (3) Wisdom is contrasted with folly, which often issues in simplicity and scorning. (4) Wisdom is personified, as if it were God speaking about the practical, moral, intellectual and religious duties of men. (5) Christ finds Himself in the book, Lu. 24:27, and if Christ be substituted for wisdom, where it is found, a new and wonderful power will be seen in the book.

Scheme of the Considerations Found in Proverbs. The first sphere-the home, father and children, 1:8-9 and Chs. 2-7. Key-word here is "my son." The second sphere-friendship; companions is the important word. 1:10-19. The third sphere-the world beyond.

Analysis.

I. Praise of Wisdom. Chs. 1-9. This is shown by contrast with folly.

1. The design and some fundamental maxims, 1:1-19.

2. Wisdom's warnings, 1:20 end.

3. Wisdom will reveal God and righteousness and save one from wicked men and strange women, Ch. 2.

4. Description of the life of wisdom, Ch. 3.

5. Wisdom the best way, Ch. 4.

6. The strange woman, Ch. 5.

7. Against various evils, Ch. 6.

8. Wisdom's warnings against the seductions of an adulterous, Ch. 7.

9. Wisdom makes an appeal, Ch. 8.

10. Wisdom gives her invitations, Ch. 9.

II. Practical Proverbs of Solomon. 10:1-22:16. These are separate and cannot be classified.

III. Words of the Wise. 22:17-24 end. Sometimes called commendations of justice. There are several authors, but no common topic.

IV. Proverbs of Solomon, copied by the scribes of Hezekiah, Chs. 25- 29.

V. Words of Agur. Ch. 30. From one who has tried "to find out God unto perfection and found the task above him."

VI. Words of Lemuel, Ch. 31.

1. The duty of Kings, 1-9.

2. The praise of a virtuous woman or good wife, 10-31.

For Study and Discussion. (1) Collect passages that tell of the rewards of virtue and piety. (2) Cite passages that show the evils of: sloth or indolence, of wine-drinking and drunkenness, of tale-bearing, of family contentions. (3) Make a list of the chief thoughts of the book concerning God, man, and other great religious teachings of our day. (4) What is said of a man who rules his own spirit, of a good name, of obedience to parents, of fitly spoken words, of a beautiful woman who lacks discretion, of a liberal soul, of a false balance, of a soft answer, of a wise son. Find where the answers are found (5) The Peril of following an unchaste love (woman), chapter 5. (6) Folly of yielding to the wiles of an harlot, chapter 7. (7) The description of a worthy woman, 31:10 end.

14
ECCLESIASTES AND THE SONG OF SOLOMON.

Ecclesiastes.

Name. The Hebrew word means preacher and refers to or signifies one who calls together and addresses assemblies.

The Personal or Human Element. Such expressions as "I perceived," "I said in my heart," "I saw," etc., indicate that it is not the will of God that is developed but a man is telling of his own ventures and utter failure.

The General View or Key-phrase is "under the sun," with the sad refrain, "vanity of vanities, all is vanity", and shows how a man under the best possible conditions sought for joy and peace, trying at its best every human resource. He had the best that could be gotten, from human wisdom, from wealth, from worldly pleasure, from worldly honor, only to find that all was "vanity and vexation of spirit." It is what a man, with the knowledge of a holy God, and that He will bring all into judgment, has learned of the emptiness of things "under the sun" and of the whole duty of man to "fear God and keep his commandments."

Purpose of the Book. The purpose, then, is not to express the doubts or skepticism of the writer, not to record the complaining of a bitter spirit. It is not the story of a pessimist or of an evil man turned moralist. But it is intended to show that, if one should realize all the aims, hopes and aspirations of life, they would not bring satisfaction to the heart. His experience is used to show the result of successful worldliness and self-gratification in contrast with the outcome of the higher wisdom of the Godly life. We are shown that man was not made for this world alone and not for selfish achievement or gratification, but to fulfill some great plan of God for him which he will accomplish through obedience and Divine service.

The Date and Authorship. The opening verse and certain other passages such as some of the conditions as well as the characters of the persons represented in the book give the impression that Solomon wrote it, but there are other evidences that point to some other author. Neither the author nor the date of writing has been definitely determined.

Analysis.

I. The Vanities of Life. Chs. 1-4. seen in both experience and observation.
 1. The Vanity of what he has experienced, 1-2.
 2. The Vanity of what he has observed, 3-4.
 II. Practical Wisdom, Chs. 5-7.
 1. Some prudential maxims, Chs. 5.
 2. Some Vanities, Ch. 6.
 3. The best way to get along in life, Ch. 7.

III. Rules for a Happy Life, Chs. 8-11.

IV. Conclusion of the Whole Matter, Ch. 13.

For Study and Discussion. (1) Make a list of all the different things enumerated as a failure or vanity. (2) Make a list of the different things coming to us as God's gift of providence. (3) Make a list of prudential maxims or rules which teach how to live rightly and to lift us above the tribulations and defeat of life. (4) Does the author think seeking pleasure is the real business of life? (5) Does he deny the value of altruistic service? (6) Does he believe in the future life and in future rewards?

Song of Solomon.

Name. Song of Songs which is Solomon's. It is also called Canticles, meaning Song of Songs and is so-called, perhaps, because of its very great beauty.

The Subject. The subject is faithful love, seen in a woman who though subjected to the temptations of an oriental court, remains faithful to her old lover. She, a country girl of the north, attracts the attention of the king who brings her to Jerusalem and offers her every inducement to become the wife of the king. But upon final refusal she is allowed to return home to her lover, a country shepherd lad.

Meaning of the Story. (1) To the Jews of that time it was a call to purity of life, for a return to those relations which God had ordained between man and woman. It was a protest against polygamy which had become almost universal. Indeed, they regarded it as setting forth the whole history of Israel. (2) To the Christian it sets forth in allegory, Christ and his church as Bridegroom and Bride and the fullness of love which unites the believer and his Savior. (3) To all the world there is shown the purity and constancy of a woman's love and devotion to her ideals. It furnishes ideal which, if properly held up, would cast out of human society all those monstrous practices that come from unworthy ideals.

The Style. It is part dialogue and part monologue. Their love on both sides is expressed in that sensuous way common among the oriental peoples. Many of the allusions give rise to the belief that it was written to celebrate the nuptials of Solomon and the daughter of Pharaoh.

Analysis of Song of Solomon..

I. The King's first attempt to win the Virgin's love, 1:1-2:7.

1. She converses with the ladies of the court, 1:1-8.

2. The King's first attempt fails to win her, 1:9-2:7.

II. The King's second effort to win her love, 2:8-5:8.

1. The virgin recalls her former happiness when with her lover at home, 2:8-17.

2. In a dream she goes in search of him, 3:1-5.

3. The King shows her his glory and greatness, 3:6-11.

4. She again rejects his love in spite of his praise of her beauty, 4:1-7.

5. She longs for her absent lover, 4:8-5:1.

6. She dreams of seeking in vain for him, 5:2-8.

III. The King's third attempt to win her, 5:9-8:4.

1. The ladies of the court cannot understand her faithfulness to her old lover, 5:9-6:3.

2. The King's third effort to win her is met with

the declaration of her purpose to remain true to her absent lover, 6:4-8:4.

VI. The Triumph of the Maiden, 8:5-14.

She returns to her home among the hills of the north and is reunited with her shepherd lover.

For Study and Discussion. (1) Make a list of the passages by which the woman's beauty is described. (2) Passages that suggest the relation of the saved soul to Christ. (3) Passages that suggest the glory of the church. (4) Some of the passages by which the love of the woman and of the king is expressed. (5) The basis of human love. 2:2-3. (6) The strength of human lover, 8:6-7. (7) The interpretation of human love in terms of divine love.

15
ISAIAH.

Prophet. In the study of the messages of the prophets we should understand that the meaning of the term prophets may be: (1) A person employed in the public utterance of religious discourse, very much as the preacher of today. This was the most common function of the prophet. Some were reformers while others were evangelists or revivalists. (2) One who performed the function of the scribes and wrote the history and biography and annals of their nations. In this capacity they compiled or wrote large portions of the books of the Old Testament. (3) One who was able to discern the future and foretell events which would transpire afterward.

The Prophetical Books. All take their name from the Prophets whose messages they bear. They are written largely in the poetic style and are usually divided into two divisions. (1) The major prophets which include Isaiah. Jeremiah, Lamentations, Ezekiel and Daniel. (2) The minor prophets, including the other twelve. This division is based on the bulk of material in the books and is unscientific and misleading, since it suggests that some are more important than others. They are more appropriately divided according to their place in the prophetic order or the period of Israel's history when they prophesied, somewhat as follows: 1. *The Pre-exilic prophets*, or those who prophesied before the exile. These are, (1) Jonah, Amos and Hosea, prophets of Israel. (2) Obadiah, Joel, Isaiah, Micah, Nahum, Habakkuk, Zephaniah, and Jeremiah, prophets of Judah. 2. *The exilic prophets*, Ezekiel and Daniel. 3. *The Post-exilic prophets*, prophets who prophesied after the captivity. All are of Judah and are Haggai, Zechariah and Malachi.

Jeremiah's ministry perhaps extended into the period of the captivity. There is great uncertainty about the chronology of Obadiah, Joel and Jonah. There is differences of opinion as to whether certain of the prophets belong to Judah or Israel. Micah is an example. The teacher will be able to give reasons for this difference.

The Study of the Prophets. The student should hold in mind that the prophet deals primarily with the moral and religious conditions of his own people at the time of his ministry. His denunciations, warnings and exhortations are, therefore, not abstract principles, but are local and for Israel. The prophet was then first of all a Jewish patriot and revivalist filled with the Holy Ghost and with zeal for Israel.

The predictive elements of the prophetic books must be interpreted in the light, (1) of a nearby or local fulfillment, such as of the dispersion and restoration, and (2) of a far off and greater fulfillment of which the first is only a forerunner, such as the advent of the Messiah and his glorious reign over the whole earth. The interpretation of prophecy should generally be in the literal, natural and unforced meaning of the words. The following passages will show how prophecy, already fulfilled, has been fulfilled literally and not allegorically. Gen. 15:13-16; 16:11-12; Dt. 28:62-67; Ps. 22:1, 7, 8, 15-18; Is. 7:14; 53:2-9; Hos. 3:4; Joel 2:28-29: Mic. 5:2; Acts 2:16-18; Matt. 21:4-5; Lu. 1:20, 31; Acts 1:5; Matt. 2:4-6; Lu. 21:16.17, 24; Acts 21:10-11.

In a given book of prophecy, the book should be read carefully and all the different subjects treated, noted. This should be followed by a careful study to find what is said about the several topics already found. To illustrate, the prophet may mention himself, Jerusalem, Israel, Judah, Babylon or Egypt, etc. One should learn what is said of each. This will make necessary the student's learning all he can of the history of the different subjects mentioned that he may understand the prophecy about it.

The Prophet Isaiah. Several things are known of him. (1) He was called to his work the last year of the reign of Uzziah. (2) He lived at Jerusalem during the reigns of Uzziah, Jotham, Ahaz and Hezekiah, and most of his life seems to have been spent as a sort of court preacher or chaplain to the king. (3) He is the most renowned of all the Old Testament prophets, his visions not being restricted to his own country and times. He spoke for all nations and for all times, being restricted to his own country and times. "He was a man of powerful intellect, great integrity and remarkable force of character." (4) He is quoted more in the New Testament than any of the other prophets and, because of the relation of his teaching to New Testament times and teachings, his prophesies have been called the "Bridge between the old and new covenants." (5) He married and had two sons.

The Nature of His Teachings. In his inaugural vision recorded in the sixth chapter Isaiah has impressed upon him some truths that shaped his whole career. He saw: (1) The holiness and majesty of God; (2) The corruption of those about him; (3) The certainty of awful judgment upon the wicked; (4) The blessing of those whose lives are approved of God; and (5) The salvation of a remnant that was to be the seed of a new Israel. With these truths burning in his soul he pressed the battle of righteousness into every sphere of life. He strove to regenerate the entire national life. He tried to make not only religious worship, but commerce and politics so pure that it could all become a service acceptable to God. He, therefore, became a religious teacher, preacher, social reformer, statesman and seer.

Conditions of Israel (The Northern Kingdom). Isaiah began to prophecy when it was outwardly rich and prosperous under the rule of Jereboam II. Inwardly it was very corrupt. It soon went to pieces, however (621 B. C.), being conquered and carried into captivity by the Assyrians.

Conditions of Judah (The Southern Kingdom). During the reigns of Ahaz, Jotham and Uzziah, oppression, wickedness and idolatry existed everywhere. Ahaz made an alliance with Assyria, which finally brought destruction to Israel, but Hezekiah listened to Isaiah and made reforms, and God destroyed the Assyrian army before Jerusalem was destroyed.

Nature of the Contents of the Book. The contents of the Book have been said to include: (1) Warnings and threats against his own people because of their sins. (2) Sketches of the history of his times. (3) Prophesies of the return of Israel from captivity. (4) Prophesies concerning the coming of the Messiah. (S)

Predictions of the judgment of God on other nations. (6) Discourses that urge upon Israel moral and religious reformation. (7) Visions of the future glory and prosperity of the church. (8) Expressions of thanksgiving and praise.

The Center of Interest. The prophet deals primarily with the nation and not with the individual. He speaks primarily of the present and not of the future. These two facts must be kept constantly in mind as we read and interpret the book.

Analysis.

I. Discourses Concerning Judah and Israel, Chs. 1-12.
 1. Some promises and rebukes, Chs. 1-6.
 2. The book of Immanuel, Chs. 7-12.
II. Prophesies against Foreign Nations, Chs. 13-23. III. The Judgment of the World and the Triumph of God's People, Chs. 24-27.
 1. The judgments. Ch. 24.
 2. The triumph. Chs. 25-27.
IV. Judah's Relation to Egypt and Assyria, Chs. 38-32.
V. The Great Deliverance of Jerusalem, Chs. 33-39.
VI. The Book of Consolation, Chs. 40-66.
 1. God's preparation for certain deliverance, Chs. 40-48.
 2. Jehovah's servant, the Messiah, will bring this deliverance. Chs. 49-57.
 3. The restoration of Zion and the Messianic Kingdom, with promises and warnings for the future. Chs. 58-66.

For Study and Discussion. (1) The sins of Israel

and Judah that he rebukes. (2) Other nations against which he makes predictions and what he said of each. (3) Isaiah's call. Ch. 6. (4) Isaiah's errand to Ahaz, Ch. 7. (5) The way in which Isaiah rests the sole deity of Jehovah upon his ability to predict a future, Ch. 41. Give other illustrations. (6) The express predictions of the Messiah as we find them fulfilled in Jesus. (7) Point out the passages portraying the future glory of the church and the spiritual prosperity of the race. (8) Passages predicting the restoration of the Jews from captivity. (9) Some predictions already fulfilled: (a) God's judgments on the kings of Israel and the nation of Israel, Ch. 7. (b) The overthrow of Sennacherib, Chs. 13 and 37. (c) Disasters which should overtake Babylon, Damascus, Egypt, Moab and Idumea, Chs. 13, 15, 18, 19 and 34. (d) Vivid and marvelous descriptions of the final fate of Babylon and Idumea, 13:19-22; 34:10-17. (10) The theology of Isaiah or his views on such subjects as the moral condition of man, the need of a redeemer, the consequences of redemption, Divine Providence, the majesty and holiness of God, the future life, etc.

16
JEREMIAH AND LAMENTATIONS.

The Author. (1) His name means "Exalted of Jehovah," and he is ranked second among the great Old Testament writers. (2) He lived the last of the sixth and the first of the fifth centuries before Christ. His ministry began in 626 B. C., the thirteenth year of Josiah (1:2), and lasted about forty years. He probably died in Babylon during the early years of the captivity. (3) He was of a sensitive nature, mild, timid, and inclined to melancholy. He was devoutly religious and naturally shrank from giving pain to others. (4) He was uncommonly bold and courageous in declaring the message of God, it was unpopular and subjected him to hatred and even to suffering wrong. He was unsparing in the denunciations and rebukes administered to his nation, not even sparing the prince. (5) He is called the weeping prophet. He was distressed both by the disobedience and apostasy of Israel and by the evil which he foresaw. Being very devoutly religious, he was pained by the impiety of his time.

Condition of the Nations. (1) Israel, the northern kingdom, had been carried into captivity and Judah stood alone against her enemies. (2) Judah had fallen into a bad state, but Josiah, who reigned when Jeremiah began his ministry, attempted to bring about reforms and restore the old order. After his death, however, wickedness grew more and more until, in the later part of the life of Jeremiah, Jerusalem and the temple were destroyed by Nebuchadnezzar and Judah was led away in captivity. (3) The world powers of the time of Jeremiah's birth were Assyria and Egypt. They were contending for supremacy. But Jeremiah lived to see both of them subdued and Babylon mistress of the world. He foresaw also how Babylon would fall and how a kingdom greater than all would rise wherein there would be righteousness and peace.

Jeremiah.

The book of Jeremiah is composed principally of sketches of biography, history and prophecy, but the events and chapters are not in chronological order. It closes the period of the monarchy and marks the destruction of the holy city and of the sanctuary and tells of the death agony of the nation of Israel, God's chosen people. But he saw far beyond the judgments of the near future to a brighter day when the eternal purpose of divine grace would be realized. The book, therefore, emphasizes the future glory of the kingdom of God which must endure though Israel does perish. He made two special contributions to the truth as understood in his time. (1) The spirituality of religion. He saw the coming overthrow of their national and formal religion and realized that, to survive that crisis, religion must not be national, but individual and spiritual. (2) Personal responsibility (31:29-30). If religion was to be a spiritual condition of the individual, the doctrine of personal responsibility was a logical necessity. These two teachings constitute a great step forward.

Analysis.

I. The Prophet's Call and Assurance, Ch. 1.
II. Judah Called to Repentance, Chs. 2-22.
1. Her sins set forth, Chs. 2-6
2. The call to repentance, Chs. 7-10.
3. The appeal to the covenant, Chs. 11-13.
4. Rejection and captivity foretold, Chs. 14-22.
III. The Book of Consolation, Chs. 23-33.
1. The restoration of the remnant, Chs. 22-29.
2. The complete restoration, Chs. 30-33.
IV. The Doom of Jerusalem Due to the People's Wickedness, Chs. 34-36.
V. The History of Jeremiah and His Times, Chs. 37-45.
VI. Prophecies Against Foreign Nations, Chs, 46-51.
VII. Historical Appendix, Ch. 52.

Lamentations.

The name means elegies or mournful or plaintive poems. It was formerly a part of Jeremiah and represents the sorrows of Jeremiah when the calamities which he had predicted befell his people, who had often despised and rejected him for his messages. He chose to live with them in their suffering and out of his weeping pointed them to a star of hope. There are five independent poems in as many chapters. Chapters 1, 2, 4 and 5 have each 22 verses or just the number of the Hebrew alphabet. Chapter 3 has 66 verses or just three times the number of the alphabet. The first four chapters are acrostic, that is each verse begins with a letter of the Hebrew alphabet. In chapter three, each letter is used in order and is three times repeated as the initial letter of three successive lines.

Analysis.

I. The Misery of Jerusalem, Ch. 1.
II. The Cause of the People's Suffering, Ch. 2.
III. The Basis of Hope, Ch. 3.
IV. The Past and Present of Israel, Ch. 4.
V. The Final Appeal for Restoration, Ch. 5.

For Study and Discussion. (1) Make a list of the evils predicted against the people because of their sins. (Example 19:7-9). (2) Make a list of the different sins and vices of which Jeremiah accuses Israel. (Example 2:12; :3:20, etc.) (3) Point out all the prophesies of Divine judgment against other nations and analyze the punishment foretold. (Example 5:18-25). (4) Study the case of fidelity to parents given in Ch. 35. (5) Collect all passages in both books which tell of the Messiah and of Messianic times and make a study of each (as 23:5-6). (6) Select a few of the striking passages of Lamentations and show how they apply to the facts of history. (6) The sign and type of the destruction of the land. Chs. 13-14. (8) The potter an illustration of God's power over nations, Chs. 18-19. (9) The illustration of the return, seen in the figs, Ch.

24. (10) Jeremiah's letter to the captive, Ch. 29. (11) Jeremiah's love for Judah-it saw their faults, rebuked them for their sins, but did not desert them when they were in suffering, because they despised his advice.

17
EZEKIEL AND DANIEL.

Ezekiel.

The Prophet. His name means "God will strengthen". He was a priest and was carried into captivity by Nebuchadnezzar. B. C. 597. He had a home on the river Chebar where the Elders of Judah were accustomed to meet. His wife died in the ninth year of his captivity. He was a man of very powerful intellect and apparently from the better classes of those carried into captivity. He is less attractive than Isaiah and less constant in the flow of his thought than Jeremiah. He is not so timid or sensitive as Jeremiah but has all his horror for sin and all of his grief, occasioned by the wickedness of his people and the suffering which they endured. In his boldness of utterance he was not surpassed by his predecessors.

Nature of the Prophecy. The nature of the prophecy or the methods by which he exercised or manifests his prophetic gift differs from that of the other prophets. He does not so much predict as see visions of them. Allegories, parables, similitudes and visions abound, some of them symbolic of the future and others of existing facts and conditions. The prophet remains on the banks of Chebar and in spirit is transported to Jerusalem and the temple. Much of the book is in character similar to Revelation and while the general subjects are very plain, much of the meaning of the symbols is obscure. There are, however, powerful addresses and eloquent predictions of Divine judgments on the nations. It was probably due to the services of Ezekiel that Israel's religion was preserved during the exile.

The Main Aspects of his Teaching. (1) Denunciation of Judah's sins and the downfall of Jerusalem, Chs. 1-24. (2) Judgments upon foreign nations, Chs. 25-32. (3) Repentance as a condition of salvation, 18:30-32. (4) The glorious restoration of Israel, li:16ff; 16:60ff; 27:22-24; 20:40ff; Chs. 33-48. (5) The freedom and responsibility of the individual soul before God. 18:20-32. (6) The necessity of a new heart and a new spirit, 11:19: 18:31; 36:26.

Condition of the Jews. (1) *Political and social condition*. They are captives living in Babylon but are treated as colonists and not as slaves. They increased in numbers and accumulated great wealth and some of them rose to the highest offices. (2) *The religious condition or outlook*. They had religious freedom and in this period they forever gave up their idolatry. They sought out the books of the law, revised the cannon, wrote some new books and perhaps inaugurated the synagogue worship which became so powerful afterward.

Analysis.

I. Ezekiel's Call, Chs. 1-3.
1. Preliminary vision, Ch. 1.
2. The call, Chs. 2-3.
II. The Destruction of Jerusalem, Chs. 4-24.
1. The siege and certain judgment of the city, Chs. 4-7.
2. The condition of the city and the sins of the people, Chs. 8-19.
3. Renewed proofs and predictions of the doom of Judah and Jerusalem, Chs. 20-24.
III. Predictions against Foreign Nations and Cities. Chs. 25-32.
IV. Prophecies concerning the Restoration, Chs. 33-48.
1. The restoration of Judah to the promised land, Chs. 33-39.
2. The Messianic times, Chs. 40-48.

For Study and Discussion. (1) The condition, the particular sin and the judgment promised upon each of the nations mentioned-has the prediction been fulfilled? (2) The duties and responsibilities of a preacher as illustrated by Ezekiel's watchman, Ch. 33. (3) The vision of dry bones. Ch 37. (4) Judah and Israel under the figure of an evil woman, Ch. 23. (5) The healing river, 47:1-12. (6) The teachings about the Restoration, in the following passages: 36:8, 9, 29, 30, 34, 35, 25-27; 37:1-14; 24:11-24; 37:22; 26,27; 43:11-12. (7) The symbols and types of the book.

Daniel.

Name. The name is taken from its leading character, Daniel, which means "God is my Judge."

Author. It was very probably Daniel, though some think it may have been one of his companions, and still others think the history may have been gotten together and written about 166 B. C.

The Date. The date then would have been between the captivity, 605 B. C., and the death of Daniel, 533 B. C., perhaps late in his life, or if by some other (which I do not think likely) about 166 B. C.

The Prophet. He was probably born in Jerusalem and was one of the noble young captives first carried into captivity by King Nebuchadnezzar. He was educated by order of the king and soon rose to great favor and was chosen to stand before the king in one of the highest government positions under the Chaldean, Median and Persian dynasties. He lived through the whole period of the captivity and probably died in Babylon. It is said that not one imperfection of his life is recorded. The angel repeatedly calls him "greatly beloved."

World Empires of the Book. (1) *The Babylonian Empire* (625-536 B. C.) with Nebuchadnezzar as the leading king and the one who carried Israel captive. (2) *The Persian Empire* (536-330 B. C.) which became a world power through Cyrus, under whom the Jews returned to Jerusalem. (3) *The Grecian Empire*, which, under the leadership of Alexander the Great, subdued the entire Persian world. (4) *The Roman Empire*, which was anticipated by and grew out of the Syrian Empire.

Purpose of the Book. The purpose of the book seems to be: (1) To magnify Jehovah, who delivers his servants, who is God of all nations, and who will punish idolatry, who is pure, righteous, etc. (2) To encourage his countrymen to resist the forces that threaten the foundation of their faith. This was done by the example of Daniel and his companions whom Jehovah saved. (3) To give a prophecy or vision of all times from the day of Daniel to the Messianic period. (4) To outline the religious philosophy of history which would issue in a great world state, which the Messianic King would rule by principles of justice and right, and which would subdue all kingdoms and have everlasting dominion. The main idea is the ultimate triumph of the kingdom of God. As compared with former prophetic books there are two new teachings. (1) Concerning angels. (2) Concerning a resurrection from the dead.

Analysis.

I. Daniel's History, Chs. 1-6.

1. His youth and education, Ch. 1.

2. Interpretation of Nebuchadnezzar's image dream. Ch. 2.

3. In the fiery furnace. Ch. 3.

4. Interpretation of Nebuchadnezzar's tree dream, Ch. 4.

5. Interpretation of the hand-writing on the wall for Belshazzar, Ch. 5.

6. In the Lion's den, Ch. 6.

II. Daniel's Vision of the Kingdom, Chs. 7-12.

1. The four beasts, Ch. 7.

2. The ram and the he-goat, Ch. 8.

3. The seventy weeks, Ch. 9.

4. The final vision, Chs. 10-12.

For Study and Discussion. (1) Make a list of the various visions of Daniel and become familiar with the contents of each. (2) Make a list of all the passages that refer to the fact of Daniel's praying and point out some of the specific prayers with their answers. (3) Point out the different attempts to overthrow or kill Daniel and tell the cause, by whom he was opposed and how he escaped. (4) Make a list of the different symbols such as the lion and learn the description given of each symbolic animal. (5) Point out the several decrees made by the different kings and learn what led to the decree, how it affected Daniel, how it bore upon the worship of the people of his nation, how it affected the worship of Jehovah, etc. (6) The difficulty and possibility of right living in bad surroundings. (7) The openness of Daniel's conduct. (8) The elements of strength of character displayed by Daniel. (9) The inevitable conflict between good and evil.

18
HOSEA AND JOEL.

Hosea.

The Prophet. He is called the "Prophet of Divine Love." His name, Hosea, means "Deliverance." He was a native and citizen of Israel and followed Amos whom he may have heard in Bethel. He was a contemporary with Isaiah and bore faithful testimony to corrupt Israel in the North while Isaiah prophesied at Jerusalem and was to Israel what Jeremiah became to Judah. He was prepared for his work through the lessons which he learned from the sins of his unfaithful wife. (1) Through the suffering which he endured because of her sins, he understood how God was grieved at the wickedness of Israel and how her sins were not only against God's law but an insult to divine love. (2) In love and at great cost he restored his wayward wife and in that act saw a hope of the restoration and forgiveness of Israel. His ministry extended over more than sixty years and was perhaps the longest of any on record. It continued 786-726 B.

C., covering the last few years of the reign of Jereboam II, to which Chs. 1-3 belong and the period of anarchy following.

The Style and Method. His style is "abrupt, uneven, inelegant," but also poetical, figurative and abounding in metaphors. His writings must be interpreted with great care to get what is meant by his symbolic speech. He reminds one of modern reformers and revivalists. Through all the anger which the book reveals we see also the surpassing beauty of reconciling love. One sees everywhere that the supreme goal to which Hosea moves is the re-establishment of Israel's fellowship of life and love with Jehovah.

Conditions of Israel. *Outwardly* there was prosperity. Syria and Moab had been conquered; commerce had greatly increased; the borders of the land had been extended and the temple offerings were ample. *Inwardly* there was decay. Gross immoralities were being introduced; worship was being polluted and the masses of the people crushed, while the Assyrian Empire was advancing and ready to crush Israel, whom, because of her sins, God had abandoned to her fate.

They countenanced oppression, murder, lying, stealing, swearing, etc. They had forgotten the law and their covenant to keep it and had substituted the worship of Baal for that of Jehovah, thereby becoming idolaters. They no longer looked to God in their distress but turned to Egypt and Assyria for help, and thereby put security and prosperity on a basis of human strength and wisdom instead of resting them upon a hope of divine favor.

Analysis.

I. Israel's Sin. illustrated by the tragedy of Hosea's unfortunate marriage, Chs. 1-3.

1. His evil wife and their children, Ch. 1.
2. Israel's unfaithfulness and return to God seen in the evil women, Ch. 2.
3. God's love restores Israel as Hosea does his wife, Ch. 3.

II. The Prophetic Discourses, Chs. 4-14.

1. Israel's sin, Chs. 4-8.
2. Israel's coming punishment, Chs. 9-11.
3. Israel's repentance and restoration, Chs. 12-14.

For Study and Discussion. (1) Make a list of all the exhortations to penitence and reformation and study them. (2) Point out the different utterances of judgment upon the people. (3) Make a list of all the different sins condemned. (4) Make a list of the expressions of tender love for the wayward and backsliding one. (5) Make a list of all passages indicating grief and suffering because of the sin and danger of the one loved. (6) Political and religious apostacy. (7) Sin as infidelity to love-as spiritual adultery. (8) The invitations of the book.

Joel.

The Prophet. His name means "Jehovah is God," but his birth-place and conditions of life are unknown. He very probably prophesied in Judah (2:15-17) and the time of his ministry is commonly thought to have been during the reign of Joash, king of Israel, and Amaziah, king of Judah. It seems certain his is one of the earliest (some think the very earliest) of the prophetic books, and his references to the temple and its services have caused some to conclude he was a priest.

The Prophecy. (1) The occasion of the prophecy was four successive plagues of insects, particularly the locusts (2:25) and a drouth (2:23) which had been unprecedented. These calamities the prophet declares are the results of their sins and should call them to repentance, that God may bless instead of curse their land. (2) The people repent and the calamity is removed. This is used by the prophet to foreshadow the coming destruction and restoration of Israel and this restoration is also doubtless used to prefigure Christian church and its triumph on earth. (3) The great subject is the terrible judgments of God which were to come upon the people because of their sins. (4) His great distinctive prophecy is 2;28-32 which was fulfilled on the day of pentecost, Acts 2:16-21. (B) In it all, he is emphasizing the rewards of the righteous and certain punishment of the wicked and thus he appealed to both the hopes and the fears of men. But the relief value of the book is its optimism. There was victory ahead, the righteous would finally triumph and be saved and God's enemies will be destroyed. The conflict of good and evil and of Israel and her enemies will end in entire and glorious triumph for Israel and right.

Analysis.

I. The Call to Repentance, Chs. 1:1-2:17.

1. By the past scourge of locusts and drought, Ch. 1.

2. By the scourge to come, 2:1-17.

II. Israel's Repentance and Jehovah's Promised Blessing, 2:18-3:21.

1. Material blessing, 2:18-27.
2. In the world Judgment, Ch. 3.

For Study and Discussion. (1) Point out the different statements about the drouth and locusts that indicate their severity and ruinous effects. (2) Collect the passages referring to the Messianic age and try to see how or what each foretells of that age. (3) Point out all references to the sins of Israel. (4) Collect evidences of the divine control of the universe as seen in the book.

19
AMOS AND OBADIAH.

Amos.

The Prophet. His name means "Burden," and he is called the prophet of righteousness. His home was at Tokea, a small town of Judea about twelve miles south of Jerusalem, where he acted as herdsman and as dresser of sycamore trees. He was very humble, not being of the prophetic line, nor educated in the schools of the prophets for the prophetic office. God called him to go out from Judah, his native country, as a prophet to Israel, the Northern Kingdom. In obedience to this call he went to Bethel, where the sanctuary was, and delivered his bold prophecy. His bold preaching against the land Of Israel while at Bethel aroused Amaziah the leading idolatrous priest, who complained of him to the king. He was expelled from the kingdom, after he had denounced Amaziah who had perhaps accused him of preaching as a trade, 7:10-14, but we know nothing more of him except what is in this book, which he perhaps wrote after he returned from Tekoa.

The Time of the Prophecy. It was during the reign of Uzziah, king of Judah and of Jereboam II, king of Israel, and was outwardly a very prosperous time in Northern Israel. But social evils were everywhere manifest, especially the sins that grow out of a separation between the rich and poor, 2:6-8, etc. Religion was of a low and formal kind, very much of the heathen worship having been adopted.

The Significance of the Prophecy. One need but read the book of Amos to see that he expects doom to come upon foreign nations, that he foretells the wickedness of the Jews and their coming doom, showing how the nation is to be dissolved and sold into captivity and that he predicts the glory and greatness of the Messianic kingdom. He thinks of Jehovah as the one true God, an all wise, all-powerful, omnipresent, merciful and righteous person whose favor can only be secured by a life of righteousness. He sees that justice between men is the foundation of society, that men are responsible for their acts, that punishment will follow failure to measure up to our responsibility, that worship is an insult to God, unless the worshiper tries to conform to divine demands.

I. The Condemnation of the Nations. Chs. 1-2.

1. Introduction, 1:1-2.

2. Israel's neighbors shall be punished for their sins. 1:3-2:5.

3. Israel's sins shall he punished, 2:6-16.

II. The Condemnation of Israel, Chs. 3-6.

1. For civil iniquities, Ch. 3.

2. For oppression of the poor and for idolatry, Ch. 4.

3. Repeated announcements of judgment with appeals to return and do good, Chs. 5-6.

III. Five Visions Concerning Israel, Chs. 7:1-9:10.

1. The locusts, 7:1-3.

2. The fire, 7:4-6.

3. The plumb line (a testing), 7:7-9, a historical interlude (the conflict with Amaziah), 7:10-17.

4. A basket of summer fruit (iniquity ripe for punishment), Ch. 8.

5. The destruction of the altar (No more services), 9:1-10.

IV. Promised Restoration and Messianic Kingdom, 9;11-15.

For Study mid Discussion, (1) Gather from the book a list of illustrations, sayings, etc., that are taken from the rustic or agricultural usages. (2) Make a list of the different nations against which he prophesies and point out the sin of each and the nature of the punishment threatened. (3) Make a list of the different illustrations used to show the greatness and power of God. (4) The sin of wrong inter-relation of nations. (5) The responsibility of national enlightenment. (6) Repentance as seen in this book. (7) The book's evidence of the luxury of the time.

Obadiah.

The Prophet. His name means "servant of the Lord," but we know nothing of him except what we can gather from his prophecy.

The Time. It was doubtless written after the fall of Jerusalem under Nebuchadnezzar, 587 B. C. and before the destruction of Edom, five years later, which would make the date about 585 B. C. This would make him a contemporary of Jeremiah.

The Occasion of the prophecy is the cruelty of the Edomites in rejoicing over the fall of Judah.

The Jews. It is said to be a favorite book with the Jews because of the vengeance which it pronounces upon Edom, their brother. Its chief importance lies in its predictions of doom upon Edom the descendants of Esau, the twin brother of Jacob and the type of the unchangeable hostility of the flesh to that which is born of the spirit.

The Teachings. (1) Jehovah is especially interested in Israel. (2) He will establish a new kingdom, with Judea and Jerusalem as the center and with holiness as the chief characteristic.

Analysis.

I. Edom's punishment, 1-9.
1. She must fall, 1-4.
2. Her allies will desert her, 5-7.
3. Her wisdom will fail her, 8-9.
II. Edom's sin, 10-14
III. Guilt of the nations, 15-16.
IV. Judah shall be restored,

For Study and Discussion. (1) The sin of pride. (2) The sin of rejoicing in another's misfortune. (3) Punishment according to our sin and of the same kind as was our sin.

20
JONAH AND MICAH.

Jonah.

The Prophet. His name means "done," and he is the son of Amittai. His home was Gath-hepher, a village of Zebulun, and he, therefore, belonged to the ten tribes and not to Judah. He is first mentioned in 2 Kings 14:28, where he prophesied the success of Jeroboam II, in his war with Syria, by which he would restore the territory that other nations had wrested from Israel. He very likely prophesied at an early date, though all attempts to determine the time of his prophecy or the time and place of his death have failed.

The Prophecy. It differs from all the other prophecies in that it is a narrative and more "the history of a prophecy than prophecy itself". All the others are taken up chiefly with prophetic utterances, while this book records the experiences and work of Jonah, but tells us little of his utterances. The story of

Jonah has been compared to those of Elijah and Elisha (1 Kings 17-19, and 2 Kings 4-6).

Although full of the miraculous element, the evident purpose is to teach great moral and spiritual lessons, and it is unfortunate that its supernatural element has made this book the subject of infidel attack. But the facts, though extraordinary, are in no way contradictory or inconsistent. Indeed, Mr. Driver has well said that "no doubt the outlines of the narrative are historical." Christ spoke of Jonah and accredited it by likening his own death for three days to Jonah's three days in the fish's belly.

It is the most "Christian" of all the Old Testament books, its central truth being the universality of the divine plan of redemption. Nowhere else in the Old Testament is such stress laid upon the love of God as embracing in its scope the whole human race.

Analysis.

I. Jonah's First Call and Flight from Duty, Chs. 1-2.
 1. The call, flight and punishment, 1:1-16.
 2. The repentance and rescue, 1:17-2:10 (end).
II. Jonah's Second Call and Preaching at Nineveh, Ch. 3.
 1. His second call. 1-2.
 2. His preaching against Nineveh. 2-4.
 3. Nineveh repents, 5-9.
 4. Nineveh is spared, 10.
III. Jonah's Anger and God's Mercy, Ch. 4.
 1. Jonah's anger, 1-4.
 2. The lessons of the gourd. 5-11.

For Study and Discussion. (1) The different elements of character noticeable in Jonah. (2) The dangers of disobedience, to self and to others. (3) The possibilities of influence for the man commissioned of God. Jonah's influence on the sailors and on Nineveh. (4) God's care for heathen nations (4-11), and its bearing upon the Foreign Mission enterprise. (5) The nature of true repentance and God's forgiveness. (6) The prophet, or preacher-his call, his message and place of service.

Micah.

The Prophet. His name means "who is the Lord?" and he was Moresheth. a small town of Gath. He was a younger contemporary of Isaiah and prophesied to both Israel and Judah during the time of Jotham, Ahaz and Hezekiah, kings of Judah; and of Pekah and Hoshea, the last two kings of Israel. He sympathized deeply with the common people, being moved by the social wrongs of his time (Ch. 2-3), and became the people's advocate and defender as well as their accuser. He clearly sets forth the wickedness of Judah and Israel, their punishment, their restoration and the coming Christ. As compared with Isaiah, he was a simple countryman, born of obscure parentage and recognized as one of the peasant classes, while Isaiah was a city prophet of high social standing and a counselor of kings.

The Great Truths of the Prophecy Are: (1) The destruction of Israel (1:6-7) (2) The desolation of Jerusalem and the temple (3:12 and 7:13). (3) The carrying off of the Jews to Babylon (4:10). (4) The return from captivity with peace and prosperity and with spiritual blessing (4:1-8 and 7:11-17). (5) The ruler in Zion (Messiah) (4:8). (6) Where and when he should be born (5:2). This is his great prophecy and is accepted as final in the announcement to Herod.

I. The Impending Calamity, Ch. 1.

II. The Sins That Have Brought on This Calamity. Chs. 2-3.

1. In their wickedness they refuse to hear the prophets and are led into captivity, 2:1-11.

2. The promised restoration, 2:12-13.

3. The sins of the rich and of those in authority. Ch. 3.

III. The Promised Restoration and Glory, Chs. 4-5.

1. The promised restoration of the city Zion, 4:1-5.

2. The restoration and glory of Israel, 4:6-13 (end).

3. The mighty messianic king to be given, Ch. 5.

IV. God's Controversy With Israel. Chs. 6-7.

1. God's charge and threat against them, Ch. 6.

2. In lamentation and patience the righteous must wait for a better time, 7:1-13.

3. God will have mercy and restore, 7:14-20.

For Study and discussion. (1) The several accusations and threatenings against Israel and Judah. (2) The different things mentioned to describe the coming prosperity of Israel and of the Messianic period. (3) The false authority of civil rulers, of moral leaders, of spiritual teachers.

21
NAHUM AND HABAKKUK.

Nahum.

The Prophet. His name means "consolation", and he was a native of Elkosh, a small town of Galilee. We do not know where he uttered his prophecy, whether from Philistia or at Nineveh. It is thought that he escaped into Judah when the Captivity of the Ten Tribe began and that he was at Jerusalem at the time of the Assyrian invasion.

The Prophecy. The date, if the above conclusions are to be relied upon, would be in the reign of Hezekiah, King of Judah, which would be between 720 and 698 B. C. Others put it between the destruction of Thebes, 664 B. C. and the fall of Nineveh, 607 B. C. claiming that it might be either during the reign of Josiah, 640-625 B. C. or in the reign of Manasseh, 660 B. C. The theme of the book is the approaching fall of Nineveh, the capital of Assyria, which held sway for centuries and has been regarded as the most brutal of the ancient heathen nations.

The purpose, in keeping with the name of the author, was to comfort his people, so long harassed by Assyria, which was soon to fall and trouble them no more. The style is bold and fervid and eloquent and differs from all the prophetic books so far studied in that it is silent concerning the sins of Judah. It is a sort of outburst of exultation over the distress of a cruel foe, a shout of triumph over the downfall of an enemy that has prevented the exaltation of the people of Jehovah.

Analysis.

I. The Doom of NinevehPronounced, Ch. 1.
II. the Siege and Fall of Nineveh, Ch. 2.
III. The Sins Which Will Cause Nineveh's Ruin, Ch. 3.

For Study and Discussion. (1) The striking features of the Divine character seen in the book. How many in 1:2-3? (2) The description of Nineveh-not only her wickedness, but her energy and enterprise. (3) The doom predicted for Nineveh-analyze the predictions to the different things to which she is doomed. (4) Pride as a God-ward sin and its punishment. (5) Cruelty, The man-ward sin and its punishment.

Habakkuk.

The Prophet. His name means "embracing," and he very likely was a contemporary of Jeremiah and prophesied between 608 B. C. and 638 B. C. at a time of political and moral crisis. He may have been a Levite connected with the Temple music.

The Prophecy. As Nahum prophesied the fall of

Assyria for its oppression of Israel, Habakkuk tells of God's judgments upon the Chaldeans because of their oppression. The style is poetical and displays a very fine imagery. (1) There is a dialogue between the prophet and the Divine ruler. (2) There is a prayer or psalm which is said not to be excelled in any language in the grandeur of its poetical conceptions and sublimity of expression.

Its purpose grew out of the fact that they were no better off under the rule of Babylon (Chaldeans) which had overthrown Assyria than they were formerly while Assyria ruled over them. It intended to answer the questions: (1) How could God use such a wicked instrument as the Chaldeans (Barbarians) to execute his purposes? (2) Could the Divine purpose be justified in such events? God's righteousness needed vindicating to the people. (3) Why does wickedness seem to triumph while the righteous suffer? This is the question of Job, applied to the nation.

Analysis.

I. The Problem of the Apparent Triumph of Sin, Ch. 1.

1. Why does sin go unpunished? 1-4.
2. God says he has used the Chaldeans to punish sin, 5-11.
3. Are they confined to evil forever, 12-17.

II. The Impending Punishment of the Chaldeans, Oh. 2.

1. Waiting for the vision, 1-3.
2. Vision of five destructive woes, 4-20.

III. An Age of Confidence in God, Ch.3.

1. Prayer of the disquieted prophet, 1-2.

2. Past history has shown that God will finally destroy Israel's enemies, 3-15.

3. The prophet must joyously trust God and wait when in perplexity, 16-19.

For Study and Discussion. (1) The morals of the people. (2) The character and deeds of the Chaldeans. (3) The Universal supremacy of Jehovah. (4) The proper attitude amid perplexing problem. (5) Faith and faithfulness as a guarantee of supremacy and life.

22
ZEPHANIAH AND HAGGAI.

Zephaniah.

The Prophet. He is a son of Cushi, a descendant of Hezekiah, and prophesied about 630 B. C. during the reign of Josiah. His prophesies may have aided in inaugurating and in carrying to success the reforms of Josiah. His name means "hid of the Lord" in he is supposed to have been a contemporary of Habakkuk.

The Prophecy. The prophecy seems to be based upon the ravages of the Scythians, whom the nations had come to fear and whom Egypt had bribed, and looks to the judgment of the Lord which cannot be escaped. Its theme, therefore, is "The great day of the Lord" in which suffering will come upon all nations with which the prophet is familiar, Jerusalem and all Judea included. Converts would be won from all parts of the world and these could worship Jehovah, "every one from his place".

Analysis.

I. The Coming Day of Wrath. Ch. 1.
1. The destruction of all things, 1-6.
2. The severe punishment of Judah, 7-18.
II. Judgment Upon Evil Nations, 2:1-3:7.
1. A plea for repentance, 2:1-3.
2. The doom that shall engulf the nations, 2:4-end.
3. Judah's obstinacy in sin, 3:1-7.
III. Promised Blessing for the Faithful Remnant, 3:8-20.
1. Because of Israel's sin, the nation will be cleansed by punishment and converted to God, 3:3-10.
2. Purified Israel shall be honored in all the earth, 3:11-20.

For Study and Discussion, (1) Gather a list of all that is said to induce repentance or the turning away from evil. (2) What sins are condemned in Judah and other nations. Make a list of them. (3) Name the special classes that are condemned, as princes. (4) Make a list of the blessings promised for the coming Messianic days. (5) The purpose of the Lord's judgments.

Haggai.

The Prophet. Haggai was born in Babylon and was one of those who returned from captivity, under Zerrubbabel, according to the decree of Cyrus. He prophesied during the period of the rebuilding of the temple, as recorded in Ezra and he was the first prophet called to prophesy after the Jews returned from the captivity in Babylon. He began his teaching sixteen years after the return of the first band to Jerusalem.

The Conditions Out of Which Grew the Prophecy. Under the decree of Cyrus. King of Persia, Zerrubbabel, a descendant of King David, had led a company of captives back to Jerusalem. They had set up the altar and work on the temple had been begun, but the work had been interrupted by the hostile Samaritans and others and for about fourteen years almost nothing had been done. These years of inactivity had dulled their zeal and they were rapidly becoming reconciled to the situation and by reason of their weakness, compared with the great task before them, they were beginning to despair of seeing their people and beloved city and Temple restored to that glory pictured by former prophets.

The Prophecy. Its purpose was to restore the hope of the people and to give them zeal for the cause of God. This was accomplished by means of four distinct visions, each of which shows their folly in not completing the work, mid promises divine blessing. They hear God say, "I am with you, and will bless you." The result is seen in that they are enabled, in spite of opposition, to finish and dedicate it in about four years.

Analysis.

I. The Appeal to Rebuild the Temple, Ch. 1.
1. The appeal, 1:11.
2. The preparations to build, 12-15.
II. The New Temple, 2:1-19.
1. The superior glories of it, 2:1-9.
2. The blessing of its holy service, 2:10-19.
III. The Messianic Kingdom, 2:10-23.

For Study and Discussion, (1) The rebukes uttered by the prophet. (2) The encouragements he offers. (3) The historical confirmation of the facts of this book found in Ezra. (4) False content and discontent. (5) Basing conclusions upon the comparative strength of the friends and enemies of a proposition, while leaving God out of the count.

23
ZECHARIAH AND MALACHI.

Zechariah.

The Prophet. His name means "Remembered of the Lord" and like Haggai he appears to have been among the captives who returned from Babylon with Zerubbabel. He was a co-laborer with Haggai, beginning his work two mouths later and continuing into the second year following him. The conditions of the times were the same as those described in Haggai.

The Prophecy. The purpose is the same as that of Haggai. The time of the first eight chapters is that of the rebuilding of the temple while the remaining chapters, 9-14, are thought to have been written thirty years later. It is distinguished for: (1) The symbolic character of its visions. (2) The richness of his Messianic predictions found in the second part. (3) The large place given to angelic mediation in the intercourse with Jehovah.

The Contents. The contents have been said to contain: (1) Encouragements to lead the people to repent and reform; (2) Discussions about keeping up the days of fasting and humiliation observed during the captivity; (3) Reflections of a moral and spiritual nature; (4) Denunciations against some contemporary nations; (5) Promises of the prosperity of God's people; (6) Various predictions concerning Christ and his kingdom.

Analysis.

I. Eight Visions Encouraging the Rebuilding of the Temple, Chs. 1-6. Introduction, 1:1-6.
   1. The horseman among the myrtle trees, 1:7-17.
   2. The four horns and four carpenters, 1:18-21.
   3. The man with the measuring line, Ch. 2.
   4. Joshua, the High Priest, and Satan, Ch. 3.
   5. The Golden Candlestick, Ch. 4.
   6. The Flying Roll 5:1-4.
   7. The woman and ephah, 5:5-11 end.
   8. The four war chariots, 6:1-8.
   Appendix: Joshua crowned as a type of Christ, 6:9-15.
II. Requirement of the Law and the Restoration and Enlargement of Israel, Chs. 7-8.
   1. Obedience better than fasting. 7:1-7.
   2. Disobedience the source of all their past misery, 7:8-14 end.
   3. The restoration and enlargement which prefigure Christ "The Jew," Ch.8.
III. Visions of the Messianic Kingdom. Chs. 9-14.
   1. The Messianic King, Ch. 9-10.
   2. The rejected Shepherd, Ch. 11.
   3. The restored and penitent people, Chs. 12-13.
   4. The divine sovereignty, Ch. 14.
For Study and Discussion. (1) The symbols and

figures used in the several visions. (2) The different ways of expressing or planning the success of God's people and the overthrow of their enemies. (3) The discussion of fasting, should they keep it up? What is superior to it? etc. (4) The promises of these prophesies. (5) The denunciations and judgments found in the book.

Malachi.

The Prophet. His name means "Messenger of the Lord." or "My Messenger". He was connected with the reform movement of Nehemiah and Ezra and condemned the same sins which they condemned. He must, therefore, have lived about 100 years after Haggai and Zechariah, or about 430-420 B. C. He was the last of the Old Testament inspired prophets.

The Condition of the Time. The people had been restored to Jerusalem and the temple and walls rebuilt. They had become sensual and selfish and had grown careless and neglectful of their duty. Their interpretation of the glowing prophecies of the exilic and pre-exilic prophets had led them to expect to realize the Messianic kingdom immediately upon their return. They were, therefore, discouraged and grew skeptical (2:17) because of the inequalities of life seen everywhere. This doubt of divine justice had caused them to neglect vital religion and true piety had given place to mere formality. They had not relapsed into idolatry but a spirit of worldliness had crept in and they were guilty of many vices such as we see today in professedly Christian communities.

The Prophecy. The purpose of this prophecy was to rebuke the people for departing from the worship of the law of God, to call the people back to Jehovah and to revive their national spirit. There are in it: (1) Unsparing denunciations of social evils and of the people of Israel. (2) Severe rebukes for the indifference and hypocrisy of the priests. (3) Prophecies of the coming of the Messiah and the characteristics and manner of his coming. (4) Prophecies concerning the forerunner of the Messiah.

Analysis.

Introduction: Jehovah's love of Israel. 1:1-5. This is seen in the contrast between Israeli and Egypt.
    I. Israel's Lack of Love of God, 1:6-2:16. It is proved.
    1. By their polluted offerings, 1:6 end.
    2. By the sins of the priests. 2:1-9.
    3. By their heathen marriages and by their divorces, 2:10-16.
    II. God Will Come and Judge His People, 2:17-4:6 end.
    1. His messenger will separate the righteous from the wicked, 2:17- 4:6.
    2. This is seen in the effect of their withholding or paying tithes. 3:7-12.
    3. Faithful services will be rewarded. 3:13-4:6 end.
For Study and Discussion. (1) Make a list of the particular sins rebuked. (2) Make a list of all the different things said about the Messiah and his mission and also that of the forerunner. (3) Analyze and study each of the seven controversies. 1:2, 7; 2:13, 14, 17; 3:7, 8, 14. (4) Compare the future destinies of the righteous and wicked as revealed in this book, making a list of all that is said of each. (5) Make a list of all the promises of the book.

24
MATTHEW.

Each Gospel was written with a view to creating a definite result and written to a particular people and they differ accordingly. In this book, therefore, each Gospel is discussed with the hope of so outlining its purpose and consequent peculiarities as to stimulate a thorough study of the questions raised.

Date. Written about 60 A. D., but after Mark.

The Author. The Author always speaks of himself as "the publican," which may indicate his sense of humility, felt in having been exalted from so low an estate to that of an apostle. He was the son of Alpheus (Mar. 2:14; Lu. 5:27), and was called Levi until Jesus called him and gave him the name Matthew, which means "Gift of God." We know nothing of his work except his call and farewell feast (9:9-10), and that he was with the apostles on the day of Pentecost. Thus silent and observant and qualified by former occupation, he could well undertake the writing of this book. It might be possible that he was chosen by the others for this great task. We know nothing of his death.

Characteristics and Purpose.

1. It is not a Chronological but a Systematic and Topical Gospel. There is order in the arrangement of materials so that a definite result may be produced. Materials are treated in groups, as the miracles in chapters eight and nine and the parables of chapter thirteen. There is order and purpose also in the arrangement of these groups of miracles and parables. The first miracle is the cure of leprosy, and is a type of sin; while the last one is the withering of the fig tree, which is a symbol of judgment. The first parable is that of the seed of the kingdom, which is a symbol of the beginning or planting of the kingdom; the last is that of the talents and prophesies the final adjudication at the last day. This same orderly arrangement is also observed in the two great sections of the book. The first great section 4:17-16:20, especially sets forth the person and nature of Jesus, while the second section, 16:20 end, narrates his great work for others as seen in his death and resurrection.

2. It Is a Didactic or Teaching Gospel. While giving the account of a number of miracles, the book is marked by several discourses of considerable length, as The sermon on the Mount, chapters 3-7, the denunciation of the Pharisees, chapter 23, the prophecy of the destruction of Jerusalem and the end of the world, chapters 24-25, the address to the apostles, chapter 10; and the doctrines of the kingdom, 17:24-20:16. These portions and the parables noted above will indicate how large a portion of the book is taken up in discourses. The student can make lists of other and shorter sections of teaching.

3. It Is a Gospel of Gloom and Despondency. There are no songs of joy like those of Zacharias,

Elizabeth, Mary, Simeon, Anna and the Angels, recorded in Luke. Nor do we see him popular and wise at the age of twelve. Instead, we have his mother almost repudiated and left in disgrace by Joseph and only saved by divine intervention. Jerusalem is in trouble, the male children are killed and mothers are weeping for them. The child Jesus is saved only by the flight into Egypt, his whole life after the return from Egypt is covered in oblivion and he is a despised Nazarite. The cross is one of desolation with no penitent thief nor sympathy from any one, with his enemies reviling, smiting their breasts and passing by. Nor is there much optimism or expectation of success. The disciples are to be rejected and persecuted even as their Lord; many are to be called and but few are chosen; only a few are to find the narrow way; many are to claim entrance into the Kingdom because they have prophesied in His name and be denied. Even Matthew himself is a despised and rejected publican.

4. It Is a Kingly Gospel. The genealogy shows the royal descent of Jesus. The Magi came seeking him that was "born king of the Jews," and John the Baptist preaches that the "Kingdom of heaven is at hand." Here we have the parables of the kingdom, beginning with "the Kingdom of heaven," etc. In Luke a certain man made a great supper and had two sons, while in Matthew it was a certain king. In the other evangelists we always have the term gospel while, with one exception, Matthew always puts it "the gospel of the Kingdom". The "keys of the kingdom" are given to Peter. All the nations shall gather before him as he sits on the throne and "the king say" unto them, and the "king shall answer," etc. (Matt. 25:34, 40).

5. It Is an Official and an Organic Gospel. This is suggested in that Matthew represents Satan as head of a kingdom; also, in that those connected with Jesus' birth are official persons and most of the acts are official in their nature. Pilate, the judge, washed his hands of the blood of Jesus, the Roman guard pronounces him the Christ, and the guards say he could not be kept in the tomb, Jesus denounces the officials and calls his own disciples by official names. It is Peter, not Simon, and Matthew, the apostolic name, and not Levi as in Luke. Jesus indicates his official capacity in his rejection of the Jews, telling them that the kingdom is taken away from them (21:43). He makes ready for the establishing of his own kingdom and tells them who is to wield the keys of the kingdom which is not to be bound by time or national relations as was the former kingdom. In Matthew alone do we find full instructions as to the membership, discipline and ordinances of the church. Here alone are we given in the gospels the command to baptize to administer the communion and the beautiful formula for baptism in the name of the Father, Son and Holy Ghost, and here we have his official command to "Go" backed by all the authority of heaven and earth.

In the further pursuit of this official work, we find Jesus giving especial recognition to the Gentile believers-giving them full place in his kingdom. The genealogy through grace and faith includes Gentiles; the second chapter shows how the Gentile Magi do him honor; the Roman centurion displays a faith superior to any Israelite; the great faith of the Canaanite woman led him to heal her daughter, and the Gentile wife of Pilate because of her dreams sends a warning that he have "nothing to do" with

145

him. All this tended to show the official and organic way in which Jesus worked.

6. It Is a Gospel of Jewish Antagonism and Rejection. On the one hand the Jews antagonize and reject Jesus. On the other the Jews, especially the scribes and Pharisees, are exposed and rejected by Jesus. The Pharisees plotted against Jesus and resented his violation of their regulations and customs concerning the Sabbath and their ceremonies about eating and washing and his associations with publicans and sinners. Their opposition culminated in their putting him to death. On the other hand Jesus also rejects the Jews. John calls them a generation of vipers and Jesus designated them with such terms as hypocrites, blind guides and whited sepulchers, the climax being reached in chapter 23. It is here that in their wickedness they are unable to discern between the work of God and of Beelzebub. They are told of the application of Isaiah's prophecy, that they have ears and hear not and that on account of their unworthiness, the kingdom is taken from them. The blasting of the fig tree with which the miracles of Matthew ends shows what is to be the fate of the Jewish nation.

7. It Is a Jewish Gospel. This is seen in his use of Jewish symbols, terms and numbers without explanation. He never explained the meaning of a Jewish word, such as Corban, nor of a custom, such as to say that the Jews eat not except they wash. The other evangelists do. He calls Jerusalem by the Jewish terms, "City of the great king," and "Holy City," and Christ the "Son of David" and the "Son of Abraham." He speaks of the Jewish temple as the temple of God, the dwelling place of God and the holy place. The genealogy is traced to Abraham by three great Jewish events of history. All this would be

calculated to win the Jews, but, much more, the sixty-five quotations from the Old Testament and the oft repeated attempt to show that deeds and sayings recorded were that the "Scripture (or saying) might be fulfilled." And, while not seeing as much in the numbers as Plummer and others, one can hardly believe that all numbers, so characteristic of Jews, are accidental here. The genealogy has three fourteens being multiples of seven. There are fourteen parables, seven in one place and seven in another. There are seven woes in chapter 23. There are twenty miracles separated into two tens. The number seven usually, if not always, divides into four and three, the human and the divine. Of the seven parables in chapter 13, four touch the human or natural while three refer to the divine or spiritual side of his kingdom. There are seven petitions in the Lord's prayer, the first three relating to God and the last four to man. A like division is perhaps true in the beatitudes.

Subject. The Kingdom of God or of Heaven.

Analysis.

I. The Beginning of the Kingdom, 1:1-4:16.

1. Jesus, the King, is the Old Testament Messiah, chs. 1-2.

2. Jesus, the King, is prepared for his work, 3:1-4:16.

II. The Proclamation of the Kingdom, 4:17-16:20.

1. The beginning of the proclamation, 4:17 end.

2. By the Sermon on the Mount, chs. 5-7.

3. By the miracles and connected teachings, chs. 8-9.

4. By the sending of the Twelve and subsequent teachings and miracles, chs. 10-12.

5. By the seven parables and subsequent miracles, chs. 13-14.

6. By the denunciation of the Pharisees with attendant miracles and teachings, 15:1-16:12.

7. By the Great Confession, 16:12-20.

III. The Passion of the Kingdom, 6:21-27 end.

1. Four predictions of the passion with intervening discourses and miracles, 16:21-26:2.

(A) At Caesarea Philippi, 16:21-17:21.

(B) In Galilee near Capernaum, 17:22-20:16.

(C) Near Jerusalem, 20:17-22 end.

(D) At Jerusalem, 23:1-26:2.

2. The events of the Passion, 26:3-27 end.

IV. The Triumph of the Kingdom, Ch. 28.

1. The resurrection of the King, 1-15.

2. Provision for the propagation of the Kingdom, 16-20.

For Study and Discussion. (1) Some events of Christ's childhood, (a) The story of the Magi. (b) The massacre of the infants, (c) The flight to Egypt, (d) The return to Nazareth. (2) Two miracles, (a) Cure of the blind man, 9:27-31. (b) Fish with money in its mouth, 17:24-27. (3) Ten Parables, (a) The Tares, 13:24-30. (b) The draw net, 13:47-50. (c) The unmerciful servant. 18:23-25. (d) The laborers in the vineyard, 20:1-16. (e) The two sons, 21:28-32. (f) The marriage of the king's son, 22:1-14. (g) The hidden treasure. 24:44. (h) The pearl, 24:45-46. (i) The ten virgins. 25:1-13. (j) The talents, 25:14-30. (4) Ten passages in Christ's discourses: (a) Parts of the Sermon on the Mount, chs. 5-7. (b) Revelation to babes, 11:25-27. (c) Invitations to the weary, 11:28-30. (d) About idle words, 12:36-37. (e) Prophecy to Peter,

16:17-19. (f) Humility and forgiveness, 18:14-35. (g) Rejection of the Jews, 21:43. (h) The great denunciation, ch. 23. (i) The judgment scene, 23:31-46. (j) The great commission and promise, 28:16- 20. (5) Some terms by which Jesus is designated in Matthew should be studied. Let the student make a list of the different places where each of the following terms are used and from a study of the passages compared with any others form opinions as to the significance of the term, (a) Son of Abraham, (b) Son of David, (c) Son of man, (d) Son of God, (e) Christ, the Christ, (f) Jesus, (g) Lord, (h) Kingdom of heaven or Kingdom of God. (6) Make a list of all the places where the expression "That the saying (or scripture) might be fulfilled" and tabulate all the things fulfilled. (7) Show how many times and where the phrase "The Kingdom of Heaven" (or of God) occurs and from a study of these passages tabulate in list the nature, characteristics and purpose of the Kingdom. (8) Make a list of all the places mentioned and become familiar with the history and geography of each and memorize the leading events connected with each.

25
MARK.

Date. Probably written about A. D. 60, and before Matthew.

The Author. He was not an apostle and was variously designated as follows; (1) John, whose surname was Mark, Acts 12:12, 25; 15:37; (2) John only, Acts 13:5. 13; (3) Mark only, Acts 15:39; (4) always Mark after this, Col. 4:10, Philemon 24, 2 Tim. 4:11, 1 Pet. 5:13. He was a son of Mary, a woman of Jerusalem (Acts 12:12). Her home was the gathering place of the disciples, whither Peter went after he was delivered from prison. On this or some other visit Mark may have been converted through the preaching of Peter, and this may have been the cause of Peter calling him "his son" (1 Pet. 5:13), which doubtless means son in the ministry. He returns with Paul and Barnabas from Jerusalem to Antioch (Acts 12:25), and accompanies them, as minister (Acts 13:5) on the first great missionary journey as far as Perga (Acts 13:13). There he left them and returned home. On the second missionary tour Paul declined to take him and separated from Barnabas, Mark's cousin (Col. 4:10), who chose Mark for his companion (Acts 15:37-39). Ten years later he seems to be with Paul in his imprisonment at Rome and was certainly counted a fellow worker by Paul (Col. 4:10, Philemon 24). Paul found him useful and asked Timothy to bring him to him in his last imprisonment (2 Tim. 4:11). He was with Peter when he wrote his first epistle (1 Peter 5:13).

What he knew of the work of Jesus directly we do not know, probably not much. The early Christian writers universally say that he was the interpreter of Peter and that he based his gospel upon information gained from him.

Characteristics and Purpose.

1. It Is a Gospel of Vividness and Details. He shows the effect of awe and wonder produced upon those present by the works and teaching of Jesus. He tells the details of the actions of Jesus and his disciples and the multitudes. Jesus "looks around," "sat down," "went before". He is grieved, hungry, angry, indignant, wonders, sleeps, rests and is moved with pity. The cock crows twice: "it is the hour", "a great while before day," or "eventide," "there are two thousand swine", the disciples and Jesus are on the sea, on Olivet, or in the court yard or in the porch. Everything is portrayed in detail.

2. It Is a Gospel of Activity and Energy. There is no story of his infancy, but he starts with "The beginning of the gospel of Jesus Christ". He portrays the active career of Jesus on earth. He, however, lays emphasis upon the works rather than the words of Jesus. Few discourses of any length and only four of the fifteen parables of Matthew are given and those in the

briefest form, while eighteen of the miracles are given in rapid review. The rapid succession is indicated by one Greek word, translated by the seven words "immediately", "anon", "forthwith", "by and by", "as soon as", "shortly", and "straightway", which occur forty-one times in this gospel. The last meaning, straightway, is truest to the Greek idea and may be called Mark's characteristic word. It indicates how with the speed of a racer he rushed along and thereby furnishes us a breathless narrative which Farrar says makes us "feel like the apostles who, among the press of the people coming and going, were twice made to say they 'had no leisure so much as to eat'." It moves as the scenes of a moving picture show.

3. It Is a Gospel of Power Over Devils. Here as in no other gospel the devils are made subject to Jesus. They recognize him as the "Son of God" and acknowledge their subordination to him by pleading with him as to what shall be done with them (5:7, 12).

4. It Is a Gospel of Wonder. Everywhere Jesus is a man of wonder that strikes awe and terror and causes to wonder those who see and hear him. Some of these may be studied, especially in the Greek, in 1:27; 2:13; 4:41; 5:28 6:50; 51; 7:37. As Archbishop Thompson puts it, "The wonder-working Son of God sweeps over his Kingdom swiftly and meteor- like" and thus strikes awe into the hearts of the on-lookers. He is "a man heroic and mysterious, who inspires not only a passionate devotion but also amazement and adoration".

5. It Is a Gospel for the Romans. The Romans were men of great power, mighty workers who left behind them great accomplishments for the blessing of humanity. So that Mark would especially appeal to

them by recording of Jesus his mighty deeds. He lets them see one who has power to still the storm, to control disease and death, and even power to control the unseen world of spirits. The Roman, who found deity in a Caesar as head of a mighty Kingdom, would bow to one who had shown himself King in every realm and whose kingdom was both omnipotent and everlasting, both visible and unseen, both temporal and spiritual.

Then, too, the Roman cared nothing for Jewish Scripture or prophecy and so he omits all reference to the Jewish law, the word law not being found in the entire book. He only once or twice refers in any way to the Jewish scriptures. He omits the genealogy of Jesus which could have no value to a Roman. Then, too, he explains all doubtful Jewish words, such as "Boanerges" (3:17), "Tabitha cumi" (5:41), "corban" (7:11), "alba" (15:36). He reduced Jewish money to Roman currency (12:42). He explains Jewish customs as not being understood by them. (See 7:3; 13:3; 14:12; 15:42).

And once more by the use of terms familiar to him such as centurion, contend, etc. "Mark showed the Roman a man who was a man indeed". He showed them manhood crowned with glory and power; Jesus of Nazareth, the Son of God; a man but a Man Divine and sinless, among sinful and suffering men. Him, the God-man, no humiliation could degrade, no death defeat. Not even on the cross could he seem less than the King, the Hero, the only Son. And as he gazed on such a picture how could any Roman refrain from exclaiming with the awe-struck Centurion, "Truly this was the Son of God".

Subject. Jesus the Almighty King.

Analysis.

I. The Almighty King is Exhibited as the Son of God, 1:1-13.
 1. In the baptism and teaching of John, 1-8.
 2. In the baptism of Jesus, 9-11.
 3. In the temptation, 12-13.

II. The Almighty King at Work in Galilee, 1:14-9 end.
 1. Begins his work, 1:14 end.
 2. Reveals his Kingdom, Chs. 2-5.
 3. Meets opposition, 6:1-8:26.
 4. Prepares his disciples for the end, 8:27-9 end.

III. The Almighty King Prepares for Death 10:1-14:31.
 1. He goes to Jerusalem, 10:1-11:11.
 2. In Jerusalem and vicinity, 11:12-14:31.

IV. The Almighty King Suffers at the Hands of His Enemies. 14:32- 15:46.
 1. Agony of Gethsemane, 14:32-42.
 2. Arrest, 14:43-52.
 3. Jewish trial and denial of Peter, 14:53 end.
 4. Trial before Pilate. 15:1-15.
 5. The Crucifixion. 15:16-41.
 6. The Burial, 15:42 end.

V. The Almighty King Triumphs Over His Enemies, Ch.16.
 1. The resurrection, 1-8.
 2. The appearances, 9-18.
 3. The ascension, 19-20.

For Study and Discussion. (1) Sections peculiar to Mark, (a) Growth of the seed, 4:26-29. (b) Jesus' compassion on the multitudes, 7:32-37. (c) The blind men healed gradually, 8;22-26. (d) Details about the ass, etc., 11:1-14. (e) Concerning watching, 13:33-37. (f)

Details concerning Christ's appearances. 16:6-11. (2) The spiritual condition of those affected by Jesus' miracles. Keeping in mind their condition before and after the miracle: (a) Were they saved as well as well as healed? (b) Did they or their friends exercise faith, or did Jesus act voluntarily without any expression of faith? (3) What did Jesus do in performing the miracle? (a) Did he use the touch? (b) Was he touched? (c) Did he simply give command, etc? (4) From the following scriptures 2:35; 1:45; 3:7-12; 6:6; 6:21-32; 6:46; 7:34-25; 8:27; 9:2; 11:11; 11:19; 14:1-12, make a list of the different places to which Jesus retired and in connection with each indicate (in writing): (a) Was it before or after a victory or conflict? (b) Was it in preparation for or rest after the performance of a great work? (c) Indicate in each case whether he went alone or was accompanied and, if accompanied, by whom? (e) In each case also tell what Jesus did during the period of retirement. Did he pray, teach, perform miracles or what? (5) List the phrases "Son of man" and "Kingdom of God" and point out the appropriateness and meaning of each. (6) List all references to demons and to demon possessed people and study their nature, the nature of their work, their power, wisdom, etc. (7) The facts concerning the death of Jesus. 14:1-15:14. List them.

26
LUKE.

Date. It was probably written about A. D. 60 or 63, certainly before the fall of Jerusalem, A. D. 70, and likely while Luke was with Paul in Rome or during the two years at Caesarea.

Author. The author is Luke, who also wrote Acts, and was a companion of Paul on his second missionary journey (Acts 16:11-40). He rejoins Paul at Philippi (Acts 20:1-7) on the return from the third missionary journey, remaining with him at Caesarea and on the way to Rome (Acts Chs. 20-28), He is called the "Beloved physician" (Col. 4:14) and Paul's "fellow laborer" (Philemon 24).

From the context of Col. 4:4 we learn that he was "not of the circumcision" and, therefore, a Gentile. From his preface (Lu. 1:1) we learn that he was not an eye witness of what he wrote. He is thought to be "the brother" whose praise is in the gospel throughout all the churches (2 Cor. 8:18), and, by tradition, is always declared to be a Gentile and proselyte. As is indicated by the gospel itself, he was the most cultured of all the gospel writers.

Characteristics and Purpose.

1. It Is a Gospel of Song and Praise. There are a number of songs such as the song of Mary (1:46-55), the song of Zacharias (1:68-79), the song of the angels (2:14) and the song of Simeon (2:29-33). There are many expressions of praise such as (2:2; 5:29; 7:16; 13:13; 17:15; 18:43; 23:47).

2. It Is a Gospel of Prayer. Jesus prays at his baptism, (3:21), after cleansing the leper (5:16), before calling the twelve (6:12), at his transfiguration (9:28), before teaching the disciples to pray (11:1), for his murderers as he was on the cross (23:34), with his last breath (23:46). Luke gives us Christ's command to pray (21:36) and two parables, the midnight friend (11:5-13) and the unjust judge (18:1-8) to show the certain and blessed results of continued prayer.

3. It Is a Gospel of Womanhood. No other gospel gives her anything like so large a place as Luke. Indeed, all of the first three chapters or a greater part of their contents may have been given him, as he "traced out accurately from the first" (1:3), by Mary and Elizabeth. He gives us the praise and prophecy of Elizabeth (1:42-42), the song of Mary (1:46-55). Anna and her worship (2:36-38), sympathy for the widow of Nain (7:12-15), Mary Magdella the sinner (7:36-50), the woman associates of Jesus (8:1-3), tender words to the woman with an issue of blood (8:48), Mary and Martha and their disposition (10:38-42). sympathy and help for the "daughter" of Abraham (13:16), the consolation of the daughters of

Jerusalem (23:28). These references have been collected by others and are the most conspicuous ones and serve to show how large a place woman is given in this gospel.

4. It Is a Gospel of the Poor and Outcast. More than any other of the evangelists Luke reports those teachings and incidents in the life of our Savior which show how his work is to bless the poor and neglected and vicious. Among the more striking passages of this character are the oft repeated references to the publicans (3:12; 5:27, 29, 30, etc.), Mary Magdella, who was a sinner (7:36-50), the woman with an issue of blood (8:43-48), the harlots (15:30), the prodigal son (13:11-32), Lazarus, the beggar (16:13-31), the poor, maimed, halt and blind invited to the supper (14:7-24). the Story of Zacchaeus (19:1- 9), the Savior's business declared to be to seek and save the lost (8:10), the dying robber saved (23:39-43).

5. It Is a Gentile Gospel. The book is everywhere filled with a world wide purpose not so fully expressed in the other evangelists. Here we have the angels, announcement of great joy which shall be to all people (2:10) and the song about Jesus as "a light for revelation to the Gentiles" (2:32). The genealogy traces Christ's lineage back to Adam (2:38) and thus connects him not with Abraham as a representative of humanity. The fuller account of the sending out of the seventy (10:1-24). the very number of whom signified the supposed number of the heathen nations, who were to go, not as the twelve to the lost sheep of the house of Israel, but to all those cities whither Jesus himself would come, is suggestive of this broader purpose of Luke. The good Samaritan (10:25-37) is Christ's illustration of a true neighbor and in some

way also intends to show the nature of Christ's work which was to be without nationality. Of the ten lepers healed (17:11-19) only one, a Samaritan, returned to render him praise, thus showing how others than the Jews would not only be blessed by him but would do worthy service for him. The Perean ministry, across the Jordan (9:51- 18:4, probably 9:51-19:28). is a ministry to the Gentiles and shows how large a place Luke would give the Gentiles in the work and blessings of Jesus.

6. It Is a Gospel for the Greeks. If Matthew wrote for Jews and Mark for Romans, it is but natural that some one should write in such a way as to appeal, specially, to the Greeks as the other representative race. And, such the Christian writers of the first centuries thought to be Luke's purpose. The Greek was the representative of reason and humanity and felt that his mission was to perfect humanity. "The full grown Greek would be a perfect world man", able to meet all men on the common plane of the race. All the Greek gods were, therefore, images of some form of perfect humanity. The Hindu might worship an emblem of physical force, the Roman deify the Emperor and the Egyptian any and all forms of life, but the Greek adored man with his thought and beauty and speech, and, in this, had most nearly approached the true conception of God. The Jew would value men as the descendants of Abraham; the Roman according as they wielded empires, but the Greek on the basis of man as such.

The gospel for the Greek must, therefore, present the perfect man, and so Luke wrote about the Divine Man as the Savior of all men. Christ touched man at every point and is interested in him as man whether low and vile or high and noble. By his life he shows the folly of sin and the beauty of holiness. He brings God near enough to meet the longings of the Greek soul and thereby furnish him a pattern and brother suited for all ages and all people. The deeds of Jesus are kept to the background while much is made of the songs of others and the discourses of Jesus as they were calculated to appeal to the cultured Greek. If the Greek thinks he has a mission to humanity, Luke opens a mission ground enough for the present and offers him an immortality which will satisfy in the future.

7. It Is an Artistic Gospel. Renan calls Luke the most beautiful book in the world, while Dr. Robertson says "the charm of style and the skill in the use of facts place it above all praise". The delicacy and accuracy, picturesqueness and precision with which he sets forth the different incidents is manifestly the work of a trained historian. His is the most beautiful Greek and shows the highest touches of culture of all of the gospels.

Subject. Jesus the World's Savior.

Analysis.

Introduction. The dedication of the gospel, 1:1-4.
  I. The Savior's Manifestation, 1:5-4:13.
    1. The announcement of the Forerunner, 1:5-25.
    2. The announcement of the Savior. 1:26-38.
    3. Thanksgiving of Mary and Elizabeth, 1:29-56.
    4. The birth and childhood of the Forerunner, 1:37 end.
    5. The birth of the Savior, 2:1-20.
    6. The childhood of the Savior. 3:1-4:13.

II. The Savior's Work and Teaching in Galilee, 4:14-9:50.
  1. He preaches in the synagogue at Nazareth. 4:14-30.
  2. He works in and around Capernaum, 4:31-6:11.
  3. Work while touring Galilee, 6:12-9:50.
III. The Savior's Work and Teaching After Leaving Galilee Up to the Entrance Into Jerusalem, 9:31-19:27.
  1. He journeys to Jerusalem, 9:51 end.
  2. The mission of the Seventy and subsequent matters, 10:1-11:13.
  3. He exposes the experience and practice of the day, 11:14-12 end.
  4. Teachings, miracles warnings and parables, 13:1-18:30.
  5. Incidents connected with his final approach to Jerusalem, 18:31- 19:27.
IV. The Savior's Work and Teaching in Jerusalem, 19:28-22:38.
  1. The entrance to Jerusalem, 19:28 end.
  2. Questions and answers. Ch. 20.
  3. The widow's mites, 21:1-4.
  4. Preparation for the end, 21:5-22:38.
V. The Savior Suffers for the World, 22:39-23 end.
  1. The agony in the garden, 22:39-46.
  2. The betrayal and arrest, 22:47-53.
  3. The trial. 22:54-23:26.
  4. The cross, 23:27-49.
  5. The burial, 23:30 end.
VI. The Savior is Glorified, Ch. 24.
  1. The resurrection, 1-12.
  2. The appearance and teachings, 13-49.

3. The ascension, 50 end.

For Study and Discussion.

1. Six miracles peculiar to Luke. (1) The draught of fishes, 5:4-11. (2) The raising of the widow's son, 7:11- 18. (3) The woman with the spirit of infirmity, 13:11-17. (4) The man with the dropsy, 14:1-6. (5) The ten lepers, 17:11-19. (6) The healing of Malchus' ear. 22:50-51.

2. Eleven parables, peculiar to Luke. (I) The two debtors, 7:41-43. (2) The good Samaritan, 10:25-37. (3) The importunate friend, 11:5-8. (4) The rich fool, 12:16-19. (5) The barren fig-tree, 13:6-9. (6) The lost piece of silver, 15:8-10. (7) The prodigal son, 15:11-32. (8) The unjust steward, 16:1-13. (9) The rich man and Lazarus, 18:19-31. (10) The unjust judge, 18:1-8. (11) The Pharisee and publican, 18:9-14.

3. Some other passages mainly peculiar to Luke. (1) Chs. 1-2 and 9:51- 18:14 are mainly peculiar to Luke. (2) John the Baptist's answer to the people. 3:10-14. (3) The conversation with Moses and Elias, 9:30- 31. (4) The weeping over Jerusalem, 19:41-44. (5) The bloody sweat, 22:44. (6) The sending of Jesus to Herod, 23:7-12. (7) The address to the daughters of Jerusalem, 23:27-31. (8) "Father forgive them", 23:34. (9) The penitent robber, 23:40-43. (10) The disciples at Emmaus, 24:13-31; (11) Particulars about the ascension. 24:50-53.

4. The following words and phrases should be studied, making a list of the references where each occurs and a study of each passage in which they occur with a view of getting Luke's conception of the term. (1) The "son of man" (23 times). (2) The "son of God" (7 times). (3) The "kingdom of God" (32

times). (4) References to law, lawyer, lawful (18 times). (5) Publican (11 times). (6) Sinner and sinners (16 times). Mr. Stroud estimates that 59 percent of Luke is peculiar to himself and Mr. Weiss figures that 541 have no incidences in the other gospels.

27
JOHN.

The Author. From the evidence found in the gospel, we may learn several things about the author. (1) *That he was a Jew.* This is seen in his evident knowledge of Jewish opinions concerning such subjects as the Messiah, and his knowledge of their customs, such as the purification. (2) *He was an eye-witness to most of what he relates.* This is seen in his exact knowledge of time, as to the hour or time of day a thing occurred; in his knowledge of the number of persons or things present, as the division of his garments into four parts; in the vividness of the narrative which he could hardly have had without first having seen it all. (3) *He was an apostle.* This is seen in his knowledge of the thoughts of the disciples (2:11, 17); in his knowledge of the private words of the disciples to Jesus and among themselves (4:31, 33, etc.); in his knowledge of the private resorts of the disciples (11:54. etc.); and in his knowledge of the Lord's motives, etc. (2:24-25, etc.); and in his knowledge of Christ's feelings (11:33). (4) *He was the son of Zebedee*

(Mar. 1:19-20), and was probably one of John's two disciples whom he turned to Jesus (1- 40). (5) *He is one of the three most prominent of the apostles*, being several times especially honored (Matt. 17:1-3. etc.), and is prominent in the work of the church after Christ's ascension, as well as in all their work before his death: (6) *He also wrote three epistles and Revelation.* He outlived all the other apostles and is supposed to have died on the Isle of Patmos as an exile about 100 A.D.

The Times and Circumstances of the Writings. These are so different from those which influenced the other evangelists that one can hardly escape the feeling that John's gospel is colored accordingly. The gospel had been preached in all the Roman empire and Christianity was no longer considered a Jewish sect, attached to the Synagogue. Jerusalem had been overthrown and the temple destroyed. Christians had been sorely persecuted, but had achieved great triumphs in many lands. All the rest of the New Testament except Revelation had been written. Some had arisen, who disputed the deity of Jesus and while the gospel is not a mere polemic against that false teaching, it does, by establishing the true teaching thoroughly undermine the false. He perhaps wrote to Christians of all nationalities, whose history had by this time been enriched by the blood of martyrs for the faith. Instead of the Messiah in whom Jews would find a Savior or the mighty worker in whom the Roman would find him, or the Ideal Man in whom the Greeks would find him. John wrote concerning the eternal, Incarnate Word in whose Spiritual Kingdom each, having lost his narrowness and racial prejudice, could be forever united.

The Style and the Plan.

This gospel differs from the others in language and plan. It is both profound and simple and has several elements of style as follows: (1) Simplicity. The sentences are short and connected by coordinate conjunctions. There are but few direct quotations, and but few dependent sentences, and most of them show the sequence of things, either as a cause or a purpose. (2) Sameness. This arises from the method of treating each step in the narrative as if isolated and separate from all the rest rather than merging it into the complete whole. (3) Repetition, whether in the narrative proper or in the quoted words of the Lord, is very frequent. The following examples will illustrate this: "In the beginning was the word and the word was with God and the word was God." "The light shineth in darkness and the darkness comprehendeth it not." "I am the Good Shepherd; the Good Shepherd giveth his life." "Jesus then, when he saw her weeping and the Jews that were weeping with her." "If I bear witness of myself my witness is not true. There is another that beareth witness of me; and I know that the witness which he witnesseth of me is true." Let the student gather a list of all such repetitions. (4) *Parallelism*, or statements expressing the same or similar truths, such as the following are common. "Peace I leave with you, my peace I give unto you"; "Let not your heart be troubled, neither let it be afraid"; "I give unto them eternal life and they shall never perish." This parallelism, which at the same time becomes repetition, is seen in the way a subject or conclusion is stated and, after elaboration, restated in a new and enlarged view, thus teaching the truth in a gradually unfolding beauty and force. An illustration is found in the statement, "I will raise him up in the last day," 6, 39, 70, 44. (5) *Contrasts*. The plan is more simple and more easily seen all along than is that of any other of the Evangelists. On the one hand, he shows how love and faith are developed in the believer until, in the end, Thomas, who was the most doubtful of all, could exclaim, "My Lord and my God." On the other hand, he shows the unbeliever advanced from mere indifference to a positive hatred that culminated in the crucifixion. This purpose is carried out by a process of contrasting and separating things that are opposites, such as (a) Light and darkness, (b) Truth and falsehood, (c) Good and evil, (d) Life and death, (e) God and Satan. In all of these he is convincing his reader that Jesus is the Christ, the son of God.

Characteristics and Purpose.

1. It Is a Gospel of the Feasts. Indeed, if subtract from it those miracles and teachings and other works performed in connection with the feasts, we should have only a few fragments left. The value of the book would be destroyed and the most beautiful and the profoundest teachings of the gospel lost.

The student will do well from the following list of feasts to endeavor to group around each all that John records as occurring in connection with it. (1) The Feast of the Passover (2:13, 23), First Passover, A. D. 27. (2) A Feast of the Jews (5:1), probably Purim. (3) Passover a Feast of the Jews (6:4), Second Passover, A. D. 28. (4) Feast of the Tabernacles (7:2). (5) Feast of the Dedication (10:22). (6) Passover (11:55-56; 12:1, 12, 20; 13:29; 18:28). Third Passover, A. D. 29.

2. It Is a Gospel of Testimony. John writes to

prove that Jesus is the Christ. He assumes the attitude of a lawyer before a jury and introduces testimony until he fells certain of his case and then closes the testimony with the assurance that much more could be offered if it seemed necessary. There are seven lines of testimony. (1) The testimony of John the Baptist. (2) The testimony of certain other individuals. (3) The testimony of Jesus' works. (4) The testimony of Jesus himself (see the I am's). (5) The testimony of the scripture. (6) The testimony of the Father. (7) The testimony of the Holy Spirit.

3. It Is of Gospel of Belief. The purpose being to produce belief there are given: numerous examples of belief, showing the growth of faith; the secret of faith, such as hearing or receiving the word; the results of faith, such as eternal life, freedom, peace, power, etc.

4. It Is a Spiritual Gospel. It represents the deeper mediations of John, which are shaped so as to establish a great doctrine which, instead of history, became his great impulse. To John "history is doctrine" and he reviews it in the light of its spiritual interpretation. It furnished a great bulwark against the Gnostic teachers, who had come to deny the diety of Jesus. He also emphasized and elaborated the humanity of Jesus. His whole purpose is "not so much the historic record of the facts as the development of their inmost meaning."

5. It Is a Gospel of Symbolism. John was a mystic and delighted in mystic symbols. The whole book speaks in the language of symbols. The mystic numbers three and seven prevail throughout the book not only in the things and sayings recorded but in the arrangement of topics. Each of the Eight Miracles is used for a "sign" or symbol, as the feeding of the five

thousand in which Jesus appears as the bread or support of life. The great allegories of the Good-Shepherd, the sheep-fold and the vine; the names used to designate Jesus as the Word, Light, the Way, the Truth, the Life, etc., all show how the whole gospel is penetrated with a spirit of symbolic representation.

6. It Is the Gospel of the Incarnation. "Matthew explains his messianic function; Mark his active works and Luke his character as Savior." John magnifies his person and everywhere makes us see "the word made flesh." God is at no great distance form us. He has become flesh. The word has come as the Incarnate Man. Jesus, this Incarnate Man, is God and as such fills the whole book, but he, nevertheless, hungers and thirsts and knows human experience. God has come down to man to enable him to rise up to God.

Subject: Jesus, the Christ, God's Son.

Analysis.

Introduction or prologue, 1:1-18.
(1) The divine nature of the word. 1-5.
(2) The manifestation of the word as the world's Savior, 6-18.
   I. The Testimony of His Great Public Ministry, 1:19-12 end.
   1. He is revealed, 1:19-2:12.
   2. He is recognized, 2:13-3 end.
   3. He is antagonized, Chs. 5-11.
   4. He is honored, Ch. 12.
   II. The Testimony of His Private Ministry with His Disciples, Chs. 13-17.
   1. He teaches and comforts his disciples, Chs. 13-16.
   2. He prays for his disciples, Ch. 17.

III. The Testimony of His Passion. Chs. 18-19.
1. His betrayal, 18:1-11.
2. The Jewish or ecclesiastical trial, 18:12-27.
3. The Roman or civil trial, 18:28-19:16.
4. His death and burial, 19:17 end.

IV. The Testimony of His Resurrection and Manifestation, Chs. 20-21.
1. His resurrection and manifestation to his disciples, Ch. 20.
2. Further manifestations and instructions to his disciples, Ch. 21.

For Study and Discussion.

(1) The events and discourses connected with each feast mentioned above. (2) The seven lines of testimony mentioned above. List examples of each. (3) The following miracles as "signs," pointing out what they symbolize about Jesus: (a) The Cana miracle, 2:1-11; (b) The nobleman's son, 4:48-54; (c) The impotent man, 5:1-16; (d) Feeding five thousand, 6:3-14; (e) Walking on the sea, 6:16-20; (f) Healing the blind man, 9:1-16; read all the chapter; (g) Raising Lazarus, Ch. 11; (h) The draft of fishes, 21:1-11. (4) The following discourses: (a) The conversation with Nicodemus, Ch. 3; (b) The conversation with the woman at the well, Ch. 4; (c) The discourse on the shepherd and the sheep, Ch. 10; (d) The discussions of chapter 13; (e) The discourse on the vine, Ch. 15; (f) The Lord's prayer, Ch. 17. (5) From the following passages find the cause or explanation of unbelief, 1:45; 3:11, 19, 20; 5:16, 40, 42, 44; 6:42, 52; 7:41, 42, 48; 8:13, 14, 45; 12:26, 44; 20:9. (6) From the following study the results of unbelief, 3:18, 20, 36; 4:13, 14; 6:35, 53, 58; 8:19, 34, 55; 14:1, 28; 15:5;

16:6, 9. (7) Make a list of all the night scenes of the book and study them. (8) Study each instance of someone worshiping Jesus. (9) Name each chapter of the book so as to indicate some important event in it- as the vine chapter or Good Shepherd chapter. (10) Find where and how many times each of the following words and phrases occurs and study them as time will admit. (1) Eternal life, 17 times, only 18 in all the other gospels, (2) believe, (3) believe on, (4) sent, (5) life, (6) sign or signs (Revised version), (7) work or works, (8) John the Baptist, (9) verily, always double and used by Jesus, (10) receive, received, etc., (11) witness, or testify, testimony, etc.. (12) truth, (13) manifest, manifested, (14) "I am" (spoken by Jesus).

28
ACTS.

Chs. 1-9.

The Author. The author is Luke who wrote the gospel of Luke. Facts concerning him may be found in chapter twenty-seven. He wrote this book about A. D. 63 or 64.

The Purpose. It was addressed to an individual as a sort of continuation of the former thesis and aims to chronicle the growth and development of the movement inaugurated by Jesus as it was carried on by the apostles after the resurrection and ascension of Jesus. It is taken up largely with the history of Christian work among the Gentiles and only gives enough of the history of the Jerusalem church to authenticate the work among the Gentiles. The chief purpose, therefore, seems to be to give an account of the spread of Christianity among the Gentiles. This view is further strengthened in the fact that Luke himself was a gentile (Col. 4:10) and that he was a companion of Paul (Col. 4:14) and the "we" section of Acts. The book does not, therefore, claim to be a complete account of the labors of the early apostles. But it does give in a simple, definite and impressive manner an account of how the religion of Jesus was propagated after his death and of how it was received by those to whom it was first preached.

The Spirituality. In the Old Testament God the Father was the active agent. In the gospels God the Son (Jesus) was the active agent. In Acts (and ever after) God the Holy Spirit is the active agent. He is mentioned about seventy times in Acts. The Savior had told the apostles to wait at Jerusalem for the power of the Holy Ghost. Until they were endued with His power they were very ordinary men. Afterward they were pure in their purpose and ideals and were always triumphant in their cause. The book is a record of mighty spiritual power seen in action everywhere.

Analysis.

Introduction, 1:1-3.
I. The Church Witnessing in Jerusalem, 1:4-8:11.
1. Preparation for witnessing, 1:4-2:4.
2. First witnessing, 2:4-47 end.
3. First persecution, 3:1-4:31.
4. Blessed state of the church, 4:32-5:42.
5. First deacons, 6:1-7.
6. The first martyr, 6:8-8:1.
II. The Church Witnessing in Palestine, 8:2-12:25.
1. The witnesses are scattered abroad, 8:2-4.
2. Philip witnesses in Samaria and Judea, 8:5-40.

    3. The Lord wins new witnesses, 9:1-11:18.

    4. Center of labor changed to Antioch, 11:19-30.

    5. The witnesses triumph over Herod's persecution, 12:1-25.

    III. The Church Witnessing lo the Gentile World, 13:1-28:31.

    1. Witnessing in Asia, Chs. 13-14. Paul's First Missionary Journey.

    2. The first church council, 15:1-35.

    3. Witnessing in Europe, 15:36-18:22. Paul's Second Missionary Journey.

    4. Further witnessing in Asia and Europe, 18:23-21:17. Paul's Third Missionary Journey.

    5. Paul, the witness, rejected and attacked by the Jews at Jerusalem, 21:18-23:35.

    6. Two years imprisonment at Caesarea, Chs. 24-26.

    7. Paul, the witness, carried to Rome, 27:1-28:15.

    8. Paul, the witness, at Rome, 28:16-31.

For Study and Discussion. (1) The first church conference for business, 1:15-26. (2) The coming of the Holy Spirit, 2:1-4. (3) Peter's sermon on the day of Pentecost, 2:5-47. (4) The first miracle, ch. 3. (5) The first persecution, 4:1-31. (6) Death of Annanias and Sapphira, 5:1-11. (7) The first deacons, 6:1-7. (8) The first martyr, ch.7. (9) Philip's work in Samaria, 8:5-40. (10) Conversion of Saul, 9:1-31. (11) Conversion of Cornelius, 10:1-11:18. (12) List the principal churches of the book, their location and what makes them notable. (13) List the principal preachers of the book and note the sermons or miracles, etc., that make them prominent. (14)The sermons and addresses of the book, to whom each was delivered, its purpose, etc.(15) The chief elements of power of these early disciples. (16) The growth of Christianity and the hindrances it had to overcome. (17) The great outstanding teachings of these early Christians. (18) The tact and adaptation of the apostles (give examples). (19) The different plans to kill Paul and the way by which he escaped each. (20) The missionary journeys of Paul and his journey to Rome as a prisoner.

29
ROMANS.

The Author. Paul, the author, was a Hebrew by descent, a native of Tarsus in Cilicia, and educated by Gamaliel, the great Pharisaic teacher. He was one of the most unmerciful persecutors of the early Christians, but was converted by the sudden appearance to him of the risen Lord. He began preaching at Damascus, but on account of persecution went into Arabia. Returning from Arabia he visited Jerusalem and Damascus, and then went to Cilicia, where he doubtless did evangelistic work until Barnabas sought him at Tarsus and brought him to Antioch, where he worked a year with Barnabas. After this they went up to Jerusalem with contributions for the brethren. Upon return to Antioch he was called by the Holy Ghost to mission work in which he continued till his death, making at least three great missionary journeys, during which and afterward he suffered "one long martyrdom" till his death.

Paul's Epistles. Paul's epistles are commonly put into four groups as follows: (1) *The Eschatological group,* or those dealing with the second coming of Christ. These are I. and II. Thessalonians and were written from Corinth about 62 to 63 A. D. (2) *The Anti-Judaic group*, or those growing out of controversy with Judaistic teachers. They are I. Corinthians. II. Corinthians, Galatians and Romans, written during the third Missionary journey, probably at Ephesus, Philippi, and Corinth. (3) *The Christological group*, which center their teachings around the character and work of Jesus, and were written during the imprisonment at Rome. They are Philippians, Colossians, Philemon, Ephesians, and Hebrews (many think Paul did not write Hebrews). (4) *The Pastoral Group*, or those written to young preachers touching matters of church organization and government and practical instructions concerning evangelists, pastors, and other Christian workers. They are 1 Timothy, 2 Timothy and Titus.

All of Paul's epistles, unless it be Hebrews, fall very naturally into five sections, as follows: (1) An introduction, which may contain a salutation, usually including the subject of the epistle and the name of those with Paul as co-laborers at the time of the writing, and a thanksgiving for the good character or conduct of those whom he addresses. (2) A Doctrinal Section, in which he discusses some great Christian teaching, which needs special emphasis as the case of the church or individual addressed. (3) A Practical Section, in which he sets forth the practical application of the principles discussed in the doctrinal section to the life of those addressed. (4) A Personal Section, in which are personal messages and salutations sent to and by various friends. (5) A Conclusion, in which may be found a benediction or autograph conclusion to authenticate the letter, maybe both, with other closing words.

The Occasion of the Roman Epistle. (1) Paul longed to go to Rome (Acts 19:21) and now hoped soon to do so (Romans 15:24-33). He may, therefore, have wished them to know of his doctrine before his arrival, especially as they had perhaps heard some false reports of it. (2) It was just after he wrote Galatians and Paul's mind was full of the doctrine of justification, and he may have desired to write further upon the subject, giving special emphasis to the Divine side of the doctrine as he had given to the human side of it in Galatians. (3) Then, too, he may have been misunderstood in Galatians and desired to enlarge upon his teaching. In Galatians man is justified by believing, in Romans God gives his own righteousness to the believer for his justification. (4) Phoebe, a woman of influence and Christian character, a friend of Paul, was about to go to Rome from the coasts of Corinth, and Paul not only had a good opportunity to send the letter, but could do her a service by way of introducing her (16:1-2).

The Church at Rome. It was doubtless in a very prosperous condition the time of Paul's writing. It was perhaps organized by some Jews heard and believed while at Jerusalem, probably on the day of Pentecost. While its membership included both Jews and Gentiles (1:6- 13; 7:1), it was regarded by Paul as especially a Gentile church (1:3- 7; 13-15).

Some Errors of Doctrine and Practice Had Crept in Which Needed Correction. (1) They seem to have misunderstood Paul's teachings and to have charged that he taught that the greater the sin the greater the glory of God (3:8). (2) They may have thought him to teach that we should sin in order to get more grace (6:1) and, therefore, may have made his teaching of justification by faith an excuse for immoral conduct.

(3) The Jews would not recognize the Gentile Christians as equal with them in Christ's Kingdom (1:9, 29, etc.). (4) Some of the Gentile brethren, on the other hand, looked with contempt upon their narrow and prejudiced and bigoted Jewish brethren (14:3). (5) Paul, therefore, aimed to win the Jews to Christian truth and the Gentiles to Christian love.

Paul's Connection With the Church. He had never been there up to this time (1:11, 13, 15) and it is not likely that any other apostles had been there. For then Paul would have not have been planning to go since his rule was not to go where another had worked (15:20; 2 Cor. 10:14-16). This strikes a heavy blow at Catholicism, claiming that Peter was first bishop of Rome. If Paul would not have followed him, then Peter had not been there, and the most important test of papacy is overthrown. Paul had, however, many intimate friends and acquaintances at Rome, many of whom were mentioned in chapter 16. Among them were his old friends, Aquila and Priscilia.

The Argument of the Book. The doctrines of the book are considered and discussed under four main propositions: (1) All men are guilty before God (Jews and Gentiles alike). (2) All men need a Savior. (3) Christ died for all men. (4) We all, through faith, are one body in Christ.

Date. Probably from Corinth, about A. D. 58.

Theme. The gift of the righteousness of God as our justification which is received through faith in Christ, or justification by faith.

Analysis.

Introduction, 1:1-17.

I. All Men Need of Righteousness, 1:18-3:20.

II. All Men May Have Righteousness by Faith in Christ (justification) 3:21-4 end.

III. All Who Are Thus Justified Will Be Finally Sanctified, Chs. 5-8. The believer's final redemption is thus guaranteed.

1. By the new relation to God which this righteousness gives. Ch. 5.

2. By the new realms of grace into which it brings him, Ch. 6 (no death in this realm).

3. By the nature given him, Ch. 7. This wars against the old nature and will win.

4. By the new possession (the Holy Spirit) which it gives, Ch. 8:1- 27.

5. By the foreordained purpose of God for them, 8:28-39.

IV. This Doctrine as Related to the Rejection of the Jews, chs. 9-11.

1. The justice of their rejection, 9:1-29.

2. The cause of their rejection, 9:30-10 end.

3. The limitations of their rejection, ch. 11.

V. The Application of This Doctrine to Christian Life, 12:1-15:13.

1. Duty to God-consecration, 12-12.

2. Duty to self-a holy life, 12:3 end.

3. Duty to state authorities-honor, 13:1-7.

4. Duty to society-love all, 13:8-10.

5. Duty as to the Lord's return-watchfulness, 13:11-14.

6. Duty to the weak -helpfulness and forbearance, 14:1-15:13.

Conclusion. 15:14-16 end. (1) Personal matters, 14:14 end. (2) Farewell greetings and warnings, ch. 16.

For Study and Discussion. (1) The greeting (1:1-

7). What does it reveal about, (a) The call, duty and standing of an apostle or preacher? (b) The standing, privileges and duties of a church, or individual Christian? (c) The relation of the old dispensation to the new? (d) Christ's diety or his Messiahship in fulfillment of prophecy? (e) The different persons of the Trinity? (2) Study sin as described in 3:10-18, and what can be learned concerning: (a) The state of sin, (b) The practice of sin, (c) The reason for sin. (3) Abraham as an example of justification by faith, ch. 4. (4) The plan and method by which God rescues men from sin, 5:6-11. (5) The contrast between Adam and Christ. 5:12-31. Do we get more in Christ than we lost in Adam? (6) Why a matter under grace should not continue in sin, 6:1-14. (7) A converted man's relation to the law. 7:1-6. (8) The different things done for us by the Holy Spirit, 8:1-27. (9) The practical duties of a Christian, ch. 12. (10) Make a list of the following "key-words," showing how many times and were each occurs, and outline form the scripture references the teachings about each. Power, sin and unrighteousness, righteousness, justification, faith and belief, atonement, redemption, adoption, propitiation, election, predestination.

30
FIRST AND SECOND CORINTHIANS.

The City of Corinth. It contained 400,000 inhabitants and was the chief city of Greece when Paul visited it, being situated on a large isthmus where the commerce of the world passed. The inhabitants were Greeks, Jews, Italians and a mixed multitude from everywhere. Sailors, merchants, adventurers and refugees from all the world crowded the city, bringing with them the evils of every country, out of which grew many forms of human degradation. Religion and philosopy had been prostituted to low uses. Intellectual life was put above moral life, and the future life was denied that they might enjoy the present life without restraint.

The Church at Corinth. It was founded by Paul on the second missionary journey (Acts 18:1-18). His spirit in founding the church is seen in 1 Cor. 2:1-2. While there Paul made his home with Aquila and Priscilla, Jews who had been expelled from Rome (Acts 18:2-3), but who now became members of the church. Apollos preached to this church and aided it in Paul's absence (18:24-28; 19:1). Both Epistles are full of information as to the condition of the church and the many problems which hit had to face from time to time. It must be remembered that Corinth was one of the most wicked cities of ancient times and that the church was surrounded by heathen customs and practices. Many of its members had but recently been converted from heathenism to Christianity and the church was far from ideal.

First Corinthians.

The Occasion and Purpose of the Letter. Unfavorable news had come to Paul concerning the Corinthian church and he had written them a letter (5:9) which has been lost. In that letter he seems to have commanded them to give up their evil practices and promised to visit them. In the meantime, members of the household of Chloe(1:11) and other friends (16:17) came to him at Ephesus and brought news of their divisions and of the evil practices of certain of their members. Finally, they wrote him a letter asking his advice on certain matters (7:1). From all this we learn (1) that there were four factions among them, 1:2; (2) that there was gross immorality in the church as in the case of the incestuous person, Ch. 5; (3) that they went to law with each other, Ch. 6; (4) that many practical matters troubled them. Paul, therefore, wrote to correct all these errors in doctrine and practice.

Content. This letter contains some of the greatest passages in the New Testament. It is, however, remarkable especially for the very practical nature of its contents. It deals with many of the problems of every day life and has been said not to discuss but one great doctrine, that of the resurrection.

Date. From Ephesus in the spring of A. D. 57.

Analysis.

Introduction, 1:1-9.
I. Concerning Divisions and the Party Spirit. 1:10-4.
Divisions are prevented:
1. By Christ as the center of Christianity, 1:10 end.
2. By spiritual mindedness, 2:1-3:4.
3. By a right view of preachers, 3:5-4 end.
II. Correction of Moral Disorders, Chs. 5-6.
1. The incestuous person, Ch. 5.
2. Lawsuits, 6:1-11.
3. Sins of the body, 6;12 end.
III. Answers to Questions and Cognate Matters, 7:1-16:4.
1. Concerning marriage and celibacy, Ch. 7.
2. Concerning things offered to idols. 8:1-11:1.
3. Concerning head dress, 11:2-16.
4. Concerning the Lord's supper, 11:17 end.
5. Concerning spiritual gifts, Chs. 12-14.
6. Concerning the resurrection, Ch. 15.
7. Concerning collections for the saints, 16:1-4.
IV. Personal Matters and Conclusion, 16:5 end.

For Study and Discussion. (1) Earthly wisdom and heavenly foolishness, 1:18-25. (2) Spiritual wisdom, 2:7-16. (3) Paul's apostolic labors, 4:9-13. (4) The scripture estimate of the human body, 6:12-20. (5) Marriages and divorce, 7:25-50, letting "virgin" mean any single person, male or female. (6) Paul's practice in the matter of his rights, 9:1-23. (7) The Christian race, 9:24-27. (8) Love and its nature, Ch. 13. (a) Superior to other gifts, 1-3. (b) Its ten marks, 4-6. (c) Its power, 7. (d) Its permanence, 8-13. (9) Spiritual gifts, Chs. 12-14. Name and describe them. (10) The resurrection, Ch. 15. (a) Calamities to result, if there were none-or the other doctrines here made to depend on the resurrection; (b) The nature of the resurrected body.

Second Corinthians.

The Occasion and Purpose of the Letter. From suggestions found here and there in these two epistles it appears that much communication passed between Paul and the church and that the two letters that have come down to us are only some of a series. He suffered much perplexity and grief because of the conditions of the church. He met Titus in Macedonia on the third missionary journey (he had hoped for him with news from Corinth while he was at Troas). He wrote this letter in response to the messages brought by Titus. He expresses solicitude for them, defends himself against the charges of his enemies, warns them against errors, instructs them in matters of duty and expresses joy that they have heeded his former advice.

The Character and Content. It is the least systematic of all Paul's epistles. It abounds in emotion, showing mingled joy, grief and indignation. It is intensely personal and from it we, therefore, learn more of his life and character than from any other source. This makes it of great value in any study of Paul himself. Section one has as its great topic tribulation and consolation in tribulation, and has in it an undercurrent of apology, darkened by a suppressed indignation. Section two is colored by a sorrowful emotion. Section three everywhere teems with a feeling of indignation. Through the whole letter there runs an undercurrent of self-defense. The "key-note" of this book, as well as of First Corinthians, is loyalty to Christ.

Date. It was written from Macedonia (probably Philippi) fall of A.D. 57.

Analysis.

Introduction, 1:1-7.
I. Paul's Trials, Principles and Consolation as a Preacher, 1:8- 7:16.
 1. His interest in the Corinthian church. 1:8-2:11.
 2. His service both to God and men, 2:12 end.
 3. His appointment by the Holy Spirit, Ch. 3.
 4. His power given by God, Ch. 4.
 5. His hope of future blessedness, 5:1-19.
 6. His exhortation and appeal to the church. 5:20-7:4.
 7. His joy at their reception of the word, 7:5 end.
II. The Collection for the Poor Saints, Chs. 8-9.
 1. The appeal for liberality, 8:1-15.
 2. The sending of Titus and two other brethren, 8:16-9:5.
 3. The Blessedness of liberality, 9:6 end.
III. Paul's Apostolic Authority. 10:1-13:10.
 1. He vindicates his apostolic authority, 10:1-12:13.
 2. He warns them that his coming will be with apostolic authority, 12:14-13:10.
Conclusion, 13:11 end.

For Study and Discussion. (1) Paul's reasons for not going to Corinth, 1:15-2:4. (2) The glory of the gospel ministry, 4:1-6. (3) His affectionate injunction, 6:11-18. (4) The grace of liberality, Chs. 8-9. Make a list of (a) ways of cultivating this grace, (b) the blessings it will bring to the possessor, to others and to the whole church. (5) Paul's boasting, 11:16-12:20. (a) Of what things did he boast? (b) When is boasting justifiable? (6) Paul's self-defense? When should we defend ourselves? (7) The vision of the third heaven, 12:1-4. (8) The thorn in the flesh, 12:7-9. (9) The personal attacks on Paul. Note the hints in 2:17; 4:3; 5:3; 10:8; 10:10; 11:6.

31
GALATIANS AND EPHESIANS.

Galatians.

The Country. (1) *Politically* it was the Roman province which included Lycaonia, Isauria, and parts of Phrygia and Pisidia. (2) Geographically it was the center of the Celtic tribes, and in this sense it seems to be used in this epistle and in Acts (Gal. 1:1; Acts. 13:14; 14:6; 16:6).

The Celtic People. They were descended from the Gauls who sacked Rome in the fourth century B. C. and in the third century B. C. invaded Asia Minor and northern Greece. A part of them remained in Galatia. predominating in the mixed population formed out of the Greek, Roman and Jewish people. They were quick-tempered, impulsive, hospitable and fickle people. They were quick to receive impressions and equally quick to give them up. They received Paul with enthusiastic joy, and were then suddenly turned from him (Gal. 4:13-16).

The Churches of Galatia. Just how and by whom

these churches were established we do not know. The great highway from the East to Europe passed through this region, making it possible for some of those present at Pentecost to have sown the seed of the gospel there. It could have sprung up from work done by Paul while at Tarsus from the time of his return from Arabia to his going to Antioch with Barnabas. But the scripture gives us no word about this.

On the second missionary journey Paul visited them (Acts 16:6) and seems to have been taken sick while passing through and to have preached to them while unable to travel (Gal. 4:14-15). They gladly received his teaching, and churches seem to have sprung up. Paul also visited them while on the third missionary journey (Acts 18:23) and instructed and established them in the faith. The churches were running well when Paul left them, but Judaizing teachers had now come in and, acting upon their fickle and unstable nature, had greatly corrupted the simplicity of their faith.

The Occasion of the Epistle. (1) Judaizing teachers had gone among the Galatians, claiming that the Jewish law was binding upon Christians, admitting that Jesus was the Messiah, but claiming that salvation must, nevertheless, be obtained by the works of the law. They especially urged that all Gentiles be circumcised. (2) In order to gain their point and turn the Galatians from their belief, they were trying to weaken their confidence in Paul, their spiritual teacher. They said he was not one of the twelve, and therefore, not one of the apostles, and his teachings were not of binding authority. They suggested that he had learned his doctrine from others, especially from the apostles who were pillars of the church.

The Purpose of the Epistle. The purpose of the

epistle was to root out the errors of doctrine introduced by the Judaizers and to hold the Galatians to their earlier faith. To do this it was necessary to establish his apostolic authority and the divine origin of his gospel. He also desired to show the practical value or application of his teaching. He especially shows the value of Christian freedom and at the same time shows that it is not license. In fulfilling these purposes he gave us an inspired classic upon the fundamental doctrine of justification by faith and forever settled the disturbing question of the relation of Christians to the Jewish law.

Author and Date. It was written by Paul, probably from Corinth in A.D. 57.

Analysis.

Introduction, 1:1-10.

I. Authoritativeness of Paul's Gospel, 1:11-2 end.

1. It is independent of man, 1:11 end.

2. It is the gospel of an apostle, Ch. 2.

II. Teaching of Paul's Gospel, Chs. 3-4. Justification by faith.

1. Their experience proves it, 3:1-5.

2. The example of Abraham attests it, 3:6-8.

3. The scripture teaches it, 3:10-12.

4. The work of Christ provides for it, 3:13-14.

5. Its superior results demonstrate it. 3:15-4:20.

6. The experiences of Sarah and Hagar and their sons illustrate it, 4:21 end.

III. Application of Paul's Gospel to Faith and Conduct, 5:1-6:10.

1. He exhorts them to stand fast in the liberty of Christ; 5:1-12; 5:12. This liberty excludes Judaism.

2. He exhorts them not to abuse their liberty, 5:13-6:10.

Conclusion, 6:11 end.

For Study and Discussion. (1) The dangers of fickleness (1:6; 4:9; 15:16). (2) The methods of false teachers: (a) Their chief method is to attack men prominent in the movement, (b) They usually put forward some one else for leader; They would supplant Paul with Peter, (c) One may well consider how a man will often allow the influence of another to be undermined if he is himself exalted. (3) The reasons Paul gives to show that his teaching is not of man, 1:11 end. (4) The confirmation of Paul's divine call, 2:1-10. (5) Difference between one under law and under faith, 4:1-7. (6) The lusts of the flesh, sins of body and mind are included, 5:19-21. (7) The fruits of the spirit, 5:22-23. (8) The words, liberty, lust, flesh, spirit, works of the law, live and die, servant and bondage, justified, righteousness, faith and believe. (9) For more advanced study list and study passages in Galatians that coincide with or correspond to passages in Romans.

Ephesians.

The City. It was the capital of pro-consular Asia, being about a mile from the sea coast, and was the great religious, commercial and political center of Asia. It was noteworthy because of two notable structures there. First, the great theatre which had a seating capacity of 50,000 people, and second, the temple of Diana which was one of the seven wonders of the ancient world. It was 342 feet long and 164 feet wide, made of shining marble, supported by a forest of columns 56 feet high, and was 220 years in building. This made it the center of the influence of Diana worship, of which we read in Acts 19:23-41. The statue with its many breasts betokened the fertility of nature.

Next to Rome, Ephesus was the most important city visited by Paul. It has been called the third capital of Christianity, it being the center of work in Asia through which were founded all the churches of Asia, especially the seven churches of Asia to which Jesus sent the messages of Revelations. Jerusalem, the birth place of power, is the first, and Antioch, the center of mission work, is the second capital.

Paul's Work at Ephesus. (1) Revisited there on the return from the second missionary journey (Acts 18:18-21). and left with them Aquila and Priscilla. (2) On the third missionary journey he spent about three years there, (Acts 20:31). (3) During this second visit he had such influence as to check the worship of Diana to such an extent as to arouse the opposition of her worshippers and make it necessary for him to depart into Macedonia (Acts 20:1). (4) On the return from the third missionary journey he stopped at Miletus, thirty miles away, and sent for the elders of Ephesus to whom he delivered a farewell address (Acts 20:16-38).

The Epistle. The contents are much akin to those of Colossians, but also differ greatly from them. (1) In each book half is doctrinal and half practical. (2) Colossians discusses Christ-hood or Christ the head of the church, while Ephesians discusses church-hood or the church as the body of Christ. (3) In Colossians Christ is "All and in all", in Ephesians the ascended Christ is seen in his church. (4) In Colossians we have Paul in the heated arena of controversy; in Ephesians he is quietly meditating upon a great theme.

It has been said to contain the profoundest truth revealed to men, and the church at Ephesus was, perhaps, better prepared than any other to be the custodian of such truth, since Paul's long stay there had so well prepared them to hear and understand it. It may have been written as a circular letter to be sent in turn to several churches of which the church at Ephesus was one.

Date. By Paul, probably from Rome, A. D. 62 or 63.

Theme. The church, Christ's mystical body.

Analysis.

Salutation, 1:1-2.
I. The Spiritual Blessings of the Church. 1:3-14.
1. The origin of these blessings, v. 3.
2. The blessings enumerated, 4-14.
II. Prayer for the Readers, 1:15 end.
1. That God may grant them the spirit of wisdom, the Holy Spirit, 15-17.
2. That they may know what they have in Christ, 18-33.
III. The Great Work Done for Them, Ch. 2. Both Jews and Gentiles.
1. They were regenerated, 1:10.
2. They were organized, 11 end.
IV. Paul's Mission and Prayer for Them, Ch. 3.
1. His mission to preach the mystery of Christ. 1-13.
2. His prayer for them and doxology of praise to God, 14 end.
V. The Duty of the Churches as the Body of Christ, 4:1-6:20.
1. Duty of individual members in relation to

other members and to the world. 4:1-5:21.

2. Duties of individuals in their home relations, 5:22-6:9.

3. Duties of individual members in their relation to the organized efforts of the church. 6:10-20.

Conclusion, 6:21 end.

For Study and Discussion. (1) The Christian's standing before God, Chs. 1-2. Such words as sealed, chosen, quickened. (2) The blessings of the church, make a list, 1:3-14. (3) The elements and characteristics of the new life, 4:25-32. (4) The different things done in an intelligent Christian life, 5:3-17. (5) The exalted nature and office of Christ, 1:2-33; 2:13-22. (6) The eternal purpose of God, 2:3-5; 2:4-7; 3:9-12. (7) Principles of Christian sociology seen in the home relations such as husband and wife, child and parents, and servant and master. (8) The Christian's relation to Christ as seen in these relations.

32
PHILIPPIANS AND COLOSSIANS.

Philippians.

The City. It belonged to Thrace until 358 B. C., when it was seized by Philip, king of Macedon, father of Alexander the Great It was the place where Marcus Antonius and Octavius defeated Brutus and Cassius (42 B. C.). which defeat overthrew the Roman Oligarchy, and Augustus (Octavius) was made Emperor. Is was on the great highway through which all trade and traders going eastward and westward must pass, and was, therefore, a fit center of evangelism for all Europe. It was the place where the first church Of Europe was established by Paul on his second missionary journey, A. D. 52.

Paul's Connection with the Church. By a vision from God he went to Philippi on the second missionary journey (Acts 16:9-12). He first preached at a woman's prayer-meeting, where Lydia was converted. She furnished him a home while he continued his work in the city. After some time there arose great opposition to him and he and Silas were beaten and put in prison, but through prayer they were released by an earthquake which also resulted in the conversion of the jailer (Acts ch. 16). He perhaps visited them again on his journey from Ephesus to Macedonia (Acts 20 2 Cor 2:12-13; 7:5-6). He spent the Passover there (Acts 20:6) and received messages from them (Phil. 4:16). They also sent him assistance (Phil. 18) and he wrote them this letter.

The Character and Purpose of the Letter. It is an informal letter with no logical plan or doctrinal arguments. It is the spontaneous utterance of love and gratitude. It is a tender, warm-hearted, loving friend and brother presenting the essential truths of the gospel in terms of friendly intercourse. He found in them constant reasons for rejoicing, and now that Epaphroditus who had brought their aid to him was about to return from Rome to Philippi, he had an opportunity to send them a letter of thanks (Phil. 4:18). It is remarkable for its tenderness, warnings, entreaties and exhortations and should be read often as a spiritual tonic.

Date. It was written by Paul during his imprisonment at Rome, about A. D. 62.

Analysis.

Introduction, 1:1-11.
I. Paul's Present Situation and Feeling. 1:12-26.
II. Some Exhortations, 1:27-2:18.
III. He Plans to Communicate with Them, 2:19 end.
IV. Some Warnings, ch. 3.
  1. Against Judaizers, 1-16.
  2. Against false professors, 17 end.

V. Final Exhortation. 4:1-9.

VI. Gratitude for Their Gifts, 4:10-19.

Conclusion, 4:20 end.

For Study and Discussion. (1) Paul as a good minister, 1:3-8. Paul's prayer for the Philippians, 1:9-11. (3) The choice between life death, 1:19-26. (4) Humble-mindedness and its rewards as seen in Jesus 2:5-11. (5) An upright Christian life, 2:12-18. (6) Paul's sense of imperfection, 3:12-16. (7) Worthy meditations, 4:8-9. (8) Outline the information the book gives concerning Paul's condition at the time of the writing. (9) Point out all the teachings of the book on the necessity of cultivating unselfishness and the blessing derived from it. (10) The expression of joy and rejoicing. (11) The number of times our Lord, under different names, is referred to.

Colossians.

The City. It was situated about 100 miles east of Ephesus, and was of little importance at the time of this epistle, though it had once been of considerable influence. It was one of a group of three cities, Laodicia and Hierapolis being the Other two, situated on the Lycus river near where it flows into the famous Meander.

The Church of Colossae. It was perhaps founded by Epaphras (1:6-7; 4:12-13) who was directed by Paul in his work there "for us" "on our behalf", (1:7). Paul though having a very vital connection with it. had never visited the church (1:7; 2:1). He seems to have kept posted about conditions in the church (1:3; 4, 9, 2:1), and to have approved the work and discipline of the church (1:5-7, 23, 2:5-7; 4:12-13). He was loved by them (1:8) and knew and loved some of them. See also Phile 9.

Condition of the Church and Occasion for the Epistle. False teachers or a false teacher, had come among them and had greatly hindered the prosperity of the church. The main source of all their false teaching lay in an old eastern dogma, that all matter is evil and its source also evil. If this were true, God, who is in no wise evil, could not have created matter. And since our bodies are matters they are evil and God could not have created them. From this notion that our bodies are evil two extremes of error arose: (1) That only by various ascetic practices, whereby we punish the body, can we hope to save it, 2:20- 23. (2) That since the body is evil, none of its deeds are to be accounted for. License was, therefore, granted to evil conduct, and evil passions were indulged at pleasure and without impunity (3:5-8).

In seeking to find relief from this condition they formulated two other false doctrines. (1) An esoteric and exclusive theory which was a doctrine of secrets and initiation (2:2, 3, 8). By this doctrine they declared that the remedy for man's condition was known to only a few, and to learn this secret one must be initiated into their company. (2) That since God could not have been creator of these sinful bodies, they could not, therefore, come to him for blessing, and so they formulated, in their theory, a series of intermediary beings or Aeons, such as angels, that must have created us and whom we must worship (2:18), especially as a means of finally reaching God.

All these false theories conspired to limit the greatness and authority of Jesus Christ, and to limit the efficiency of redemption in him (2:9-10). They are called by the one name, Gnosticism, and present four aspects of error in this book. (1) Philosophic, 2:3, 4, 8. (2) Ritualistic, or Judaistic, 2:11, 14, 16-17. (3) Visionary, or angel-worship, 1:16; 2:10, 15, 18. (4) Ascetic practices, 2:20-23. There are three modern applications of the Colossian heresy. (1) Ceremonialism, or ritualism. (2) Speculation. (3) Low standards of righteousness.

The Epistle. The news of these false teachings was brought to Paul probably by Epaphras. 1:7-8, and he wrote to combat them. It is polemic in spirit and argues that we have everything in Christ, that he is the source and Lord of all creation and that he alone can forgive sins and reconcile us to God. It, therefore, represents more fully than any other of Paul's epistles his doctrine of the person and preeminence of Christ.

Analysis.

I. Doctrinal Teachings, Ch. 1.
1. Introduction, 1-14.
2. Christ in relation to creation, 15-17.
3. Christ in relation to the church, 18 end.
II. Polemic Against False Teachings, ch. 2.
1. Introduction, 1-7.
2. Polemic against the general false teachings, 8-15.
3. Polemic against the particular claims of the false teachers, 16 end.
III. Hortatory Section, 3:1-4:6.
1. To a lofty Christian life, 3:1-4.
2. To exchange the old vices for the Christian graces, 3:5-14.
3. To make Christ sovereign over the whole of life, 3:15-17.

4. To the Christian discharge of relative duties, 3:18-4:1.

3. To a proper prayer life, 4:2-6.

IV. Personal Section, 4:7 end.

For Study and Discussion. (1) Paul's prayer for them, 1:9-14. (2) The preeminence of the Savior, 1:5-20. (3) The false and true philosophy of religion, 2:8-15. (4) The worldly vices, 3:5-8. (5) The Christian graces, 3:9-14. (6) The lofty Christian life, 3:15-17. (7) All references to the false teachings as in the words mystery, head, body, Lord, fullness, etc. Note 2:3, 8, 11, 16, 18, and many others. (8) Paul's view of Jesus. Study every reference to him.

33
FIRST AND SECOND THESSALONIANS.

The City of Thessalonica. It was founded by Cassander, King of Macedon 315 B. C., and was about a hundred miles west of Philippi. It was a great commercial center of Paul's time, the inhabitants being Greeks, Romans and Jews. It still exists under the name of Saloniki, and has a population of from 75,000 to 85,000 about half of whom are Jews.

The Church of Thessalonica. Upon being delivered from prison at Philippi. Paul continued his second missionary journey to Thessalonica, having also Silas and Timothy with him (Acts 17:1-5). He spent three Sabbaths there, but on account of the persecution of the Jews, went from there to Berea, then to Athens, and then to Corinth where he spent 18 months. The first letter bears testimony to the splendid Christian character of these new converts from heathenism.

First Thessalonians.

This is probably the first epistle written by Paul and perhaps the first written document of the Christian religion. It is not doctrinal, has no element of controversy and is one of the most gentle and affectionate of Paul's letters. It is notable for its special salutations and refers to their expectations of the immediate return of Jesus. Its main idea is *consolation* (4:17-18), its keynote *hope* and its leading words *affliction and advent*. Its purpose was: (1) to send affectionate greetings, (2) to console them in their afflictions, (3) to correct their wrong, their mistaken views of Christ's second coming, (4) to exhort then to proper living as against certain immoral tendencies.

Date. From Corinth A. D. 53.

Analysis.

I. The Spiritual Condition of the Church, Ch. 1.
1. Introduction. 1.
2. Their faith, love and hope, 2-3.
3. The cause of these, 4-5.
4. The result of these, 6-10.

II. Paul's Character and Conduct While With Them, 2:1-16.
1. How he brought them the gospel, 1-12.
2. How they received it, 13-16.

III. Paul's Interest in the Church Since Leaving Them. 2:17-3 end.
1. Desired to visit them, 2:17 end.
2. He sent Timothy to them and rejoices in his report of them, 3:1- 10.
3. Benediction upon them, 3:11 end.

IV. Exhortation for the Future, 4:1-5:11.

1. To purity, 4:1-8.
2. To brotherly love, 4:9-10.
3. To honest industry, 4:11-12.
4. To be comforted in the loss of their dead in Christ, 4:13-5:11.

Conclusion, 5:12.

For Study and Discussion. (1) Things in the church for which Paul is thankful, 1:2-6. (2) What is said about how the gospel was preached to them, 2:1-16. (3) Paul's longing to know about them, 3:1-9. (4) The duties enjoined, 4:1-12. (5) The second coming of Christ and the resurrection, 4:13-18. (6) How we are prepared for the great day of his coming, 5:3-10. (7) The several exhortations in 5:12-22. (8) The human elements or explanation of Paul's power as a preacher Ch. 2. (9) The deity of Jesus seen in the book.

Second Thessalonians.

This letter was also written from Corinth and during the same year. It is the shortest letter Paul wrote to any church and is characterized by its lack of special salutations and for its general idea of patient waiting for our Lord. The occasion seems to be to correct their wrong views of the second coming of Christ and the errors of life growing out of it. It may be that they had misunderstood his own teaching to be that the day of the Lord was already at hand (2:2).

Analysis.
Introduction, 1:1-2.

I. Thanksgiving and Prayer for in View of The Second Coming of Christ, 1:2 end.

II. Warnings about Christ's Second Coming. 2:1-12.

III. Their Escape at His Coming, 2:13 end.
IV. Practical Matters, 3:1-15.
1. Their prayers for each other, 1-5.
2. Discipline for the disorderly, 6-15.
Conclusion, 3:16 end.

For Study and Discussion. (1) Things commendable in the church, 13-14. (2) Moral disorders of the church, 3:7-11. (3) How to deal with the disorderly, 3:6, 14, 15. (4) How to deal with the idle, 3:12. (5) Facts concerning Christ's second coming, from the whole book. (6) Facts concerning the judgment of the wicked.

34
FIRST AND SECOND TIMOTHY.

Timothy.

He was a native of Lycaonia. His father was a Greek, but his mother and grandmother were Jews, 2 Tim. 1:5. He was taught the scriptures from his very youth, 2 Tim. 3:15, and was probably converted during Paul's first visit to Lystra, Acts 14:8-20. He was ordained as an evangelist 1 Tim. 4:14; 2 Tim. 1:6, and, after Paul's second visit to Lystra. he spent most of his time with Paul, Acts 16:1. He did much valuable service for Paul, and was greatly esteemed by him. Acts 17:14; 18:5; 20:4; Rom. 16:21; 1 Cor. 4:17; 16:10. His name is associated with Paul in writing a number of letters, 2 Cor. 1:1; Phil. 1:1; Col. 1:1. He was pastor at Ephesus and while there received these letters, 1 Tim. 1:3-4. Paul desired to have him with him when death came, 2 Tim. 4:9; 13, 21.

First Timothy.

This epistle was written while Timothy was pastor at Ephesus, probably between A. D. 64 and 66. Its purpose was to instruct Timothy with regard to his pastoral duties. It, therefore, reflects the condition of the church and especially the errors which he would correct or against which he wished to warn his "true child in the faith."

Analysis.

Greeting, 1:1-2.
I. The True Teachings of the Gospel, 1:3 end.
1. Gnostic teachings and the true purpose of the law, 3-11.
2. Paul's salvation. 12-17.
3. Further warnings against false teachers, 18 end.
II. Public Worship. Ch. 2.
1. Prayer, 1-7.
2. Conduct of men and women in church assemblies, 8 end.
III. Church Officers. Ch. 3.
1. A bishop or pastor, 1-7.
2. Deacons and deaconesses. 8-13.
3. A personal word, 14 end.
IV. Pastoral Duties, 4:1-6:2.
1. As to the true doctrine, Ch. 4.
2. Toward the various classes of the church, 5:1-20.
3. Concerning himself, 5:21 end.
4. In teaching slaves and their masters, 6:1-2.
V. Final Warnings and Exhortations, 6:3 end.
1. Against false teachers, 3-10.
2. To be truly godly, 11-16.

3. To teach the rich aright, 17-19.
4. To be true to his charge, 20 end.

For Study and Discussion. (1) False teachings, 1:3-11; 4:1-8; 6:20-21. (2) The kind of man a pastor should be, 4:12-5:2. (3) The kind of men to select for church officers, 3:1-13. (Fifteen qualifications of a pastor and seven of a deacon). (4) Church government and services of worship, 2:1, 2, 8; 3:14, 15. (5) The word's doctrine or teaching, godliness and faith meaning doctrine.

Second Timothy.

This letter was written from Rome just before his martyrdom A. D. 67. It was written to further instruct Timothy and to explain his own personal affairs. It is the last letter written by Paul, a sort of last will and testimony and is of great importance as it tells as how he fared just before his death. It is more personal in tone than First Timothy and shows us how very pitiable was his plight in these last days.

Analysis.

Introduction, 1:1-5.
I. Exhortations to Timothy. 1:6-2 end.
1. To steadfastness in the gospel. 1:6 end.
2. To patient endurance of suffering, 2:1-13.
3. To faithfulness as a pastor, 2:14-26 end.
II. Warnings to Timothy. 3:1-4:5.
1. Concerning the perilous, 3:1-13.
2. Concerning his duties in such times, 3:14-4:5.
III. Paul's View of Death, 4:6-18.
1. His satisfaction and hope at its approach, 6-8.

2. His hope during this loneliness and need, 9-18. Conclusion, 4:19 end.

For Study and Discussion. (1) Paul's condition when he wrote,1:17; 4:7, 13-16; 6:20. (2) The desire or appeal of 1:4; 3:8; 4:5, 9, 13, 21. (3) The exhortations to Timothy, 1:6, 7, 13, 14; 2:1-6, 15, 23; 3:14; 4:5. (4) perilous times to come, Ch. 3. (5) Paul's view of death, 4:5-22.

35
TITUS AND PHILEMON.

Titus.

The Author. We do not know much of the work of Titus. But from Gal. 2:1-5; 2 Cor. 2:12-13; 7:2-16, and Titus 1:5 and 3:12 we learn: (1) that he was a Gentile whom Paul carried to Jerusalem, (2) that by the liberty of the gospel the Jerusalem council did not require him to be circumcised. (3) that he a capable and an energetic missionary, (4) that Paul had left him in Crete to finish the work which he had begun there.

The Book. The book is written to counsel Titus concerning the work Paul had left him to do (1:5). It contains: (1) the qualifications of the presbyters to be selected; (2) the method of dealing with false teachings; (3) instructions to the different classes of the church; (4) exhortations to Titus himself.

Date. Probably written from Macedonia, A. D. 66.

Analysis.

Greeting, 1:1-4.

I. Qualifications and Duties of Bishops or Pastors, 1:5 end.

1. The qualifications and duties, 5-9.
2. Reasons for needing such officers, 10 end.

II. Instruction in Practical Godliness, 2:1-3:11.

1. Proper conduct for the different classes and its basis, Ch. 2.
2. Proper conduct in the different life relations, 3:1-11.

Conclusion. 3:12-15.

For Study and Discussion. (1) Qualifications of presbyters 1:5-10. (2) Lofty moral ideals for all Christians 2:1-15. (3) Savior and salvation used seven times. (4) Good works or good things, the keyword of the epistles and used seven times. (5) Sound doctrine occurs seven times in this form or as sound in the faith, uncorruption in doctrine, sound speech or doctrine of God. (6) Sober-minded occurring six times, at least in thought. These last three constitute the Epistle's idea of real godliness.

Philemon.

Philemon lived at Colossae and was probably a convert of Paul and member of the Colossian church. Onesimus was a slave of Philemon who had robbed his master (v 18) and fled to Rome where he had been converted under Paul's preaching (v 10). It is the only individual or private letter written by Paul and is written to tell Philemon of the conversion of Onesimus and to make a plea for him. Through the kindness shown Onesimus we have revealed to us the great kindness of the Apostle's heart. He speaks to Philemon not as an apostle in authority, but as a friend to a friend, thereby showing his great courtesy. The letter is of inestimable value as showing the power of the gospel to win and transform a poor slave and to soften the harsh relations between the different classes of ancient society.

Date, From Rome about A. D. 63.

Analysis.

1. Introduction, 1-7.
2. The purpose of the letter-an appeal to Onesimus, 8-21.
3. Closing matters, 22 end.

For Study and Discussion. (1) How Christianity deals with slaves. (2) The effectiveness of the Christian religion in a life: (a) Even a fugitive slave would confess his guilt, as, no doubt, Onesimus had done to Paul; (b) It will make one desire to correct any wrongs one has done, and willing, as was Onesimus, to go to the one wronged and make confession; (c) It often raises one from worthlessness to great usefulness (v 11); (d) It will not only make one useful to others in temporal matters, but will make one profitable in things spiritual (v 13). (3) Concerning a real Christian helper, we may learn that, like Paul: (a) He wilt not try to hide or cover up a man's past faults; (b) He will sympathize with the poor fellow who has a bad record behind him; (c) He will make it as easy as possible for such a convert to right the past; (d) He will gladly use the very humblest Christian (v 13); (e) He will be courteous and recognize the rights of others, as in the case of Philemon; (f) He will not force a man to do his duty, but will use love and persuasion to bring him to it. (4) Make a list of all the persons named and learn something of each.

36
HEBREWS AND JAMES.

Hebrews.

The Author. The writer nowhere indicates his name, and there is difference of opinion as to who wrote it. I am personally inclined to the view of those who regard Paul as the author, which for a long time was the common view. The main points against his authorship are that the language and style are dissimilar to Paul's and that it is less like an epistle than any other book that bears his name. It seems clear, however, that the thoughts and course of reasoning are Pauline and the differences otherwise may be explained by the difference of purpose and spirit in writing. For the arguments for and against his authorship the student is referred to the larger commentaries and introductions to the New Testament literature.

Those To Whom It Was Written. It was, no doubt, addressed to Hebrew Christians, but whether to a special church or to those in a special locality, is a matter of dispute. Several things, however, may be learned about them. (1) They had steadfastly endured persecution and the loss of property. (2) They had shown sympathy with other Christians, 6:10; 10:32-34. (3) They had been Christians some time, 5:12. (4) They knew the writer whom they are, by their prayers, to help restore to themselves, 13:19. (5) They knew Timothy who was to visit them, 13:23. (6) They were now in danger of apostacy to Judaism but had not yet resisted to blood, 12:3-4; 5:11; 6:9. Their danger of going back to Judaism might arise from several sources. (1) There was a tendency to disbelieve Christ and his claims, 3:12. (2) The elaborate worship of the Temple compared with the simple worship of the Christian church. (3) The Jews branded them as traitors and taunted them for turning against the law, which was given by prophets, angels, and Moses, and from the sanctuary ministered to by the priests of God. (4) They were suffering persecution.

Purpose and Contents. The purpose was to prevent apostacy from Christianity to Judaism and incidentally to comfort them in their suffering and persecution. To accomplish this purpose the author shows, by a series of comparisons, that the religion of Christ is superior to that which preceded it. "Better" is the key-word, which along with other terms of comparison such as "more excellent" is constantly used to show the superiority of Christianity. It is very much like a sermon, the author often turning aside to exhort, then returning to the theme.

Date. It was written from Jerusalem, Alexandria or Rome some time before A. D. 70, since the temple was still standing, 9:6-7; 10:1.

Analysis.

I. Christianity is Superior to Judaism because Christ through Whom it was Introduced is Superior to the Messengers of Judaism, chs. 1-6.

    1. He is superior to prophets, 1:1-3.

    2. He is superior to angels. 1:4-2 end.

    3. He is superior to Moses, including Joshua, chs. 3-6.

Three points in each of these comparisons are the same.

    1. He is God's son.

    2. He is man's Savior.

    3. He is man's high priest.

Neither prophets nor angels nor Moses equal Jesus in these points. There are two notable exhortations, (a) 2:1-4; (b) 5:11-6 end.

II. Christianity in Superior to Judaism because Its Priesthood is Superior to that of Judaism, 7:1-10:18.

    1. Christ its priest is superior to the priests of Judaism, 7:1- 8:6.

    2. Its covenant is superior to that of Judaism, 8:7 end.

    3. Its tabernacle is superior to that of Judaism, ch. 9.

    4. Its sacrifice is superior to those of Judaism, 10:1-18.

III. Christianity is Superior to Judaism, because the Blessings it Confers are Superior to those of Judaism. 10:19-11 end.

    1. In the liberty of approach to God, 10:19 end.

    2. In the superior ground of faith, 11:1-12:17.

    3. In our coming to Mount Zion instead of Mount Sinai, 12:18 end.

IV. Practical Conclusion, ch. 13.

For Study and Discussion. (1) Description of Christ. 1:1-3. (2) Christ's superiority to angels. 1:3-14. (3) Christ's humiliation for our salvation, 2:9-18. (4) How is Christ superior to Aaronic priests, 3:14, 15; 5:1-7, 9; 7:28. (5) The two covenants, 8:6-12. (6) Typical character of the old ordinances. 9:1-10:4. (7) Our assurance and hope, 6:13-20. (8) The danger of rejecting Christ, 10:26-31. (9) The benefit of affliction, 12:4-11. (10) The comparisons of 12:18-29. (11) The warning of 13.-8-15, (12) The exhortations of the book, as 2:1-4. Make a list. (13) All the terms of comparison, as better and more excellent. Make a list. (14) Every reference to Christ as high priest. (15) Every reference to the Holy Spirit-What are his works and where in the book is it taught?

James.

The Author. Three persons called James are mentioned in the New Testament. One of these is James, the Lord's brother (Matt. 13:55), who did not believe on Jesus until after the resurrection, Jno. 7:2-9; Mar. 3:21, 31; Acts 1:13-14. This James occupies and important place as pastor at Jerusalem, and made an important speech at the council of the Apostles, Acts 15: 13-21. He is mentioned elsewhere, in Acts, 12:17; Gal. 1:19; 2:9-12. Josephus tells us that he was stoned to death about 62 A. D. on a charge of departing from the Jewish law. This James, the Lord's brother, is supposed to be the author of this epistle.

To Whom Written. This letter was written to the Jews scattered everywhere, 1:1, and evidently to Christian Jews, 2:1. Some of them were rich, some poor, 2:1-10. They were lustful, greedy, and proud,

4:1-12, and were omitting to do the Lord's work as they should. 1:22- 27.

The Epistle. The chief characteristic of style is abruptness. Change is made from one subject to another with no effort to connect them. There is, therefore, no general subject, and a lack of close connection between the points of analysis. "Faith without works is dead" flashes in every section as a sort of bond of unity. It is eloquent, stern and sincere, and has a distinct Jewish tone. It lacks the doctrinal emphasis found in Paul and states the Christian faith in terms of moral excellence and instructs them in the subject of Christian morals. It is notable for its omissions. It does not have the resurrection or ascension and only mentions Christ's name twice. Date and Place of Writing. It was no doubt written from Jerusalem where he was pastor, but the date is much disputed. Some put it as early as A. D. 40. Others among whom is Dr. Robertson say it was written not later than A. D. 50. Still others put it about A. D. 61 or 62, just before the martyrdom of James. It is probably safe to say that it was one of the very earliest of the New Testament books.

Analysis.

Salutation, 1:1.
I. Proper Attitude Toward Trials. 1:2-18.
II. Proper Altitude Toward God's Word, 1:19-27 end.
III. Various Warnings. 2:1-4:12.
1. Against respect of persons, 2:1-13.
2. Against barren professions of faith, 2:14-26.
3. Against the dangers of the tongue, 3:1-12.
4. Against false wisdom, 3:13-18.

5. Against quarrels, greed and pride. 4:1-12.
IV. Various Denunciations, 4:13-5:6.
V. Various Exhortations, 5:7-20 end.

For Study and Discussion. (1) From the following scriptures make a list of all the things James advises us not to do: 1;6, 13, 16, 22; 2:1, 14; 3:1. 10; 4:1, 11, 13; 5:9, 12. (2) From the following scriptures make a list of all the things James advises us to do; 1:2, 4, 5, 6, 9, 11, 22, 26; 2:8, 12; 3:13; 4:8. 5:7, 10, 12, 13, 16, 19. (3) Make a sketch of heavenly wisdom, showing the different things said about it, studying especially, 1:5-8 and 3:13-18. (4) Study the ethics of speech and of the tongue, 1:19-21 and 3:1-12. (5) Life's trial and temptations, 1:2-4, 12-15. (6) Make a list of ail the figures of speech, especially similes and metaphors as "a doubter is like a surge of the sea," 1:6. (7) James' rebuke of selfishness, 5:1- 6. (8) The utility and power of prayer, 5:13-18.

37
FIRST AND SECOND PETER.

The Author. The author was the Apostle Peter, whose name before he became a disciple, was Simon. He was born in Bethsaida and lived in Capernaum where he followed the occupation of fishing. He was brought to Jesus by Andrew, his brother, and became one of the leaders of the Apostles, both before and after Christ's death. His career should be studied as it is found in Acts. He was impetuous, brave and energetic, and after the ascension performed many miracles.

First Peter.

Those Addressed. The sojourn of the dispersion (1:1) points to Jewish Christians. They were strangers (sojourners) 1:1, 17; 2:11, who were persecuted, 3:17; 4:12-19, but whose persecution came, not from the Jews, but from pagans, 4:3-4. They had certain faults and wrong tendencies, 2:1, 11, 12, 16; 8:8-12; 4:9; 5:2-3.

Purpose. To console them in their suffering, and to exhort them to faithfulness and duty.

Date. Probably about 64-68 A. D. Certainly not after 70 A. D., as he was not doubt put to death before then.

Analysis.

Introduction, 1:1-2.

I. Thanksgiving for the Blessing of Grace, 1:3-12.

1. For a living hope and an abiding inheritance, 3-5.

2. For joyful faith during trials, 6-9.

3. For salvation, 10-12.

II. Obligations Growing out of the Blessings of Grace, 1:13-4:19.

1. A right relation of the heart toward God and man, 1:13-2:10.

2. Right conduct in life relations, 2:11-3:12.

3. Right attitude toward suffering, 3:13-4:19 end.

III. Exhortations to Particular Classes, 5:1-9.

Conclusion 5:10 end.

For Study and Discussion. (1) Peter's loyalty to Christ. (a) He makes everything depend on Christ, his cross (1:18-19; 2:24; 3:18), his suffering (2:21; 3:18; 4:13), his resurrection (1:3), his manifestation (1:7-13), his exaltation (3:22; 4:11; 5:10). (b) He calls Christ a living stone, 2:4-8. (c) He clings to Christ's teaching, submission to rightful authority (2:13-16), forgiveness of others (4:8; Matt. 18:22), humility (5:5). (2) The mercy of God our hope 1:3-7. From this passage list what is said of spiritual inheritors and their inheritance. (3) How to obtain the Christian ideal, 1:13-21. (4) Spiritual development. 2:1-10. (5) Various deities of society, 2:13-17; of domestic life 2:18; 3:1, 7; of

Christian brotherhood, 1:22, 2:1-5; 3:8-9; 4:8-11; 5:1-5. (6) The work of the different persons of the Trinity. (7) The words precious, joy and rejoicing, mercy, love and faith.

Second Peter.

The Occasion. The occasion of the epistle is found in the harm being done to the church by false teachers, who were of two classes, the libertines and the mockers about whom he warns.

Purpose. Its purpose was to exhort them to Christian growth and to warn them against false teachers.

Comparison with First Peter. It has no reference to Christ's death, suffering, resurrection and ascension. Glance through 1 Peter again to see how often these are mentioned. The spirit manifested is one of anxiety, severity, and denunciation, white in 1 Peter it is one of mildness, sweetness and fatherly dignity. It connects the second coming of Christ with the punishment of the wicked, while 1 Peter connects it with the glorification of the saints. Its key-note is knowledge, while that of 1 Peter is hope.

Some Teachings. (1) To be holy, not to secure an inheritance, but because we already have it. (2) To love the brethren, not to purify our soul, but because it is pure. (3) That we sacrifice, not as penance, but as an expression of praise.

Analysis.

Introduction, 1:1-2.
I. Progress in the Christian Life, 1:3-21 end.
1. An exhortation to growth, 3-11.
2. Reasons for these exhortations, 12-21.

II. False Teachers, Ch. 2.
1. The evil teachers and their followers, 1-3.
2. Their punishment, 5-10.
3. Their character, evil ways and end, 11-32.

III. The Second Coming of Christ, 3:1-13. He will bring both blessings and destruction.

Conclusion, 3:14-18.

For Study and Discussion. (1) What our salvation involves, 1:5-11. (2) The characteristics of the false teachers, 2:1-3, 10, 12-14. (3) The certain punishment of these false teachers, 2:4-6, 15, 16, 21, 22. (4) The exhortations of the book such as to sobriety, 1:13. (5) The predictions of the book.

38
FIRST, SECOND AND THIRD JOHN AND JUDE.

First John.

Author and Date. It was probably written from Ephesus, 80 or 85 A. D. though some put it as early as A. D. 69, while others put it as late as A. D. 95. The author nowhere indicates his name, but through all the centuries it has been attributed to John, the beloved disciple. For information concerning him see lesson twenty-eight.

The Readers. It was doubtless written primarily to the churches of Asia Minor in which John by reason of his work at Ephesus had a special interest. It is evident that those addressed were of all ages and were hated of the world. They were inclined to worldliness and to the danger of looking too lightly upon sin. They were also in danger of being led into doubt by those who denied the deity of Jesus.

The Style. It is more in the form of a sermon or pastoral address than of an epistle. It is written with a tone of conscious authority. The thought is profound and mystical, but the language is simple both in words and in sentences. The arguments are by immediate inference. Their are many contrasts, parallelisms and repetitions with no figures of speech except perhaps the words light and darkness.

The Purpose. The chief purpose was to tell them how they might know that they had eternal life, 5:13. The accomplishment of this purpose would also assure the fulfillment of the secondary purpose stated in 1:3, 4.

Theme. The evidence of eternal life.

Analysis.

Introduction, 1:1-4.

I. How Those Who Possess Eternal Life will Live, 1:5-5:12.

   1. They will dwell in the light, 1:5-2:28.

   2. They will do righteousness, 2:29-4:6.

   3. They will live a life of love, 4:7-5:3.

   4. They will walk by faith, 5:4-12.

II. What Those who Live such Lives may Know, 5:13-20.

   1. That they have eternal life. 13.

   2. That their prayers are answered, 14-17.

   3. That God's people do not live in sin, 18.

   4. Their true relation to God and to Christ, 19-20.

Conclusion, 5:21.

The following analysis made with the idea of the theme being "Fellowship with God" (1:3-4) is very suggestive.

Introduction, 1:1-4.

I. God is Light and our fellowship with him depends upon our walking in the light, 1:5-2:28.

II. God la Righteous and our fellowship with him depends upon our doing righteousness, 2-29, 4:6.

III. God is Love and our fellowship with him depends upon our having and manifesting a spirit of love, 4:7-5:3.

IV. God Is Faithful and our fellowship with him depends upon our exercising faith in him, 5:4-12.

Conclusion. 5:13-21 end.

For Study and Discussion. (1) The different things we may know and how we may know them. Make a list giving reference, as, "know Him if we keep His commandments" (2:3). (2) Make a list of the things defined in the following scriptures, and give the definition in each case: 1:5; 2:25; 3:11, 3:23; 5:3; 5:4; 5:11; 5:14. (3) The several figures and attributes of God, as light, righteousness and love. (4) The requirements of deeds of righteousness, 1:6, 7; 2:9-11; 3:17-23. (5) God's love for his children, 3:1-2; 4:8-11, 16, 19. (6) Christians' duty to love one another, 2:10; 3:10-24; 4:7-21; 5:1-2. (7) The propitiatory death of Jesus Christ, 1:7; 2:1-2; 4:10. (8) Difference between Christians and non-Christians, 3:4-10. How many times do each of the following words occur? Love, light, life, know, darkness, hate, righteousness, sin, liar and lie, true and truth.

Second John.

It is a friendly, personal letter, written some time after the first letter, to the "elect lady" who, as I think, was John's friend, and not a church or some nation as has sometimes been argued. The aim is evidently to warn his friend against certain false teachers.

Analysis.

1. Greeting, 1-3.
2. Thanksgiving, 4.
3. Exhortation to obedience. 5-6.
4. Warning against anti-Christs, 7-9.
5. How to deal with false teachers, 10-11.
6. Conclusion, 12-13.

For Study and Discussion. (1) The character of the children of the elect lady. (2) Evidence of real discipleship. (3) How to deal with false teachers.

Third John.

This also is a private letter written, some time after First John, to his personal friend, Gaius. There was some confusion about receiving certain evangelists. Gaius had received them while Diotrephes had opposed their reception. He commends Gaius for his Christian hospitality and character.

Analysis.

1. Greeting, 1.
2. Prayer for his posterity, 2.
3. Commends his godly walk, 3-4.
4. Commends his hospitality, 5-8.
5. Complaint against Diotrephes, 9-10.
6. Test of relation to God, and worth of Demetrius, 11-12.
7. Conclusion, 13-14.

For Study and Discussion. (1) The character of Gaius and Diotrephes. (2) Christian hospitality. (3) Such words as truth, sincerity and reality.

Jude.

The author is named as Jude, the brother of James. He probably means the James wrote the epistle of that name and is, therefore, the Lord's brother.

Purpose. False teachers were boldly teaching their heresies in the meetings of the congregation. These men were also very immoral in conduct and the epistle is written to expose their errors and to exhort his readers to contend for the true faith and to live worthy lives. In many points it is very similar to the second letter of Peter.

Date. It was probably written about A. D. 66. At any rate it must have been written before A. D. 70 when Jerusalem was destroyed, as Jude would hardly have failed to mention that event along with other examples of punishment, 5-7.

Analysis.

Introduction, 1-4.
I. The Fate of Wicked Disturbers, 5-16.
1. God punishes the wicked, 5-7.
2. He will destroy these men, 8-16.
II. How to Contend For the Faith, 17-23.
1. Be mindful of the enemies, 17-19.
2. Be strong (built up in the faith), 20-21.
3. Maintain an evangelistic spirit, 22-23.
Conclusion, 24-25.

For Study and Discussion. (1) Make a list of all the words and phrases occurring in threes, as mercy, love, peace, or Cain, Baalam, Korah. (2) Make a list of all the different things taught about the evil workers mentioned, 8-10, 12, 13. 16, 19. (3) What the apostles had foretold concerning them.

39
REVELATION.

Author. John, the Apostle, while in exile on the Isle of Patmos, 1:1, 4, 9; 22:8.

Date. About 95 or 96 A. D.

The Book. (1) It is a book of symbols and imagery, and constantly creates excitement and wonder. (2) It is a book of wars, but war always ends in peace. The word war occurs seven times in Revelation, and only seven times in all the rest of the New Testament. (3) It is a book of thunder, but the thunder and earthquake die away and are followed by liturgies and psalms. (4) It is a book of the rewards of the righteous. This is seen in the letters to the seven churches, and in the victories of the right in all conflicts and wars of the book. (5) It is, therefore, a book of optimism. Everywhere God overcomes Satan, the Lamb triumphs, Babylon falls, etc.

Its Interpretation. There are several classes of interpreters, as follows (1) *The Praeterist*, who thinks it has been fulfilled in its primary sense. He makes all the prophesies and visions refer to Jewish history down to the fall of Jerusalem, and to the history of Pagan Rome. (2) *The Futurist*, who interprets literally and thinks all the events of the book are to come just before or just after the second coming of Christ. (3) *The Historical or Continuous School*. These think some have been fulfilled, some are now being fulfilled, and some will be fulfilled in the future. (4) *The Spiritualist*, who objects to the other three classes of interpreters because they make so much of the time element. He lays stress upon the moral and spiritual element of the book and reads the book "as a representation of ideas rather than of events."

Value. The chief value of the book seems to lie in its testimony to the faith and hope of persecuted Christians and in the comfort and inspiration it has brought to sorrowing and oppressed souls of every age. It points outthat there will be an end of conflict, that God and the Lamb will triumph that the enemies of our souls will be punished and that the followers of God will be rewarded with eternal reward.

Analysis.

Introduction, 1-8.
I. The Seven Churches, 1:9-3 end.
1. A preparatory vision of Christ, 1:9 end.
2. The addresses to the churches, Chs. 2-3.
II. The Seven Seals, 4:1-8:1.
1. A preparatory vision of the throne, Chs. 4-5.
2. Six seals opened in order, Ch. 6.
3. An episode-sealing God's servants, Ch, 7.
4. The seventh seal opened, 8:1.
III. The Seven Trumpets, 8:11 end.
1. A preparatory vision, 8:2-6.
2. Six trumpets sounded in order, 8:7-9 end.

3. An episode-Little book, measuring the temple and two witnesses, 10:1-11:14
   4. The seventh trumpet sounded, 11:15 end.
   IV. The Seven Mystic Figures. Chs. 12-14.
   1. The sun-clothed woman, Ch. 12.
   2. The red dragon, Ch, 12.
   3. The man-child, Ch. 12.
   4. The beast from the sea, 13:1-10.
   5. The beast from the earth, 13:11-18.
   6. The Lamb on Mount Sion, 14:1-13. Three angels.
   7. The son of man on the cloud, 14:14-20. Three angels.
   V. The Seven Vials, Chs. 15-16.
   1. The preliminary vision, Ch. 15-a song of victory.
   2. Six vials poured out in order, 16:1-12.
   3. An episode, 16:13-16. The spirits of the devil gather the kings of the earth to the battle of Armageddon.
   4. The seventh vial poured out, 16:17-21 (end).
   VI. Three Final Conflicts and Triumphs, 17:1-22:5.
   1. The first conflict and triumph, 17:1-19:10.
   2. The second conflict and triumph, 19:11-20:6.
   3. The third conflict and triumph, 20:7-22:5.
   VII. The Epilogue Conclusion, 22:6-21 end.
   1. Three-fold testimony to the truth of the vision. Angel, Jesus. John, 6-8.
   2. Directions of the angels concerning the prophecy, 9-10.
   3. The moral of the book, 11-17.
   4. John's attestation and salutation, 18-21.
   For Study and Discussion. (1) The vision of Jesus, 1:9 end. (2) The letters to the seven churches: (a)

Which churches are given noting but praise? (b) Which nothing but blame? (c) Which both praise and blame? (d) What is commended and what condemned in each. (3) The twenty-four elders, four living creatures, sealed book and the Lamb, Chs. 4-5. (4) The sealing of God's servants, Ch. 7. (5) The little book, Ch. 10. (6) The measuring rod and two witnesses; 11:1-14. (7) Each of the seven mystic figures, Chs. 12-14. Describe each. (8) Mystery Babylon, Ch. 17. (9) Song of triumph over Babylon, 19:1-10. (10) The judgment of Satan, 20:1-10. (11) The description of the general resurrection and judgment, 20:11-15; 22:10-15. (12) The description of heaven, Chs. 21-22. (13) Verify the following points of similarity in the seven seals, seven trumpets and seven vials, (a) that heaven is opened and a preliminary vision before each series, (b) that the first four in each series refer especially to the present natural world, while the last three in each series refer more particularly to the future or spiritual world, (c) that in each series there is an episode after the sixth which is either an elaboration of the sixth or an introduction to the seventh. (14) Compare these three series again and note, (a) that they portray the same events in similar language, (b) that the victory of the righteous and the destruction of the wicked are portrayed in each, (c) that the victory of the redeemed predominates in the first (seals) while the destruction of the wicked predominates in the last (vials). (15) In the series note the progress in the severity of punishment, (a) one- fourth afflicted in the first (seals), (b) one-third afflicted in the second (trumpets), (c) all are destroyed in the third (vials). (16) From the following scriptures make a list allowing how nearly the same thing is affected in each of the seven trumpets and vials, (a) 8:7 and 16:2, (b)

8:8 and 16:3, (c) 8:10-11 and 16:4-7, (d) 8:12 and 16:8-9, (e) 9:9-11 and 16:10-11, (f) 9:13-21 and 16:12-16, (g) 11:15-18 and 16:17-21. (17) The contrasts and resemblances of the trumpets and vials.

Trumpets. 1. Hail, fire blood cast on earth, one-third of the trees burned.

Vails. 1. The Vial poured out on the earth, affliction upon the followers of the beast.

Trumpets. 2. One-third of the sea made blood, one-third of its creatures and of its ships destroyed.

Vails. 2. The whole sea made blood, and every soul therein destroyed.

Trumpets. 3. One-third of the rivers made bitter, many men destroyed.

Vials. 3. All the rivers made blood and vengeance upon all men.

Trumpets. 4. One-third of the sun, etc., smitten, one-third of the day darkened.

Vials. 4. The whole sun smitten, men are scorched, they blaspheme and repent not.

Trumpets. 5. The stars of heaven fall into the pit; locusts sent forth; men seek death.

Vials. 5. The throne and kingdom of the beast smitten, men suffer and blaspheme and repent not.

Trumpets. 6. One-third of the men destroyed by the armies of the Euphrates; men do not repent. Episode: God's two witnesses witness for Him and work miracles. War against them by the beasts.

Vials. 6. A way prepared for the kings beyond the Euphrates. Episode: The dragon's three unclean spirits witness for him and work miracles. War by the world at Armageddon.

Trumpets. 7. Voices in heaven, judgment, earthquake, hail, etc.

Vials. 7, Voice in heaven, fall of Babylon, earthquake, hail, etc.

(18) The benedictions and doxologies of the book. (19) Things taught about Jesus. (20) Things taught about Satan.

END.

THE BIBLE PERIOD BY PERIOD

AUTHOR'S PREFACE.

The author believes that the Bible is the word of God and that it is the inspired revelation of God's will to men and of the plan which he has provided for their redemption. He believes that it contains instructions which alone furnish the basis of wise and worthy conduct both for individuals and for nations. He, therefore, believes that all men should avail themselves of every possible opportunity to acquaint themselves with its teachings and that all Christians should be faithful and even aggressive in their efforts to teach its truths.

Moreover, several years of teaching the Bible to a multitude of students has convinced the writer that what is needed most is a study of the Bible itself rather than things about it. Having this in mind this little volume presents only a small amount of introductory discussion. It offers instead a large number of topics for study and discussion. By following the suggestions for study which they offer the student may gain a working knowledge of the contents of Biblical history.

It is suggested that these outlines will furnish a basis of work for college and academy Bible classes. It is also hoped that it may be adopted for study in many Sunday School classes. If it shall be studied in the Sunday Schools according to instructions which the author will furnish, it will be granted college entrance credit in Baylor University. Women's societies will find it well suited to their Bible study work.

The aim has been to make a companion book to the author's "The Bible Book by Book." The twenty one periods selected are only one of the many ways in which Bible history may be divided and lays no claim to superiority. If this volume shall prove as helpful as the sale of its companion book would indicate that it has been, the work incident to its preparation will be amply repaid.

J. B. Tidwell.
Waco, Texas. 1916.

1
FROM THE CREATION TO THE FALL.

Gen. Chs. 1-3

Problems Solved. This simple narrative solves some of the great problems about which philosophers have speculated and before which scientists have stood baffled. Every child of the human race has asked, "What is the origin of the material world, what is the origin of life, and what is the origin of sin?" In general the philosophers held (and most of what science says concerning these matters is not science but speculative philosophy) that matter was eternal and simply asked how it came to its present state. One group, the materialists, held that an active principle inherent in the matter working through long ages, brought about the present state of things. Another group, the pantheists, held that every thing emanated from a common divine substance, working everywhere in nature. But this brief story lets at rest all this inquiry. It informs us that matter was not eternal nor did it come into existence by chance, but it was created out of nothing by our eternal God. The story incidentally sets forth the majesty and glory of God and man's dependence upon and his obligation to God. It also explains the origin of sin and of all man's ills and death.

Creation of Man. The Story of the preparation of a residence for man is told in five brief paragraphs. For concision, picturesqueness and concreteness, this narrative is not excelled in all literature. It shows how God acting as a creating Spirit through six successive periods of light and darkness prepared the world and put man in it. In the matter of the creation of man the presence and activity of Jehovah is especially emphasized. He shaped the body out of the dust of the earth and breathed into the nostrils of that human form that which made him become a living soul. It was the breath of God that gave life to man and hence he will return again to dust when that breath is withdrawn. Concerning the creation of woman it is better to admit that her creation was supernatural just as was man's. Her creation was to provide for man a helpful companionship so that his development and happiness might be complete. Her creation out of a part of man's body and to meet an inborn need provides the eternal grounds of marriage and the basis upon which they are in marriage to become one flesh and by reason of which man must "love his wife as his own flesh." Man is created in the image of God and like the Creator has intelligence and will and is given authority to rule over the earth.

Man's Home and Occupation. No sooner was man created than was planted in the far distant east a garden that should be to him a home and provide therein for his physical and spiritual needs. Where that garden was located is not known with certainty.

Occupation was, however, provided so that he might exercise and develop each part of his nature. He exercised his mind in naming the animals and in some way the tree of good and evil was destined to be for his blessing. His soul had fellowship with Eve his helpmate and God his creator. This garden also had in it a life-giving tree that gave them the possibility of enjoying an endless life should they remain near it and continue to eat its fruit.

The Temptation. The study proceeds on the basis that there was already a race of fallen beings in the universe. Satan was the chief of these and had the mysterious power of tempting others to follow him. He assumed the form of a serpent-a creature least likely to be suspected and thereby deceived Eve the weaker. The temptation had several elements: (1) The talking serpent was to her in the nature of a miracle; (2) Eve had not heard the command of God herself (it was given before her creation) but had learned it from Adam. The devil therefore raised a doubt as to whether God really forbade it; (3) The question implies a doubt concerning the goodness and wisdom of God; (4) It appeals to the lust of flesh, to the pride of the eye and to the pride of life. It was beautiful, good for food, and to make her wise even like God; (5) In this appeal to curiosity there is an implied dare; (6) She was told that she had a mistaken idea of the penalty-that she should "not surely die."

In all this it will be noted that the temptation was to fall upward. All the motives-the satisfaction of natural appetite, the desire for knowledge and power and the love for beauty were in themselves worthy. The temptation was to better herself. Such it is always. Adam was not directly approached, but he willfully disobeyed without being beguiled as was the woman. The chief blame, therefore, fell upon him.

The Fall and Punishment. The fearful consequences of their sin are felt at once. They are changed so that they are conscious of guilt and endeavor to hide themselves from Jehovah. Thus they acknowledge their unfitness for fellowship with Him. Their soul having lost communion with God, they become corrupt. This is spiritual death. They were banished from the garden and forced to struggle for food. Their bodies became subject to pain and death by separation from the animating spirit. They could not longer eat of the life-giving tree of the garden. The earth was cursed so that instead of ministering to man's pleasure and support, it would produce much to his hurt. The woman in her unredeemed state was to be in subordination to her husband. The sad story of downtrodden women in heathen lands of all times since then, and even today wherever Christ is not known, tells something of the awful results of her sin.

The Hope Offered. The gloom of this sad story of their punishment was relieved by an element of hope. The man and his wife are not beyond the pale of God's love. There is given a promise (3:15) which assures the coming of one, who would contend with the tempter and would finally crush his head and repair the damage of the Fall. All of the rest of the Bible unfolds the plan and work of God in fulfilling this promise. There is beginning with Cain and Abel and running through the entire scripture a record of the conflict caused by the enmity between the seed of woman and that of her seducer. This conflict is to end when Christ the "seed of the woman" shall return to reign and shall cast his adversary into the bottomless pit. Along with this promise he also provided for them garments of the skins of animals such as were suited to their new and hostile environment and in which most writers find a suggestion of the covering of righteousness that comes to guilty sinners through the death of Jesus. Then too there was erected at the east of the garden an alter of worship not unlike that provided in connection with the Tabernacle later and where God dwelt in mercy and could be approached. Here was opened up a way by which they might after being forgiven again have a right to the tree of life and live forever.

Some Teachings of this Story. Back of this story are many truths worthy of most careful study. They constitute the basal facts of all history and religion. The following are put down as among the most vital: (1) Back of all nature is a personal Creator and Ruler who has the tenderest solicitude and care for man, as the highest product of his creation. (2) There was an orderly progress in creation from the more simple and less important to the most complex and most important. (3) All things were made for man and his comfort. (4) Marriage is a sacred obligation growing out of the very character of man and woman who were made for each other and each can, therefore, meet the deepest needs of the other. (5) Sin does not originate in God but in man's yielding to his baser instead of his nobler and diviner motives. (6) Sin as a cause brings its own punishment, the worst of which is the separation of the individual from harmonious relations with God, which is spiritual death.

For Study and Discussion. (1) The condition of the material universe when God began to prepare it for man's abode. (2) The six creative days or periods and what was created in each. (3) The special emphasis upon the presence and activity of God in the creation of man and woman. (4) The divine interest in and preparation for the happiness of man. (5) The home prepared for them. (6) The lessons about marriage, its purpose, basis, etc. (7) The law and place of testing in the formation of character. (8) The ills of life that are the results of some one's sin. (9) The nature and results of the curse upon the man, upon the woman, upon the tempter. (10) God's care for man after the Fall and the provisions for his recovery. (11) The revelation of God made by these three chapters. (12) The image of God in man..

2
FROM THE FALL TO THE FLOOD.

Gen. Chs. 4-8.

Cain and Abel. These two, who are apparently the oldest children of the first pair, were no doubt born soon after the expulsion from the garden. One tilled the soil and the other was a shepherd. They each appear to have been attentive to worship. Their offerings, however, were very different and no doubt revealed a difference of spirit. The superiority of Abel's offering was in the faith in which it was made (Heb. 11:4), meaning perhaps that he relied upon the promise of God and that he apprehended the truth that without shedding of blood there is no remission. (Heb. 12:24).

Because God granted to Abel a token of acceptance of his offering and failed to grant a like token to Cain, the latter became jealous and finally slew his brother. Thus early did Adam and Eve begin to reap the effects of sin. The record, in kindness to them, makes no mention of the great sorrow that must have come to them as they saw their second son murdered by their first-born. These two sons represent two types running through all the Bible and indeed through all history-the unchecked power of evil and the triumph of faith. They represent two types of religion, one of faith and the other of works. Then as in all succeeding ages the true worshipers were persecuted by false worshipers.

God showed his mercy to Cain whom he sent away from the place of worship at the east of the garden by putting upon him the divine mark so that no one should destroy him. He also allowed him to prosper and it was through his descendants that civilization began to show itself.

Cain and Seth-Two Races. Another son was born to Adam named Seth. Probably others have been born since the death of Abel but none of a like spirit to Abel and hence none worthy to become the head of a spiritual branch of mankind. Cain's descendants applied themselves to the arts and to manufactures, to the building of cities and the making those things that furnish earthly comfort, while the descendants of Seth, were selected to be the instruments of religious uplift and to have communion with Jehovah. Through inter-marriage with the descendants of Cain, however, the generation of Seth was corrupted. This led to a period of great wickedness and the destruction of the people by the flood.

The great age of those who lived in this period may have been a provision of nature for the promotion of a rapid increase of the race and for the advancement of knowledge. The revelation of God to them could thereby be the better preserved. Then, too, the body of man was not originally subject to death and when it became so because of his sin, the process of decay may have been less rapid. And, besides, the effect of hereditary disease had not begun to effect and weaken the race.

The Great Wickedness. As indicated above, this Wickedness seemed to arise from the intermarriage of the descendants of Seth and those of Cain. The descendants of Seth were called "the song of God," because they were the religious seed. When they looked upon the beautiful daughters of Cain (called the daughters of man because they represented the irreligious portion of the race), they married them and thereby brought the whole race into such corruption that "every imagination of the thought of his heart was only evil continually" (Gen. 6:5). God therefore declared "My Spirit shall not always strive with man" and set the limit when he should quit thus striving with him at one-hundred and twenty years (Gen. 6:3). After that God proposed to destroy the whole wicked race from off the face of the earth (Gen. 6:7).

Noah God's Chosen Man. The narrative tells us (Gen. 6:8) that "Noah found favor in the eyes of Jehovah." This was no doubt because his character and acts were acceptable to Him. He was the tenth and last in the Sethic line. He was the son of Lamech (Gen. 5:28), a godly man, who had felt the weight of burden because of the curse which God had pronounced upon the ground because of Adam's sin. He was called Noah by his father, because he said the child would be a source of comfort concerning their toil growing out of that curse (Gen. 5:39). He was a just and perfect man and walked with God (Gen. 6:9; 7:1). Compare also I Peter 3:20 and Heb. 11:7. He is also called a preacher of righteousness (II Peter 2:5) and it is probable that, during the one-hundred and twenty years that were likely employed in building the ark, he preached to his generation and tried to lead them to repentance. He was, however, unable to influence any save his own family. The saving of his own family was, however, a splendid monument of his life.

The Ark. Noah built the ark according to the pattern given him by Jehovah. It was a sort of box-like boat 525 ft. long 87-1/2 ft. wide and 42-1/2 ft. deep, if we count a cubit at twenty-one inches. It was three stories high, and the building of it was a huge undertaking. We need not, however, think of it as an undertaking beyond the resources of the times. All those early people seem to have been fond of colossal works. The building of this Ark was not only an object lesson to the ungodly people of the time but a satisfactory proof of the faith of the builder.

The Flood. At the command of Jehovah Noah and his household entered the Ark carrying two of every species of unclean, and seven of every clean kind of animal and creeping things. They were shut in by the hand of God. The scripture passes silently over all horrors that filled the earth as man and beast were destroyed. We may imagine them trying by strength to get out of reach of the rising waters, but no mental culture or mechanical skill or physical culture, neither tears and entreaties could deliver man from the destruction which God had determined because of sin. It was seven months before the Ark rested on Ararat and more than five more before the ransomed company departed from it.

The Sacrifice and Rainbow Covenant. Upon leaving the Ark Noah expressed his thanksgiving and devotion to God by erecting an altar to Jehovah and offering thereon a sacrifice consisting of victims of every species of clean bird and beast. The fragrance of this sacrifice, such as the world had never seen before, was pleasant to Jehovah and he visited Noah with a promise that he would not again send such a flood upon the earth. The rainbow was given as a pledge of the promise made him. It was to be the constant seal of mercy on God's part, and it is not necessary to worry over the question as to whether there had never been a rainbow before or whether it was simply appropriated as a sign. In this new covenant the earth was put under Noah, as it was under Adam at first. He was, however, allowed to eat flesh, only mans blood was not to be shed and the seasons were to continue in regularity. Thus the race started anew as a saved group, rescued through the faith of Noah.

Confirmation of Tradition and Geology. Perhaps no other event of scripture history has found so large a place in ancient traditions and legends as has the flood. It is found in each of the three great races-the Semites; the Aryan; and the Tutarian. It is found alike among savage and civilized races, and as might be expected is most accurate in the countries that were nearest to where the Ark rested. Among the most important of these early traditions are those of Babylon. Greece, China, and America. In a general way these traditions may be said to agree with the Biblical story in the following particulars: (1) That a flood destroyed an evil world; (2) That one righteous family was saved in a boat and that animals were saved with them; (3) That the boat landed on a mountain; (4) That a bird was sent out of the boat; (5) That the saved family built an altar and worshiped God with sacrifice. All these stories tend to corroborate the Biblical story and to show that the whole race must have spring from this common home from which they have been scattered abroad.

Geology has also done much to confirm the flood story. Geologists are well acquainted with facts in world history that bring the flood "entirely within the range of natural phenomena." The Scripture (Gen. 7:11) speaks of the fountains of the deep being broken, language that could refer to the inrushing of the sea upon a depression of the earth which later rose again. Such elevations and depressions have occurred many times. An example is the elevation of the coast of Chile by an earthquake in 1822. Such an explanation by no means destroys the miracle of it, since the coming just when Noah had completed the ark and entered it and just when God said it would come, provided the element of miracle. A wide-spread flood is also required by the discovery of evidence in the earth of the destruction of animal life.

Some Teachings of This Period. The teachings of this period may be divided into three groups: Those concerning Cain and Abel; those concerning Cain and Seth. or the two races; those concerning the flood.

Those concerning Cain and Abel are: (1) The mere fact of having worshiped is not a guarantee of acceptance with God. (2) Both the spirit and the form of worship must please Jehovah. (3) God tries to point out the right way to men and only punishes when man fails to give heed. (4) Man is free and though God may turn to show him a better way, he will not restrain him by force even from the worst crimes. (5) To try to shun the responsibility of being our brother's keeper is to show the spirit of Cain.

The story of Cain and Seth, or the two races show: (1) That our acts reveal our thoughts. (2) That the indulgence of our lusts and appetites disgraces the noblest people. (3) That outward culture without true religion will not save a people. (4) The noble and good will finally dominate other men.

The story of the flood teaches: (1) That Jehovah can not make men righteous against their will. (2) That men by wickedness grieve God and thwart his purposes. (3) That man has, therefore, power to cause his own destruction. (4) That God does not save because of numbers or civilization, but because of character and obedience to his laws. (5) That God is pleased with the worship of those who obey him.

For Study and Discussion, (1) The consequences of sin as seen in this period with special reference to the new truths added to those of the former period. (2) New truths about God. (3) The beginning of the arts of civilization. (4) The unity of the race. (S) The names and ages of the six oldest men and whether any one of them could have known personally both Adam and Noah. (6) The size, architecture and the task of building the Ark. (7) The flood as a whole. (8) The inhabitants of the Ark. (9) The departure from the Ark, and the new covenant. (10) The flood as a divine judgment especially in the light of the judgment put upon Adam and Cain. (11) Noah as the first man mentioned who saved others and the way in which he represents Jesus. (12) Evidences of man's freedom as seen in this and the former chapters. (13) Worship as seen in the two periods studied.

3

FROM THE FLOOD TO ABRAHAM.

Gen. Chs. 9-11.

Noah's Shame and Prophecy. Just what the vocation of Noah bad been before his call to prepare for the flood we do not know. But after the flood, perhaps compelled by necessity, he became an husbandman. He had probably settled on the slopes or in the valleys of Ararat where he planted a vineyard. On one occasion at least he fell under the intoxicating influence of the fermented wine. This man upon whom God had conferred such great favor and who alone preserved the race alive lay naked and helpless in his tent.

In this shameful condition he was discovered by his sons whose conduct led him in a spirit of prophecy to assign to his three sons the rewards and punishments which their deeds merited. The punishment and rewards fell upon the descendants of his sons. The descendants of Ham, because of his joy rather than sorrow over the sin and humiliation of his father, should always be a servile race. Out of these descendants of Ham arose the Canaanites, the Babylonians and the Egyptians who developed the three great civilizations of antiquity. Their ascendancy, however, soon passed. The Canaanites were subdued by the Israelites; the Cushites of Chaldea were absorbed by Semitic conquerors and Carthage of the Phoenicians fell before her foes. The sons of Cush, in the scripture commonly meaning the Ethiopian and now known as the black-skinned African, are the very synonym for weakness, degradation and servitude.

The descendants of Japheth and Shem like those of Ham can be traced only in part. The Japhethites probably settled around the Mediterranean and in the northwest beyond the Black Sea. From them "the great races of Europe, including the Greeks, the Romans, and the more modern nations, must have sprung." The Shemites were located, generally speaking, between the territories occupied by the sons of Ham and Japheth. Aram, one of the sons of Japheth, settled in Syria near Damascus in northern part of Mesopotamia and through his son, Uz, gave the name of Uz to the territory, thus showing how that branch of the Hebrews came from western Mesopotamia, a fact now confirmed by modern discovery. All the other sons of Shem and their descendants are dropped from the record of Chapter eleven, except that of Arphaxad from whom descended Abram.

The prophecy of Noah was not only fulfilled in the case of Ham and his punishment but in the blessing of the Others. Shem was for a long time signally blessed as is witnessed by the Asiatic supremacy and especially in the Jews who conquered the Canaanites (descendants of Ham) and in whose tents

God dwelt. During that period of the ascendancy of the Shemites not much was known of the descendants of Japheth. But now for more than two thousand years his have been the dominant race of the earth. Year by year, the Japhethites have spread over the globe, until whole continents are now peopled by him. He now rests his foot upon every soil either as a trader, colonist or national power.

The Tower of Babel. The place of this tower is in the land of Shinat, which is the name given by the early Hebrews to the land of Babylonia (Gen. 10:10; 14:19; Is. 11:1; Dan. 1:2; Zech. 5:11). This plain of Shinar had become the center of the earth's population. They threw up with infinite toil great mounds, which still stand as monuments of human achievement. Many such mounds and ruins, any of which would have seemed lofty in contrast with the level plain of Babylon, may be seen by the traveler.

The exact location of this tower cannot be determined with certainty, but it has been thought by some that a great mound on the east of the Euphrates, which probably represents the remains of the great temple of Marduk with its huge pyramid-like foundation, was the site of this tower. On the west of the Euphrates, however, is a vast mound called Birs Nimrood, which used to be regarded as the ruins of the Tower of Babel. The fact that it early gave the impression of incompleteness favors this claim. Nebuchadnezzar says on a tablet that another king began it but left it unfinished. It fell into disrepair and was completed by Nebuchadnezzar and was used as one of the great temples. It was built of brick and was oblong in form. It measured seven hundred yards around and rose to a height of from one hundred and fifty to two hundred feet high. It consisted o? seven stages or stories colored to represent the tints which the Sabeans thought appropriate to the seven planets. Beginning from the bottom they were black, orange, bright red, golden, pale yellow, dark blue and silver, representing respectively the colors of Saturn, Jupiter, Mars, the Sun, Venus. Mercury, and the Moon. These marks may indicate the prevalence of idolatry and have led some to think the tower of Babel was intended to do honor to the gods of Babylonia.

The specific purpose of this tower is difficult to determine. Josephus says the object was to save the people in case of another flood. The scripture record (11:4) indicates that they were moved by an unholy pride and selfish desire to make for themselves a great name. It also was intended to become a sort of rallying-point which would keep the people together and prevent the destruction of their glory which they thought would result from their separation. In 11:6 God says "nothing will be restrained from them which they have imagined to do." In this there is an implication that they are at cross purposes with God. It was an act that defied God and showed the need of punishment. It is not unlikely that idolatry had begun to prevail and that the tower was built in honor of those false Gods whom men were disposed to trust.

The incompleteness of the tower is attributed to divine intervention. Hitherto all the descendants of Noah had spoken the same language, but now by a direct divine interposition they are caused to speak several, and then separated so they can no longer co-operate with each other in carrying out their plans which had so displeased God. The different languages then are regarded as a punishment of the race which had rebelled against God.

Traditions of such a tower may be found in many

forms and in many countries. **In Babylonia** there was a tradition that not long after the flood men were tall and strong and became so puffed up that they defied the gods and tried to erect a tower called Babylon by means of which they could scale heaven. But when it reached the sky the gods sent a mighty wind and turned over the tower. They said that hitherto all men had used the same language, but that at this time there was sent on them a confusion of many tongues, from which confusion the tower was named Babel. **In Greece**, there was a legend in which we trace the story of the tower of Babel. According to this legend a race of giants tried to reach Mount Olympus, which was supposed to be the residence of the gods, by piling Mount Ossa upon Pelion. But the gods interfered with their plan and scattered the impious conspirators. This effort of the Titans to mount up to heaven corresponds so well to the motive of the builders of the tower as to indicate that there was a common origin for both stories.

There is also a Greek tradition that Helen had three sons: Aeolus, Dorus, and Ion, who were the ancestors of the three great branches of the Hellenic race. This again corresponds to the prophetic table of nations which were to descend from Shem, Ham, and Japheth, the three sons of Noah.

The Civilization of the Ancient World. Just when and where civilization began we have no means of telling. The Bible speaks of a very high state of civilization at a very early time (Gen. 4:20-22). In ages long before Abraham and Moses the world had made great advancement in culture, commerce, law and religion. From the monuments and engraven vases that have been found in such unearthed cities as Nippur, we now know that Abraham and Moses did not live in a crude and undeveloped age, but, as the Bible would imply, in an age of great progress. We even learn that long before their time there was a most complete and complex civilization.

Two Great Empires of Antiquity. It is impossible to tell which of two great nations, the Chaldeans and the Egyptians, first attained to a high state of civilization. They appear to have started very early in the race, the Chaldeans in the plains on the banks of the Euphrates and the Egyptians in the plains on the banks of the Nile. They seem to have made about equal progress in all the arts of civilization.

Nimrod, a descendent of Ham, is declared to be the founder of the Chaldean Empire. His exploits as a hunter seem to have aided him to the throne. He began to reign at Babel and had a number of cities in the plain of Shinar. Later he went out in the district of Assyria and built Ninevah and a number of other cities. From the Assyrian and Chaldean ascriptions, we have learned much of the Accadians, whose influence carried forward that early civilization. We thereby confirm the Biblical claim that it was under Nimrod the Cushite, and not through the Semitic race, that the Chaldean kingdom began.

Of the beginning of the Egyptian empire, the other great center of civilization, we have no certain knowledge. So far as the records of the scriptures or of the earliest records to which the monuments bear witness, Egypt comes before us full grown. The further back we go the more perfect and developed do we find the organization of the country. The activity and industry of the Egyptians, their power of erecting great buildings and of executing other laborious tasks at this early period is a marvel to all ages. It has been shown by Prof. Petrie that some of the blocks in at least one of the great pyramids were cut by tubular drills fitted with diamond points or something similar. This to us is a very modern invention.

At least thirty dynasties of kings (according to Manetho) ruled Egypt in succession. At least twelve of these must have reigned in Egypt before Jacob and his sons settled within their borders. Many of the great monuments and some of the largest of the pyramids were already to be seen before Abraham visited that country. There had been constant progress in all kinds of learning and art, and a highly advanced society and government had been attained when the Bible history first came in contact with it.

Commerce was carried on extensively on both land and sea. Long before the time of Moses a stream of caravans were on the road between Egypt and Babylon, passing through Canaan. Treaties were made between different states whereby these caravans were protected and given safe passage through the countries traversed. Three thousand years before Christ the Phoenicians sent out ships from Tyre that had intercourse with the cities of the Mediterranean and later with England and sailed around Africa and traded on the Red Sea and the Persian Gulf. Egypt sent sea expeditions to South Africa in the sixteenth century before Christ. All of this suggests how much more of geography these ancients knew than we are accustomed to think.

Language and Literature. It is impossible to say what was the original language. But that men once spoke the same language and that the varieties of human tongues arose from some remarkable cause is in some degree confirmed by the research of modern scholarship. The Bible alone states clearly what that cause was. All existing languages belong to three great families: the Aryan, the Semitic, and the Turanian. These correspond roughly to three sons of Noah: Shem, Ham and Japheth.

In the time of Abraham and long before, and on to the time of Moses there was great literary culture. Letters passed between kingdoms and cities. There were schools and colleges, great dictionaries and many books on many subjects. The Babylonian language was almost universally employed, so that the scribes could read without difficulty a letter sent anywhere in Egypt, Babylon, Canaan, or Arabia. This unity makes the translation of inscriptions on the monuments comparatively easy.

We know nothing of the origin of writing. As far back as we go into their history we find, already developed, a most complex system of writing and large libraries both in the royal cities and in small towns.

The Motive of Their Civilization. This is not difficult to find. The old Babylonian kings were called Priest Kings, and built their empires, temples, and cities, and exhibited such wonderful activities from a religious motive. The great mounds on the plain of Shinar, and the pyramids of Egypt are the eternal monuments of the religious devotion of these ancient people. Their religion was, however, filled with all sorts of idolatrous abuses and God called Abraham to be the leader of a purer religious life and to be the father of a people from whom would come the Great Revealer of all religious truth.

The Lessons of this Period. The stories of this period have for us several valuable lessons, among which the following are most vital. (I) All races had a common origin and are, therefore, vitally related. (2) By tracing the origin of the different races, we are shown Israel's place in the family of nations. (3) Since all nations are but branches of the same great family, all men are brothers. (4) The Hebrews are deeply interested in all of their neighbors, and their unique history can only be understood, in their true relation, as a part of the ancient Semitic world. (5) God exercises a common rule over all nations. (6) Civilization at this early age had reached a great advancement. (7) Men had reached a stage of great wickedness and because of their defiance of God were punished both by the confusion of tongues and by being scattered far and wide.

For Study and Discussion. (1) The genealogies of Noah's sons. (2) The different places where his descendants settled, the cities they built and the names of those connected with each. Study the geography. (3) Through which of Noah's sons the Messiah came and through which of his sons. (4) Lessons from the shame of Noah and the spirit of his sons. (5) The nature and fulfillment of his prophecies concerning his sons. (6) The universality of the race and the origin of the nations. (7) The teachings of the tower of Babel. (8) The origin of different languages and the relation of languages to the creation of separate nations. (9) The traditions of other peoples and their relation and correspondence to the stories of this section. (10) The evidence of ancient monuments that corroborate or throw light upon the meaning of this section of the scripture. (11) The civilization of that early time compared with that of our time.

4
FROM ABRAHAM TO EGYPT.

Gen. Chs. 12-50.

The Events of the Period. The events of this period may be put down somewhat as follows: (1) Abraham's call and settlement in Canaan, chs. 12-13. (2) The rescue of Lot from the plundering kings of the North, ch. 14. (3) God makes a covenant with Abraham, ch. 15. (4) The birth and disposal of Ishmael, ch. 16. (5) The Promise of Isaac, ch. 17. (8) The destruction of Sodom and Gomorrah, chs. 18-19. (7) Abraham lives at Gerar. Isaac is born and sacrificed, chs. 20-22. (8) Sarah's death, ch. 23. (9) Isaac is married, ch. 24. (10) Abraham and Ishmael die and Isaac's two sons, ch. 25. (11) Isaac dwells in Gerar and Jacob steals his brother's birthright, chs. 26-27. (12) Jacob's experiences as a fugitive and his roll and settlement in Canaan, chs. 28-36. Joseph's career and the settlement of the nation in Egypt, chs. 37-50.

The Purpose of Narrative. In this section we have given us, in brief form, the career of Abraham, Isaac and Jacob and their families and how we received the promises through them. Ages have passed since Noah and the people had grown wicked and turned from Jehovah to other gods. God had promised not to destroy the world with another flood, but he must employ other and new means. He, therefore, selects a man and in him a nation that should be his representative on earth. With this man and nation God would deposit his truth and in it the hopes of the race until the time when Christ the redeemer should come.

We pass, therefore, from the consideration of the beginnings of the history of the race and from the general history to the story of one man, Abraham and the chosen family and nation. All the rest of the Old Testament is an account of the victories and defeats of this nation.

The Conditions of the Times. At the time of Abraham three countries are of special interest, Chaldea, Egypt and Canaan. Outwardly there was a splendid civilization as is shown by the monuments. There were great cities with splendid palaces, temples and libraries. "There were workers in fabrics, metals, stones, implements and ornaments." Time was divided as now and sun-dials showed the time of day. Great systems of canals existed and the country was in a high state of cultivation. The pyramids were already old and a great stone wall had long ago been built across the isthmus of Suez to prevent the immigrants and enemies of the north from coming down upon them. In Tyre and Sidon there were great glass works and dying factories. There were also vast harbors crowded with sea going ships. Luxurious living was to be found everywhere.

Inwardly, however, there was a corrupt moral condition, which was hastening the nations to decay and to a ruin such as amazes all the world to this day. Ur of the Chaldees, the birth place and home of Abraham, was the seat of the great temple of the moon-god, and this sanctuary became so famous that the moon-god was known throughout all northern Syria as the Baal or Lord of Haran. The bad state of the times is suggested by Sodom and Gomorrah and their fate. For these cities were perhaps only typical of the entire civilization of the time.

In such a time and out of such a civilization God called Abraham, who should found a new nation that would serve him and form the basis of a new civilization. He also selected Canaan as the home of this new people. It was the geographical center of all the ancient world and a revelation of God made there would soon be know among all nations.

The Confirmations of the Biblical Record. Each new excavation made in the ruins of the ancient, long-buried, cities throws new light upon the scriptures and always confirms its statements. There are on the tablets of clay found in the old libraries statements concerning the social, commercial, religious and political conditions of the time of Abraham and before and all of them agree with the statements of Genesis. There has been found a record of the years of famine and the Pharaohs of the time have been determined.

The kings who captured Lot are now known. The Bible has suffered nothing at all from the knowledge gained from the ancient records.

The Experiences of Abraham. The call of Abraham as recorded In this section is probably from Ur of the Chaldees to Haran where his father died (11:31-32). His call is the most important event in the history of God's kingdom since the fall of man. It was indeed a new starting point for that kingdom. The call was accompanied by a promise or covenant in which God bound himself not to withdraw from Abraham (15:17-21). The call and work, together with the promises, may be put down somewhat as follows:

1. ***It was a call to separation from his home and native land.*** He was a large shepherd-farmer with large flocks and herds and a number of slaves. The family was perhaps of high rank in his country and there was a warm family affection in his family. Many others had gone from his country to the regions of the Mediterranean but always for gain or selfish betterment, Abraham went in obedience to the divine call. There was no selfishness in his move. He went for conscience' sake, somewhat as the Pilgrims, forsaking all the ties of nature that bound them to England, sailed to America in the Mayflower.

2. ***It was a call to service.*** The people of his time were falling into idolatry. Even Terah, his father, was an idolater and reputed to have been a maker of idol images. He was to serve the one true God and to stand for principle where everyone was against him. He was to enter into covenant relations with God and stand alone with him where all social and national customs were hostile.

3. ***It was a call to found a nation.*** The promise was to make of him a great nation that should have as its main purpose the service of the one God. God foresaw the ruin that was to come to all the nations of Abraham's time and prepared him and in him a new and spiritual nation which would produce a new and godly civilization. He died when Jacob was but a lad and did not see the fulfillment of the

promise of the nation that should outlast Egypt or Babylon.

4. **It was a call to be the father of a son**. In 17:16 God promised him a son, Isaac, in whom his seed should be called (21:12). Out of him was to come a blessing to all nations. This promise was fulfilled in Christ, through whom all the nations of the earth have been blessed. Just as in Isaac Abraham became the head of a great earthly seed that should be as the sand of the sea, so in Jesus he should be the head of a great spiritual seed that should be as the stars of the heaven for numbers.

God often repeats his covenant and promises with Abraham, Gen. 12:1-7; 13:14-17; 15:1-21; 17:1-8; 18:18; 22:16-18. He often renews it in the generations to come as to Isaac, Gen. 26:1-5, and to Jacob, Gen. 28:10-15.

The Character of Abraham. How great is the name of Abraham today! He is revered by Jews, Mohammedans and Christians (ch. 12:2). In all history there is not a nobler character. The story of his life shows him to have been shrewd in business, of good temper, of warm domestic affections and possessed of much calm wisdom. He was generous in his dealings with others, looking well after their interests. He often made sacrifices for the well-being of others. The most significant thing about him, however, was his attitude toward God. His chief desire was to obey God. Wherever he went he erected an altar to God and in everything he manifested reverence, confidence, love and submission toward God. This is the chief element of his greatness.

The Character and Career of Isaac. The life of Isaac has but little in it that is of special interest. He probably spent most of his life in a quiet home near, or in Hebron. This has been taken to suggest that he was of a quiet and retiring disposition. He was not a man of energy and force of character such as Abraham, his father, but he had all his father's reverence for God. His faith in God was rewarded with a renewal of the promises which Abraham had received.

Among the incidents of his life that should be noted are the following: (1) His experience on Mount Moriah, when his father in obedience to God prepared to sacrifice him in worship. Such sacrifice was common in Babylonia, Phoenicia and Canaan. The submission to his father's will and evident obedience to the divine will indicated would seem to point to his faith in God. While he does not mention the matter himself and it is not referred to again in this section, the experience must have had much influence on his whole career. (2) The second notable event of his life was his marriage. In this story there is preserved the ancient customs of his father's provision for the marriage of the son. The story also shows the overruling influence of deity in his marriage. The whole experience was calculated to show his sincere relation to God who was leading. (3) The birth of his twin sons Esau and Jacob. They were so different in type that their descendants for centuries showed a like difference and even became antagonistic. Jacob was ambitious and persevering. Esau was frank and generous but shallow and unappreciative of the best things. The birthright carried with it two advantages: (1) The headship of the family. (2) A double portion of the inheritance (Dt. 21:15-17). Jacob set great value upon it, while Esau preferred a good dinner. Isaac's latter days were made dark because of the relation of these sons.

Stories Concerning Jacob. These are calculated to

show that Jacob was clever and far-sighted and was willing to employ any mean, honorable or dishonorable, to gratify his ambition. They also show his suffering for his unfair acts and his final change to a new man. His deception of his father resulted in his becoming a fugitive from home and never again seeing his mother who aided him in his treachery. He was treated by Laban just as he himself had treated his brother. For twenty years he was deprived of the quiet and friendly life of his old home.

While away he had some religious experiences that made him a new man. His vision at Bethel taught him that Jehovah his God was also caring for him though in a strange land. He may have thought that Jehovah dwelt only among the people of his nation and that on leaving home he was also going beyond the protection of God. As a result he erected here a sanctuary that became sacred to all the Hebrews.

His struggle at the brook Jabbok made Jacob a new man. He had all along depended on his own wits. Now he is ready to return to his brother and show sorrow for his conduct. The incident is parallel to the struggle which a repentant man must wage against his lower nature. When the struggle is over he is a new man, a prince of god. Religion had become real to him and his whole future career is built on a new plan. He is still inventive and ambitious and persevering but is God's man doing God's will.

In connection with Jacob we have also the lessons concerning Esau. He was a man intent upon immediate physical enjoyment; an idle drifter without spiritual ideals. From his character and that of the Edomites, his descendants, there is taught the lesson that such an unambitious man or nation will always become degenerate and prove a failure. God himself cannot make a man out of an idle drifter.

The Stories About Joseph. The moral value of these stories is very great. They are told in a charm that is felt by all. The literary power and unity is remarkable. There is seen in them ideals of integrity and truthfulness. He is cheerful and uncomplaining and no adversity could destroy his ambitions. The study of this section will well reward a frequent review of it.

All the materials may be grouped around the following principal great periods or incidents of his life. (1) His childhood, where we find him petted and spoiled but ambitious and trustworthy and hated by his brethren. (2) His sale to the Egyptians and separation from his house and kindred, this including his slavery and the faithfulness he showed in such a position. (3) His position as overseer and his loyalty together with his temptation and unjust imprisonment. (4) His exaltation to the governorship of Egypt with his provisions for the famine and change of the whole system of land tenure, which put it all under royal control. It would also include his kindness to his father's family in providing for their preservation.

The stories have in them several elements that need to be noticed. (1) There are many sudden and striking contrasts. Such are his changes from a petted and spoiled boy in the home to a slave in Egypt; from an overseer of his master's house to a prisoner in the dungeon; for that dungeon to the governor of the powerful empire of the age. (2) His success is never based on or promoted by a miracle but is assured because he is of value to others. He wins no promotions by means of armor or conquests of power but by faithfulness to those whom he served. His is a conquest made by business sagacity. He is a hero of usefulness. (3) The use of his position to advance the interests of others is altogether out of line with the views of western students of society. We would hardly think it right for one to so earnestly promote the interests of a heathen sovereign as Joseph did in the case of his slave master and of Pharaoh. (4) The pathos and depth of feeling is not surpassed in all literature. This is especially true in the story of his relations with his brethren when they visit Egypt. Pent up emotion tugs at one's heart as one reads of the anxiety of the brothers, the fear of the fear of the father, and the burning affection of Joseph. The spirit of forgiveness and love for his humble kinsmen fill one with admiration.

The death of Jacob and Joseph. Jacob was greatly prospered and died at a ripe old age. He asked to be buried in Canaan and Joseph after having him embalmed went, accompanied by his kindred and friends, to Canaan and buried him according to his request. Before his death, he pronounced upon his sons a blessing that promised great increase in numbers and in political power.

After the death of Jacob, Joseph continued to show kindness to his brethren. Before his death, at the age of one hundred and ten years, he prophesied that God would come and lead them out of Egypt and took an oath of them that they would carry up his bones to the land of Canaan into which they would be delivered.

In Jacob's blessing on his sons and in Joseph's prophecy of their removal by God and his promises, they saw the providence of God in all the future of the race and expected its triumph.

These stories typical. The stories of this section

are commonly thought to be typical of New Testament truth. While it is probably not best to make too much of this typical idea, it is safe to say that much of it is illustrative of such New Testament teachings. The career of Abraham, Isaac and Joseph each at some point or points suggests the life and work of Jesus. Abraham is called or appointed of God to be the head of a spiritual nation, he has revealed to him the will of God, he intercedes for a wicked Sodom and saved lot, all of which suggests the attitude and work of Jesus. Isaac is an only son, is offered in sacrifice, has secured for him a bride in a most unusual manner. This again in many ways illustrates the attitude and work of the Savior. But Joseph is perhaps more highly figurative of the Redeemer. His being hated and cast out by his brethren is like the rejection of Jesus; the way his wicked brethren came to him in their extremity and received forgiveness and sustenance suggest how a sinner finds mercy and life in Jesus; his prosperity and honor gained among others and the final coming of his brethren to him is suggestive in many of the details of the way the Jews rejected Jesus and of how, after Jesus has gained great power among Gentile nations, the Jews will finally repent of their national sin and accept the crucified Savior as the Jews' Messiah; the whole story of the humiliation, sufferings and exaltation of Joseph correspond to like events in the career of Jesus.

Social and Religious Conditions of the Times. There is little to suggest anything savage or barbarous. The spirit and language of courtesy is everywhere present. There is great hospitality and the marriage relation was respected by such heathen rulers as Pharaoh and Abimelech. When property was bought and sold the contracts were formal and were held sacred even though the owner was long absent as in the case of Abraham who bought the cave of Machpelah. Rebekah had bracelets, ear-rings, jewels of silver and of gold, and fine raiment as elements of adornment. There were slaves but they were kindly treated and made almost as part of the family. Wealthy people as Jacob employed their sons in the ordinary occupations such as caring for the sheep. In Egypt and Chaldea the arts were highly developed and there was much learning.

The worship of the patriarchs was very simple. They erected simple altars and offered on them burnt offerings. The erection of such altars and making such open profession of their worship were always among their first acts when they settled in a new place. There are some evidences that they observed the Sabbath of rest. Abraham gave a tithe to Melchizedek and Jacob promised God to do the same if he would bless him. God communed with them and gave them knowledge of his will and especially promised them great future blessing, through a deliverer that would come through the line of Abraham, Isaac, Jacob and Judah.

The Book of Job. There has been a general belief that the incidents recorded in the book of Job belong to this period or even to an earlier time. There is no mention of the bondage in Egypt nor of any of the early Hebrew patriarchs. The Sabeans and Chaldeans were Job's neighbor! and he lived "in the east" where the first settlements of mankind were made. The social religious and family life as portrayed in this book correspond to those of this period. There was art and invention; there was understanding of astronomy and mining; there was a fine family affection and evidences of social kindness and benevolence; there was high development of commerce and government; there was both the true and false or idolatrous worship. This book should be read following the outline given in the author's *The Bible Book by Book*.

Lessons of the Period. It would be difficult to point out all the splendid lessons brought forward by these narratives but the following are among the more important ones. (1) God guides to a noble destiny all those who will be guided by him. (2) God reveals himself to all those who seek a revelation, no matter in what place or land, if only they are in the path of duty, (3) Unselfish service always brings a blessed reward. (4) God's blessing and guidance are not confined to Israel but are extended to other nations also. (5) A noble ambition, courage, unselfishness and childlike faith in God's leadership make men valuable to others in every age and walk of life. (6) A man or nation without spiritual ideal and bent on physical enjoyment will soon become degenerate as did Esau. (7) Even a fugitive, fleeing from his own crimes, is followed by the divine love and in his saddest moments and amidst his most discouraging surrounding circumstances is given glorious revelations. (8) In the divine providence our misfortunes of life often develop our nobler impulses of heart. (9) Unjust adversity cannot destroy a man of faith and integrity of character, if only he manifest a cheerful and helpful spirit. (10) God overrules evil for good, so that all things can bring good to them that love God. (11) Loyalty to unfortunate kindred in the time of success is a sure sign of nobility of character.

For Study and Discussion. (1) The several appearances of God to Abraham: (a) The purpose of each; (b) its influence in the life of Abraham. (2) The promises made to Abraham and renewed to Isaac and Jacob noting the progressive nature of the revelation seen in these promises. (3) Select four prominent persons besides Abraham, Isaac, Jacob, and Joseph, sketched in the section, and study them. (4) The other nations introduced in the narrative. (5) The moral condition of the times. (6) The worship of God seen in the section. (7) The points of weakness and strength in each of the patriarchs mentioned. (8) The disappointments and family troubles of Jacob as seen in the light of his early deceptions. (9) Other illustrations that a man will reap whatever he sows. (10) The strong family ties, seen especially in the matter of marriage. (11) The fundamental value of faith in life. (12) God's judgment and blessings of heathen people on behalf of his own chosen people. (13) The different immigrations of Abraham and others. (14) The places of historical importance mentioned. (15) The promises or types and symbols of Christ and the New Testament times.

5
FROM EGYPT TO SINAI.

Ex Chs. 1-19.

Israel in Egypt. The length of time the Hebrews remained In Egypt is a perplexing question. Exodus 6:16-20 makes Moses the fourth generation from Levi (See Gen. 15:16; Num. 26:57-59). This would make it about 150 years. Gen. 15:13 predicts 400 years. Ex. 12:40 says they were there 430 years and Paul (Gal. 3:17) says 430 years from Abraham to Sinai. These apparently conflicting dates may be explained because of different methods of counting generations, probably based on long lives of men of that period or they may have had a different point to mark the beginning and end of the sojourn. If the Pharaoh of Joseph was one of the Hyksos or Shepherd kings, as has been the common view, and if the Pharaoh "that knew not Joseph" was, as is the general belief, Rameses II, the period of 430 years would about correspond to the historical data.

Their oppression grew out of the fear of the king

lest they should assist some of the invaders that constantly harassed Egypt on the North. They may have assisted the shepherd kings under whom Joseph has risen and who had just been expelled. To cripple and crush them there was given them hard and exhaustive tasks of brick making under cruel task-masters. There still remains evidence of this cruelty in the many Egyptian buildings built of brick, made of mud mixed with straw and dried in the sun. When it was found that they still increased in number in spite of the suffering, Pharoah tried, at first privately then publicly, to destroy all the male children. This order does not seem to have been long in force but was a terrible blow to a people like the Hebrews whose passion for children, and especially for male children, has always been proverbial.

It is difficult to gather from this narrative the varied influence of this sojourn upon the Hebrews themselves. They doubtless gained much of value from the study of the methods of warfare and military equipment of the Egyptians. They learned much of the art of agriculture and from the social and political systems of this enlightened people. No doubt many of their choicest men received educational training that fitted them for future leadership. Their suffering seems on the one hand to have somewhat deadened them, destroying ambition. On the other, it bound them together by a common bond and prepared the way for the work of Moses, the deliverer, and for the real birth of the nations.

Moses the Deliverer. Chapters 2 and 4 tell the wonderful story of the birth of Moses, of his loyalty to his people, of his sojourn in Midian and of his final call to the task of the deliverance of Israel. His wonderful life-a life to which all the centuries are indebted-is naturally divided into three parts. (1) **His early life of forty years at the court of Pharaoh**. By faith his parents trusted him to the care of Providence and he was brought to the house of Pharoah and was taught in all the learning of the Egyptians, who conducted great universities and were highly cultured in the arts and sciences (Acts 7:22). Finally feeling it to be his duty to renounce his worldly glory and identify himself with his Hebrew brethren, he made the choice by faith (Heb. 11:24-27). He no doubt felt then the call to be their deliverer but did not find his countrymen ready to accept him as such (Acts 7:25-28). Whereupon he fled to the wilderness of Midian. (2) **Forty years in the desert** where he gained an intimate knowledge of all the wilderness through which for forty years he was to lead the Hebrews in their wanderings. Here he had opportunity to learn patience and meditate and gain the ability to wait on God. Here God finally appeared to him and gave him definite and ample instructions for his task of delivering out of bondage this crushed and ignorant slave race and for making of them a nation of the purest spiritual and moral ideals the world has ever known. (3) **Forty years as leader and lawgiver for Israel** while they tabernacled in the wilderness.

Perhaps three reasons led Moses to undertake the task of leaving Midian and championing the cause of Israel. (1) He had a vision of God the holy one of all power who would be with him. (2) The conviction that the time was ripe, because of the death of the king of Egypt and the years of weak government that followed. (3) By over-ruling all objections God gave him an overwhelming sense of his responsibility in the matter. He saw it as his personal duty.

The call of Moses consists of two elements. (1) **The human element** which consisted of a knowledge of the needs of the Hebrew people. To him, as to all great leaders and benefactors of the race, the cry of the oppressed or needy constituted the first element of a call to enlist in their service. (2) **The divine element**. God heard the cry of his people and remembered his covenant with Abraham and appeared to Moses in a burning bush and sent him to deliver them from under the tyranny of Pharaoh. Like Isaiah (Is. Ch.6) he not only saw the need of his people but also the holy God calling him to supply the need.

Moses task was three fold: (1) Religious: He was to show in Egypt weakness of the idolatrous worship and to establish in the wilderness the true worship of one and only God who is ruler of all. (2) **Political**: He was to overcome the power of the mighty Pharaoh and deliver a people of 600,000 men besides the children with their herds and flocks out of his territory. Then, too, he was to give them laws and so connect them together that as a nation they would survive the hostile nations around them and the civil strife and dissensions within. (3) **Social**: He was also called upon to provide rules by which, to keep clean not only the individual, but his family, and to teach them right relations to each other. In carrying out this program, it devolved upon him to provide an elaborate code of civil, sanitary, ceremonial, moral and religious laws.

The Great Deliverance. The deliverance may be properly considered in three sections. (1) The preparation. (2) The contest with Pharoah and the ten plagues. (3) The crossing of the Red Sea.

The preparation consists (1) in getting the people

acquainted with what God intended to do and thereby secure their full consent to enter into the plan. Then, too, it was necessary to have a very thorough organization so that the expedition could proceed in an orderly way. (2) There were various preliminary appeals to Pharaoh with the consequent added burdens laid upon the Hebrews.

The contest with Pharaoh consisted of certain preliminary demands followed by ten national calamities intended to force the king to let the people go. The struggle was all based upon the request of Moses that all Israel be allowed to go three days' journey into the wilderness to serve their God. This gave the conflict a religious aspect and showed that the struggle was not merely one between Moses and Pharaoh, but between the God of Israel and the gods of Egypt.

All the plagues, therefore, had a distinct religious significance: (1) To show them the power of Jehovah (Ex. 7:17); (2) to execute judgment against the gods of Egypt (Ex. 12:12). Every plague was calculated to frustrate Egyptian worship or humiliate some Egyptian god. For example, the lice covered everything and were miserably polluting. All Egyptian worship was compelled to cease, since none of the priests could perform their religious service so long as any such insect had touched them since they went through a process of purification. In smiting the cattle with murrain, the sacred bull of Memphis was humiliated whether stricken himself or because of his inability to protect the rest of the cattle.

These plagues grew more severe with each new one. And much effort has been made to show that one would have led to another. Much has been said also, to show that the plagues, at least most of them, were events that were common in Egypt and that they were remarkable only for their severity. Such attempts to explain away the miraculous element are based upon the wrong view of a miracle. The very occurrence in response to the word of Moses and at such time as to each time meet a particular condition, or to make a certain desired impression, would put them out of the pale of the pale of the ordinary and into the list of the extraordinary or miraculous. At all events the sacred writer, the Hebrews in Egypt at the time, and the Egyptians all believed the strong hand of Jehovah was laid bare on behalf of his people. So it must seem to all who now believe that God rules in his universe.

In connection with and just preceding the tenth plague, there was instituted the Passover to celebrate their deliverance from Egypt and especially the passing of the Hebrew homes by the angel who went abroad in Egypt to slay the first born. It was this plaque that finally showed Pharaoh and his people the folly of resisting Jehovah and assured Israel of his power. The paschal lamb, whose blood sprinkled upon the door posts and lintels of the dwelling saved the Hebrew, is a beautiful type of Christ and his saving blood. This feast became one of great joy, annually celebrated, during all future Hebrew history.

The Crossing of the Red Sea. For three days and nights God led them by a pillar of cloud by day and of fire by night. At the end of the third day they had reached the shore of the Red Sea and were shut in by mountains on each side. They were greatly frightened to find that Pharaoh with a host of chariot-warriors was in close pursuit of them. But God caused the cloud that had been leading them to remove to their rear and to throw a shadow upon their enemies while giving power to the east wind (Ex. 14:21) that caused the waters of the sea to divide so they could cross on dry ground. When Pharaoh and his hosts attempted to follow then. God caused the waters to return and overwhelm them. As in former miracles, Moses was God's instrument in performing this miracle. When they were safe across and saw the overthrow of their enemies their feelings of joy expressed themselves in a great song of victory in which they ascribe praise to God and recount the incidents of his work of deliverance.

The Journey to Sinai. It is not possible to locate all the stations at which they stopped on their journey from the Red Sea to the time of their encampment at the foot of Horeb or Sinai. The list is given in Numbers, Chapter thirty-three. For our purpose it is sufficient to notice only a few places and incidents of the journey. (1) They encamped at Marah, being the first watering place they had found. The water, however, was bitter and could not be used until God had enabled Moses by a miracle to sweeten it. This was the first example of divine support for them. (2) At Elim they found water and shade and here God gave them the manna from heaven and the quail at eventide. Thus again Jehovah demonstrated his purpose to provide for their needs while wandering through the wilderness. This food was supplied to them continuously until they reached Canaan forty years later. (3) Under the leadership of the cloud, which during all the forty years of wilderness wandering, was their guide, they next encamped at Rephidim where there was no water at all. Here Moses by the command of God smote a rock and caused them to drink of a fountain thus opened for them. This rock is a suggestive type of Christ.

It was here also that they encountered and defeated the Amalekites, a tribe of Edomites, who still kept up the enmity of Esau their father against Jacob. Here also Jethro, Moses' father-in-law came to them bringing Moses wife and sons. Upon Jethro's advice the people were thoroughly organized. From Rephidim they came to Mount Sinai where they encamped for a whole year.

Lessons of the Period. The lessons of this period might be divided into two classes. (1) Those of special value to the Hebrews themselves and lessons needed just then. (2) Those valuable for all time and all people. Among those of the first class, the following are worthy of record: (1) The authority of Moses was confirmed and the people were made ready for his teachings and leadership. (2) They were established in the popular belief in the goodness and power of Jehovah their God. Of the second and more general lessons, the following are highly important: (1) There is no chance in God's universe, but even the apparently unimportant events serve his purposes. (2) No human power whether of king or peasant or of nation can prevent the accomplishment of God's purposes. (3) Those who resist his power are overthrown as were the Egyptians, and those who act according to the divine will are elevated just as were the Israelites. (4) It is dangerous to oppose or harm God's people. He will avenge them. (5) Ample provisions are assured to those who will submit to divine leadership.

For Study and discussion. (1) The number of Hebrews that entered Egypt with Jacob, and the number that made the Exodus with Moses. (2) The Biblical story of their suffering while there, including the added burdens when Moses requested that they be allowed to go out to Egypt. (3) The birth, preservation and education of Moses. (4) Moses' forty years of wilderness training, its advantages and dangers. (5) The divine and human elements in Moses' call to be the deliverer. (6) The plagues, (a) the description of each, (b) the appropriateness and religious significance of each, (c) those imitated by Egyptian magicians, (d) those in which the Egyptians suffered and Israel did not. (7) The stubbornness of Pharaoh and his attempted compromises. (8) The miracles of this period other than the plagues. (9) God's provision and care for his people. (10) The murmurings of Israel. (11) The religious conditions of the times. (12) The geography of the country.

6

FROM SINAI TO KADESH.

Ex. 20-Num. 14.

Mount Sinai. There are differences of opinion concerning the location of this mountain. It is sometimes called Horeb (Ex. 3:1; 17:6. etc.). All the Old Testament references to it clearly indicate that it was in the vicinity of Edom and connect it with Mt. Seir (Deut. 33:3; Judg. 5:4-5). Several points have been put forward as the probable site, but there can not now be any certainty as to the exact location. All the evidence both of the scripture and of the discoveries of archaeologists seem to point to one of the southwestern spurs of Mt. Seir as the sacred mountain. The differences of opinion as to location do not affect the historical reality of the mountain nor the certainty that at its base there took place the most important event in the history of the Hebrew people.

The Sinaitic Covenant. At the foot of Sinai and in the midst of grandly impressive manifestations of Jehovah, Israel entered into solemn covenant relations with Him. It was a covenant of blood and was the most sacred and inviolable ceremony known to the ancient peoples. Half of the blood was sprinkled on the alter and half upon the people, thus signifying that all had consented to the terms of the covenant. In this covenant Israel is obligated to loyalty, service and worship, while Jehovah is to continue to protect and deliver them. This covenant is commonly called "The Law of Moses." All the rest of the Old Testament is a development of this fundamental law and shows the application of it in the experience of Israel.

The Purpose of the Mosaic Law. It should be observed that the rewards and punishments of this law were mainly confined to this life. Instead of leading them to believe that outward obedience to it would bring personal salvation and, therefore, instead of superseding the plan of salvation through a redeemer, that had been announced to Adam and Eve, and confirmed in the covenant with Abraham, it pointed to the Savior. The sacrifices foreshadowed the substitution of the Lamb of God as a means of their deliverance for sin and its punishment.

There are probably two purposes in promulgating this law. (1) To preserve the Israelites as a separate and peculiar people. To the weld the scattered fugitives from Egypt into a nation, distinct from other nations, required laws that would make them different in customs, religion and government. (2) A second purpose was to provide additional spiritual light, that they might know the way of salvation more perfectly.

The Several Parts of the Law. On the whole the law contains three parts. (1) **The Law of Duty**. This is given in the form of ten commandments (Ex. ch. 20) and relates to individual obligations, (a) The first four define one's obligations to God. (b) The fifth defines our relation to parents, (c) The last five define our relation to the other members of society. These ten words define religion in terms of life and deed as well as worship. They reach the very highest standard and, in the last command, trace crime back to the motive even to the thought in the mind of man. They point out duties arising out of the unchangeable distinctions of right and wrong.

(2) **The law of Mercy**. This law is found in the instructions concerning the priesthood and the sacrifices. Through these were seen; (a) the need of an atonement for the sinner's guilt; (b) the need of inward cleansing on the part of all; (c) the redemption of the forfeited life of the sinner by another life being substituted in its stead and only by that means; (d) the fact that God would punish wrong-doing and reward righteousness. This is also called "The Law of Holiness" or "The Ceremonial Law" and was intended to show Israel man's sinfulness and how a sinful people could approach a holy God and themselves become holy. It, therefore, deals with such matters as personal chastity, unlawful marriages and general social purity and the religious behavior by which they were to be absolved from all impurity and symbolically to be made pure again.

(3) The Law of Justice. This is composed of miscellaneous civil, criminal, humane and sanitary laws, calculated to insure right treatment of one another and thus promote the highest happiness of all: (a) There was to be kindness and justice to each other including slaves, and also to domestic animals; This is beautifully shown in the provisions for the treatment of the poor, the aged and the afflicted; (b) The rights of property were to be sacredly regarded and all violations of such rights severely punished as in the case

of fraud or theft; (c) Laws of sanitation and health guarded the imprudent against the contraction of disease and protected the wicked or careless against its spread and thereby saved Israel from epidemics of malignant disease. Thus the right of the innocent and helpless were insured; (d) The sanctity of the home and of personal virtue was held inviolable and every transgressor, such as the man who should commit adultery with another man's wife, was put to death; (e) Life was to be sacred. No man being able to give it was to take it from another and so the murderer was to pay the penalty by giving his life.

These laws were so amplified as to meet every demand of the domestic, social, civic and industrial relations of the nation. There could hardly be designed a happier life than the proper observance of all these laws would have brought to Israel. This legislation reached its noblest expression in the law of the neighbor: "Thou shall love thy neighbor as thyself" (Lev. 19:18). It is the final word in all right relation to others.

The Journey to Kadesh-Barnea. After camping before Sinai a little more than a year, during which tune they received the law and were gradually organized into a nation, the cloud by which they were always led from the time of their departure to their entrance to Canaan, arose from the tabernacle and set forward. It led them by a way that we cannot now trace but which Moses says was eleven days' journey from the sacred mountain. (Dt. 1:2).

A few notable events of this journey are recorded. (1) The fire of Jehovah that burned in the camp because of their murmuring. (2) The appointing of seventy elders to share with Moses the burden of the people. (3) The sending of the quails and the destruction of those that lusted. (4) Miriam, the sister of Moses, was smitten with leprosy because with Aaron she rebelled against Moses and spoke disrespectfully of him.

The Twelve Spies. From Kadesh Moses sent out twelve men who should investigate the condition of Canaan. These men agreed that it was an attractive and well favored land. They brought back evidences of its fruitfulness. Only two of them, believed they could conquer it. The People yielded to the opinions of the majority and refused to attempt to enter Canaan and even worse they openly resolved to return to Egypt. For this disbelief and open rebellion they were sentenced to wander forty years in the wilderness and all of them who were above twenty years old except Joshua and Caleb were not only doomed not to be allowed to enter this promised land but were to die in the wilderness.

Lessons of the Period. The more important truths taught by the records of this period may be divided into three groups. (1) Those about man and his nature: (a) He is sinful, his whole nature is out of proper attitude toward God and is a fountain of evil; (b) He is, therefore, in need of redemption and cannot have the benefit of worship to God without it; (c) He owes obedience to God. (2) There are lessons about God: (a) He is shown to be a Holy God. who hates and punishes sin; (b) He is represented as a God of mercy and forgiveness; (c) He is seen as one of power and might, able to carry forward his plans and to change the whole destiny of a people. (3) There is a many sided view of redemption: (a) It is based on blood; The victim must shed its blood before redemption can come; (b) It is by Institution as is attested by all the sacrifices; (c) It is by imputation or the putting of one's sins upon the victim; (d) It is by death and that of an innocent creature. In all of this there is a revelation of Christ who puts away sin and brings the sinner into favor with God.

For Study and Discussion. (1) The awe-inspiring ways by which Jehovah made known his presence on Sinai. (2) The several things Israel covenanted to do. (3) The worship of the golden calf and the breaking of the tables of stone. (4) The three great divisions of the law. (5) The law of mercy or of Holiness, what it teaches, and its purpose. (6) Catalogue the different laws of justice according to the outline suggested above or make a new outline and catalogue them. (7) The present day conditions that could be met and changed for good by an application of these laws. (8) The tabernacle and its material. (9) The different kinds of offering, learn what was offered and how and by whom. (10) The different scared occasions, feasts, holidays, etc. (11) The different occasions of rebellion on the part of the people and what resulted. (12) The spirit of Moses as seen in his talks to the people and in his prayers to God. (13) The rebellion of Miriam and Aaron against Moses. (14) The results of wrong influences or reports as seen in the case of the spies. (15) The rewards of righteousness as seen in the entire period.

7
FROM KADESH TO THE DEATH OF MOSES.

Num. 14-Dt. 34.

The Pathos of the Forty Years. The stories of this period have running through them an element of pathos arising especially from two sources. (1) Perhaps the experiences of Moses are most sorrowful. That he should now, after faithfully bringing this people to the very border of the land which they sought, be compelled to spend forty monotonous years in this bare and uninteresting desert must have been a disappointment very heavy to bear. During these wanderings he buried Miriam, his sister, and Aaron, his brother and helper. He was often complained of by the people he was trying to help, and because of it was led to sin in such a way as to cause God to refuse him the privilege of entering Canaan. It was necessary for him to appoint his successor and himself be buried in these lands. He was compelled to renumber the people to find that all but two of those who were above twenty when they left Egypt had perished. (2) Surely the experience of the people of Israel during these years is sufficient to arouse a feeling of pity. Forty years of suffering and unhappiness and the loss of all opportunity to enter Canaan by those who fell in the wilderness beclouds the whole story.

The Events of the Forty Years' Wandering. It is now impossible to trace exactly any except the latter portion of their journeyings. It is clear that they went from place to place, not of course marching continuously each day, but changing their location as often at least as the requirements of pasturage demanded. Of the early portion of these years we know but little. They seemed to have remained a long while at Kadesh (Dt. 1:45) and indeed may have made it a sort of headquarters. The story of the rebellion of Konah with the consequent punishment, and the budding of Aarons rod by which the appointment of the family of Aaron to the priesthood was attested are the important incidents of this period.

Final Scenes at Kadesh. After about thirty-eight years had elapsed (Dt. 2:14), and the period of wandering was nearly at an end, Israel is again found at Kadesh (Num. 20:11) on the borders of Edom where the spies had been sent out and they made their calamitous blunder. Here at this time happened three important events; (1) Miriam died and was buried, (2) Moses smote the rock and brought forth water, but because he smote it instead of speaking to it Jehovah was angry with him and told him he should not enter the land of promise. (3) Moses asked permission of the King of Edom to pass peaceably through his land and was refused. They were, therefore, compelled to take a long journey around Edom to reach there own land.

From Kadesh to the Jordan. When they were refused passage through the land of the Edomites, their kinsmen, (Num. 20:14-21), the Hebrews made a long journey around. On this journey occurred three important events. (1) The death of Aaron in Mount Hor (Num. 20:22-29). (2) The defeat of the King of South Canaan and the laying waste of his country to Hormah where they had been routed nearly forty years ago. (3) The sending of the fiery serpents and the brazen serpent as a remedy. They also passed the country of Moab and came finally to the river Arnan (Num. 21:13), which is the boundary between Moab and the Amorites. Here they came into conflict with Sihon the King of the Amorites, whom they defeated, and possessed his land. (Num. 21:23-24). The overcoming of this strong and ancient people brought Israel into contact with Og, king of Bashan, who was himself a giant and whose country was far more formidable than that of the Amorites. By defeating him and possessing his cities Israel was enabled to pass on and come to the plains of Moab beyond Jordan at Jericho. In Psalms 135 and 136, written hundreds of years later, the victory over Sihon and Og and the overthrow of Pharaoh are dwelt on together in such a way as to show that their conquest was regarded as an achievement worthy to rank along side of that of their deliverance from the power of Egypt.

The Prophecies of Balaam. (Num. Chaps. 22-24). The Moabites were greatly distressed about the settlement of the victorious Hebrews in the region just north of them and feared lest they should suffer the same fate as Shihon and Og. Balak, the King of Moab, had beard of Balaam, a famous soothsayer or wise prophet of Chaldea, whose curses and blessings were reported to carry with them extraordinary effects. He sought at any cost to have him cripple Israel by placing a curse upon them. But instead of cursing Israel and blessing the Moabites, he revealed how wonderfully Israel was blessed Of God and how a scepter would rise out of Israel and smite and destroy Moab.

This strange man Balaam seems to have had the gift of prophecy without its grace. He had the knowledge of future events but sought to use it for his own advantage instead of for the glory of God. He was a covetous, money-loving prophet and sought the rewards offered by Balak. He tried repeatedly to find some way by which he could speak good for Moab and thereby earn the much desired fee. On the other hand he was afraid to speak against Israel lest the curse should recoil on him. No other word seems to describe his course except to say that he was compelled by Jehovah to speak to Israel's advantage and to predict her future greatness. His language fittingly describes the material splendor and the splendid victories and reign of David. The spirit of Israel described is that of the united kingdom standing at the zenith of its power. In a beautiful way also he pointed to the Messiah who should put all enemies under his feet.

He may have secured his reward, however, in another way. He seems to have led Balak to entice Israel, through pretensions of friendship, to partake in the idolatrous and impure festivals of the Moabites (Num. 25:1-5; 31:15-16; Rev. 2:14). These and other acts of their own brought down upon Israel the curse of heaven and made them the subject of such calamites as Balaam could not himself pronounce against them. By suggesting this course to Balak, he may have obtained the coveted pay without directly disobeying God. This whole story would seem to imply that the Hebrew historians did not believe that divine relations were limited to seers and prophets of their own race.

The Last Acts of Moses. Events are now transpiring in rapid succession and the story hastens to the close of the career of Moses, the great leader prophet, priest and judge of Israel. Several matters are worthy of study: (1) The sending of an expedition to destroy the Midianites. (2) The final numbering of the people preparatory to their entrance into Canaan. (3) The appointing of Joshua as his successor. (4) The settlement of the two and a half tribes on the east side of Jordan. (5) The appointment of the cities of refuge. (8) The delivery of a farewell address, or of farewell addresses.

The Last Scene on Moab. There were far too many of the Israelites to hear his voice and he probably gathered together the princes and elders who listened to him from day to day, each of whom went home and repeated to his own people what he had heard from their inspired leader. In these addresses Moses recounted their wanderings and Jehovah's goodness to them. He reminded them of all that God had commanded them in his law and gave such new instructions and interpretations as would be needed in the new conditions that they would meet on coming into the Promised Land. He painted in frightful colors the fearful doom that would befall the disobedient and eloquently described the blessing of loyalty to God. After being called of God to depart into the mountains and die, he pronounced in one of the most beautiful passages in all the scripture, his farewell blessing upon each of the tribes.

And how solemn must have been the occasion. They are listening for the last time to his voice. With what veneration they must have gazed on him. He it was that Jochebed with loving hands had laid in the bulrushes when 120 years ago Pharaoh had persecuted them. He was the man that had so nobly chosen to suffer affliction with the people of God instead of the attractions of Egypt. His eyes under the shadow of Horeb had looked on the burning bush. His hand had stretched out over Egypt and overwhelmed it with the plagues. His was the face that had reflected the divine glory of the mount after forty days of fellowship with Jehovah, during which he received the substance of the law. That was the faithful and tried man that had often been wrongly accused, that had meekly borne so many trials, that had guided the people so faithfully, and advised them so wisely, and had refused honors himself because he loved them so well. How they must have hung on those last words! And the echo of his last words had hardly died away until his spirit had been called away and unseen hands had laid his dust in an unknown tomb.

The Significance of the Work of Moses. Humanly speaking, he explains the great difference between the Hebrews and the people kindred to them. He accounts for their development from a company of disheartened slaves, and from the careless habits of wandering tribes into a conquering nation, made irresistible by its belief in the guidance of Jehovah. Humanly speaking, he was the creator of Israel. (1) He was a **leader** and as such heartened and disciplined them. (2) He was a **prophet** and as such taught them ideals of social justice, purity and honor. (3) He was a **lawgiver** and as such furnished them with civil, sanitary, social and religious laws that channeled them into a sober, healthy, moral, and right-minded people.

(4) He was the *founder of a religion* and as such led them into a real loyalty to Jehovah as their God and gave them such a conception of the divine character and requirements as to stimulate in them a growth in goodness.

Lessons of the Period. The student will readily collect for himself lessons that have been brought to his attention. The following, however, should not fail of consideration: (1) God's law is inflexible. It is of universal operation and can not be evaded or revoked. Even the best men must suffer if they violate it as was the case of Moses. (2) To rebel against God's appointed leaders and to speak disrespectfully of them will subject one to the outpouring of divine wrath. (3) God never forgets his covenants as seen In the case of his refusal to give to Israel the land of Edom and of Ammon. (4) That God decides the fate of armies in battle and is therefore the God of nations as well as individuals. (5) Early hardships often fit us for a more glorious destiny later.

For Study and Discussion. (1) The rebellion of Korah. (2) The story of Balak and Balaam and the present day truth which it suggests or the problems of today to which it is applicable. (3) The story of the budding of Aaron's rod. (4) The sin of Moses because of which he was not allowed to enter Canaan. Find every reference to it. (5) The different victories of Israel recorded in the period. (6) The fiery serpents and serpent of brass. (7) The cities of refuge, their names, location, purpose and the lessons for today to be drawn from their use. (8) The principal events of Israel's past history mentioned in Dt. chs. 1-4, and find where in previous books each is recorded. (9) From Dt. chs. 27-28 list the curses and blessings, showing the sin and its penalty and the blessing and that for which it is promised. (10) The farewell blessing of Moses on the tribes (Dt. ch. 33). List the promises to each. (11) The death of Moses (Dt. chs. 32 and 34). (12) The incidents of the period that have in them a miraculous element. (13) Other prominent leaders besides Moses, Aaron and Joshua. (14) The nations mentioned with whom the Hebrews had contact. (15) The geography of the places and nations noticed in this period.

8
JOSHUA'S CONQUEST.

Joshua.

The Facts of History Recorded. The history recorded in this period follows closely upon and completes the story of the deliverance begun in the Exodus. But for the sin of Israel in believing the evil spies and turning back into the wilderness, none of the events of the last twenty-one chapters of Numbers and none of those found in Deuteronomy would have occurred and Joshua would have followed Exodus and have completed the story of Israel's deliverance out of Egypt into Canaan. As it is, this history follows close upon that of Deuteronomy. Joshua, who had been duly chosen and set apart for the work, took command of the hosts as soon as Moses died. He was trained in the school of Moses and exhibited the same devotion to Jehovah and the same dependence upon His guidance.

The Story Naturally Falls Into Three Parts. (1) The conquest of Canaan, (Chs. 1-12). In this section we have the story of the crossing of the Jordan, fall of Jericho and the conquest of the land both south and north. (2) The division of the territory of Canaan (Chs. 13-22). In this section we have the assignment of the territory of Canaan, the cities of Refuge, the cities of Levites and the return of the two and half tribes to the east of the Jordan. (3) Joshua's last counsel and death (Chs. 23-24), in which we have his exhortations to fidelity and farewell address and death.

While the war itself probably did not continue but seven years, the entire period was not less than twenty-five and may have been as much as fifty-one years. The period marks a new era in Biblical history. Instead of the experiences of Nomadic or semi-Nomadic tribes, a people with a fixed abode and with a growing body of customs and institutions is described.

The Land of Canaan. It is well to consider at least three things concerning this little, yet wonderful country. (1) **Its geography**. It is about four hundred miles long and from seventy-five to one hundred miles wide and is made up of plains, valleys, plateaus, gorges and mountains fashioned together in wonderful variety. There are many small bodies of land capable of supporting a group of people and yet so secluded as to allow them to develop their own individuality and become independent. Every traveler between Egypt and Babylonia must pass through Palestine which thereby became the bridge for the civilization and commerce of tie world. Here the Hebrew could easily keep in touch with the world events of his day. Later it became the gateway of travel from east to west. The territory naturally falls into three divisions: (a) Judah or Judea which is in the southern portion and about seventy-five miles long, (b) Ephraim or Samaria occupying the center of the country, (c) Galilee occupying the northern portion. Along the entire coast line there is a continuous coast plain. There are many mountains, the most important being Hermon, Carmel and Gerizim.

(2) ***Its inhabitants and the nations surrounding it***. That the population was very dense is indicated by the mention of about three hundred cities and towns a large number of which have been identified. While there were many war-like people crowded into Palestine, seven, the Hittites, the Girgashites, the Perizzites, the Hivites, the Jebusites, the Amorites and the Canaanites, were the most important. The Canaanites, who had been there about six centuries, and the Amorites, who had lived there about ten centuries, were the two peoples that furnished greatest resistance to Israel's occupancy of the country. They were virtually one people.

Around Palestine were many kingdoms, some large and strong, some small and weak. Among the more important were the Philistines, west of Judah, the Phoenician kingdoms on the north, Arameans or Syrians on the northeast, and on the east and southeast, the Ammonites, Moabites and Edomites, the last three being kinsmen of the Hebrews.

(3) ***Conditions favorable to its conquest***. Several circumstances conspired to make it a suitable time for the Hebrews to enter Canaan: (a) Egypt had crushed the Hittites and devastated their land; (b) Northern hordes from and through Syria had broken the power of Egypt and the Hittites and had also crushed the Canaanites; (c) Assyria had increased her borders to the coasts of Phoenicia and was feared by all other peoples; (d) Babylonia was not strong

enough to displace Assyria as an Asiatic power but strong enough to dispute her supremacy; (e) For two hundred years, therefore, their weakness together with that of Egypt and the Hittites gave the Hebrews ample time to develop and grow strong.

The Crossing of the Jordan and the Fall of Jericho. To the Hebrews these two incidents have always been of first importance. As the two great events through which they gained entrance to their permanent home, they have been given a place in Hebrew literature almost equal to that of their deliverance from Egyptian bondage. The divine share in these great accomplishments was fully recognized. He it was who caused the waters of Jordan to separate and He it was who threw down the walls of Jericho. Not only did Jericho occupy a strategic position, being somewhat apart from other Canaanite cities, but the marvelous manner of its fall both encouraged the Hebrews to expect complete victory and also caused the Canaanites to fear them and expect defeat.

The Complete Conquest of Canaan. The conquest was a sort of whirlwind campaign that crushed the active and dangerous opposition of the Canaanites, the complete occupancy being accomplished by a piecemeal process of subduing one after another of the little cities and independent tribes. The campaign was well planned. The Jordan was crossed, Jericho was taken and then by pushing forward for the heart of the land, Ai was overcome and in a short time Joshua was in the center of the land, ready to strike either way. With his central camp established at Gilgal (5:10; 9:6) and the forces of Canaan divided, Joshua could advance by two lines of invasion. Whether he made simultaneous campaigns in different directions is not certain, but he seems first to have turned his attention to the southern territory and then to have completed his conquest by an invasion of the northern districts. After bending before this storm the Canaanites still held possession of the land and the piecemeal process of subjugation began. It was not all accomplished by the sword but aided by the peaceful measures of inter-marriage and treaties with friendly neighbors. Israel contended against a far superior civilization but finally won because the religious as well as the civil and social life was involved.

The Cruelty to the Canannites. Stress has commonly been laid on the cruelty to the Canaanites and upon their being driven out of their land when it should have been put upon their character where the Scripture puts it. This is a waste of false sympathy. The Scripture always speaks of the driving out of the Canaanites as a punishment for their sins (Dt, 9:4-5; Lev. 18:24-25). Some of the abominations which they practiced are described in Lev. 18:21-30 and Dt. 12:30-32. These abominations were practiced in the name of religion and were so shocking that one shudders to read the description.

Everything evil was worshiped. The chief god was Baal, the sun, who was worshiped at different places under different names, but everywhere his worship was fierce and cruel. His consort Ashtaroth, the Babylonian goddess Istar, the goddess of love, worshiped as the morning star, Venus, fostered in her worship abominations that are almost inconceivable in our times. It was a worship of impurity and could not be cured by ordinary means. God had borne with it for hundreds of years. Their destruction was therefore justifiable just as was that of the old world and the Jews were simply God's instruments just as were the waters of the flood or the fire and brimstone in the case of Sodom and Gomorrah.

God was planning to begin, a new nation, to start a new civilization and by using this method of punishment for the Canaanites he impressed the Hebrews in a most striking way with the consequences of forsaking worship of the true God. It was a new thing in the world to have all idolatrous symbols destroyed and to worship an unseen God and yet Joshua constantly represented to them that all the evils they had inflicted upon the Canaanites, and greater evils, would be sent upon them if they should become idolaters. Little, therefore, need be said of the cruelty of the Hebrews nor of the suffering of the Canaanites. The Hebrews were the instrument of God and the Canaanites were reaping what they had sown.

The Significance of the War Against the Canannites. Of all the wars recorded in human history this was one of the greatest, if not the greatest of all. None was ever fought for a more noble purpose and none has accomplished greater ends. The fate of the world was in the balance. Old civilizations on account of their wickedness, were to soon fall and this series of conflicts was to decide whether a new civilization with a pure and holy purpose to serve God could arise in their midst. It was, therefore, a war (1) ***For purification***. The individual, the temple and the home must all be pure. (2) ***For civil liberty***. Israel was now, under God, to govern herself and thereby to give the world a pattern of government as God's free nation. (3) ***For religious liberty***. Idolatry, vice and superstition were everywhere and the people must be free to worship the one true God and Creator of all. (4) ***For the whole world***. Israel was to be a blessing to all nations. Out of her and out of this land was to come Christ, her son, who should save the nations. The war was, therefore, for us as well as for them.

The Character and Work of Joshua. The name Joshua in the Old Testament is equivalent to Jesus in the New (Heb. 4:8). His character and work were well adapted to his age and he therefore made a deep impression upon this formative period of Israel's history. He was fully prepared for the work of the conquest by his association with Moses and by such events as the defeat of Amalek which he accomplished by divine help (Ex. 17:10-16). With all he had been called of God and set apart for the work of subjugating the Canaanites. As a soldier and commander, he ranks among the first of the world. He is resourceful, brave, straightforward, fertile in strategy, and quick to strike (1:10-11; 2:1 etc.). In the councils of peace he was wise and generous. He displayed statesmanship of the highest order in mapping out the boundaries of the tribes and thus preparing the land for a permanent occupancy of the Hebrews. In the matter of religion he was actuated by a spirit of implicit obedience to God's authority. He combined in his nature both courage and gentleness and exhibited in his dealings the disposition of both the lion and the lamb. His dying charge is full of earnestness and devotion. As a type of Christ he led the people to the "rest" of Canaan, though not to the rest of the gospel which "remaineth to the people of God." A void still remained and they still had to look forward. He led them to victory over their enemies and became their advocate when they sinned and met defeat.

Lessons of the Period. Among many lessons suggested by this book the following should be considered and the student asked to suggest others. (1) God is at war with sin: (a) He thrusts out the Canaanites because of their sins; (b) He allows the defeat of Israel at Ai because sin was among them; (c) He allows Achan put to death because of it. He is, therefore, against all sin, personal, social and civic or national. (2) Religious victory and entrance upon spiritual rest is accomplished through a leader or commander and through a divine power, not through a law giver and by the works of the law. It was not Moses, the lawgiver, through whom they entered and not by their own strength. (3) God keeps his covenants in spite of all the weakness of man. (4) God decides the issues of battles and of wars with a view to the final on-going of his kingdom. Only God and not the relative strength or preparedness of the contending armies can forecast the final issues of war. (5) The fact that God is for one does not preclude the use of strategy and discretionary methods. (6) The failure or sin of one man may defeat a whole cause and that in spite of the faithful efforts of many others. (7) What is a just severity to some is often a great mercy to others. The destruction of the Canaanites was a severe penalty for their sins, but it was an unspeakable blessing to all the future ages because by it a true faith and a pure worship was preserved.

For Study and Discussion. (1) Each of the lessons suggested above. Find a basis either in incident or teaching for each. (2) The geography of the country with the principal cities mentioned. (3) The several tribes of people mentioned in the narrative. (4) The providential conditions favorable to the conquest just at that time. (5) The cruelties of the Israelites to their enemies. Select examples and discuss each. (6) The significance of the war. (7) The character and work of Joshua. Point out incidents or acts that show elements of greatness and weakness in his character; also estimate the value of his work. (8) The cooperation of the two and a half tribes in these wars. (9) The several battles described. List them and decide what contributed to the success or failure of Israel in each case. (10) The story of the fall of Jericho. (11) The sin of Achan, its results, its discovery and punishment. (12) The story of the Gibeonites, their stratagem, its embarrassment to Joshua and consequent slavery to them. (13) The portion of land allotted to each tribe and how it was secured. (14) The miraculous element running through the narrative. List and discuss each incident that tends to show or makes claim of such miraculous element. (15) The place of prayer and worship in the hook. Give incidents. (16) The element that is figurative or illustrative of truth revealed in New Testament times.

9
THE JUDGES.

Judges 1; 1 Sam. 7.

The Characteristics of the Times. This is a period of transition for Israel Nothing was quite certain, and "every man did that which was right in his own eyes" (17:6). In consequence of this there was lack of organization, cooperation or leadership. While we do not have all the history covered by the period and while we do not easily understand or explain its events, it is clear that things did not run smoothly. In Judges 2:16-19 the author gives a vivid picture of the conditions and characteristics of the time. The problems of the times may be outlined as follows: (1) **Political problems**. These arose, (a) because of the isolated conditions of the tribes, (b) because of their tribal government which lacked the bond of unity of former times, (c) because of the strength and opposition of the Canaanites. (2) **Social problems**. These grew out of: (a) the adoption of Canaanite customs and manner of life, (b) the intermarriage of the Jews with the new people. (3) **Religious Problems**. The source of these problems arose from two directions, (a) Baal worship ministered to their lusts and was therefore a snare to them, (b) the religion of Israel required purity and was, therefore, counted a burden. The problems of the times of peace were greater than those in the times of war.

The Judges. Now that there was no central stable government and no hereditary rulers the people accepted from time to time as their rulers certain military leaders whom God raised up and who, by their prowess, delivered them from the yoke of foreign oppression. It was, therefore, a period of personal efforts some of which are preserved for us in this portion of scripture. Fifteen Judges are named counting Eli and Samuel, who are by some not so named, but we know very little of any except six of the military judges and Eli and Samuel. These six are brought into prominence because of as many invasions by other nations as follows. (1) The Mesopotamians came down from the northeast and oppressed Israel until Othniel, Caleb's nephew, was raised up to deliver them. (2) The invasion of the Moabites and the deliverance through Ehud. (3) The oppression of the Canaanites, who came down from the north, was thrown off through the leadership of Deborah assisted by Barak. (4) The Midianites came in from the east and greatly oppressed Israel until Gideon defeated and destroyed these bold oppressors. (5) The invasion of the Ammonites and Israel's deliverance through Jephthah. (6) The Philistines were the next successful enemies of Israel and were enabled to do great harm to Israel until Samson arose and overthrew their power.

Eli and Samuel differed widely from the other judges and on that account are sometimes not counted among them. Eli was a good but weak man. His weakness in the control of his children ruined them and brought him to sorrow and also caused a severe defeat for Israel.

Samuel was the last of the judges and was also a priest and prophet. He is one of the outstanding Old Testament characters. Abraham founded the Hebrew race; Joseph saved them from famine; Moses gave them a home and Samuel organized them into a great kingdom which led to their glory. His birth was in answer to prayer and as judge or deliverer he won his most signal victory, that against the Philistines, by means of prayer. He founded schools for the instruction of young prophets at Gilgal. Bethel, Mizpeh and Ramah. In this he perhaps rendered his most valuable and most lasting service. These schools gave a great impetus to prophecy. After this time prophecy and prophets had a vital and permanent place in the life of the nation. Even kings had to consult them for instructions from God.

Ruth the Moabite. In contrast with the many stories of idolatry and sin of the times and especially in contrast with the story of the idolatry of Micah and the crime of Gibeah found in the last chapters of Judges, we have the beautiful little story of Ruth, the Moabite. Others had turned away from Jehovah the true God to false gods, but she turned from the false gods and received the true God.

Other Nations. Of the condition of the other nations of this period we are left largely to the monuments, but much has been discovered that throws light on the general world conditions. The following might be noted here. (1) *Egypt*. After the Exodus of Israel Egypt seems to have enjoyed several centuries of great prosperity during which the country was adorned with wonderful buildings, her religion prospered, her people were famous for their learning and, through colonization projects, she carried her civilization to many other climes. (2) **Assyria** was now a growing empire and destined to become, ere long, one of the most powerful of all. (3) **Babylonia** was now weak and generally at a disadvantage in contests with other nations. (4) **The Elamites** also became a people of considerable influence and at least on different occasions invaded Babylonia. (5) **Mesopotamia**, before being absorbed by Assyria was a powerful nation and ravaged Syria and Palestine. (6) **Phoenicia** was a country of great commercial progress with Tyre and Sidon as centers of great influence. (7) **Greece**. The most interesting of all the countries that began to show their strength during that period is Greece. The inhabitants were wonderful in physical energy, in war and conquest, in discovery and in capacity for education. They were fond of pleasure and had great capacity for the tasks of society, government, and religion. They contrived a religious system that was conspicuous for the absence of the great priestly class of the eastern systems of religion. However, it left the morally corrupt nature of man untouched and, therefore, did not contribute anything to the cause of pure religion.

Outline of The Narrative. The Scripture narrative falls into the following well-defined divisions: (1) An introduction or the condition in Palestine at the beginning of the period, Jud. 1:1-3:6. (2) The Judges and their work, Jud. 3:1:1-3:6. (2) The Judges and their work, (Jud. 3:7-16 end). (3) Micah's idolatry, Jud. Chs. 17-18. (4) The crime of Gibeah, Jud. Chs. 19-21. (5) The story of Ruth, Ruth. (6) The career of

Samuel including the judgeship of Eli, 1 Sam. Chs. 1-7.

Ethical and Religious Standards. Since this is a transitional period we may expect great difference of moral and religions standards. Some things are stressed far beyond their importance while other matters of more consequence are overlooked. The following examples will indicate to what extremes they went in some matters. (1) **Some things bad**: (a) Murdering a heathen enemy was counted a virtue; (b) It was not a crime to steal from a member of another Hebrew tribe; (c) Might was right; (d) They would keep any foolish vow to God even though it cost the life of one's child as in the case of Jephthah. (2) **Some things good**: (a) The marriage relation was held sacred; (b) A covenant was held binding and sacred as in the case of the Gibeonites; (c) They counted inhospitality a crime. (3) **Some strange inconsistencies**: (a) Micah would steal his mother's silver, then rear a family altar to Jehovah; (b) Samson would keep his Nazarite vow, preserve his hair intact and abstain from wine and unclean food but give himself over to lying and to his passions, and selfish inclinations and fail to observe the simple laws of justice, mercy and service.

Lessons of the Period. (1) **As to national decay**: (a) It is caused by religious apostasy; (b) It evidences itself in religious blindness, political folly and social immorality; (c) Its curse results in political and social disorder, chaos and ultimate ruin. (2) **As to punishment for sin**: (a) He surely sends punishment on the offender whether an individual or a nation; (b) His punishment is a matter of mercy and is intended to prepare the way for deliverance. (3) **As to deliverance**: (a) It never comes until repentance is manifested; (b) It is always through a deliverer whom we can not find but whom God must raise up for us. (4) From the book of Ruth it is shown that circumstances neither make nor mar believers.

For Study and Discussion. (1) The names of the Judges in order with the length of time each served or the period of rest after the work of each. (2) The enemy each judge had to combat. (3) What each judge accomplished against the enemy and what weapon he used-an oxgoad or what? (4) The elements of strength and weakness in the character of the principal men of the period. (5) The New Testament truths illustrated in the life and work of Gideon and Samson. (6) The lessons of practical life illustrated by the stories of Jephthah and Deborah. (7) The facts of the story of Micah and Gibeah. (8) The career of Samuel as found so far. (9) The value of a trusting soul as seen in Ruth. (10) The main element in their religion. (11) The condition of Israel at the beginning and at the end of this period. (12) The subject of good and successful parents with bad and unsuccessful children. The importance they attached to the Ark of the Covenant.

10
THE REIGN OF SAUL.

I Sam. 8-31; I Chron. 10

The Demand for a King. The last period saw one tribe after another come to the front and assert itself through some leading man as an emergency arose, but now the tribes are to be united into a monarchy and this, too, at their own request made in the form of a desire for a king. Several things no doubt influenced them to make this request. (1) From the days of Joshua there had been no strong national bond. They were only held together by the law of Moses and the annual assemblages at Shiloh. But the wise reign of Samuel had given an enlarged national consciousness and led to a desire for a stable government with the largest possible national unity. (2) The failure of the sons of Samuel, who had been entrusted with some power and who would naturally succeed him, led them to feel that provision for the welfare of the nation must be made before the death of Samuel or ruin would come. (3) The attitude of the nations around Israel suggested the need of a strong government headed by a leader of authority. The Philistines and Ammonites had already made incursions into their land and threatened at any time to further oppress them. The new organization, therefore, seemed necessary as a national protection. (4) The faith of Jehovah was threatened. The victories of the Philistines would be interpreted to mean that Jehovah was powerless or else did not care for his people. This would lead them to turn to other gods. Then too they were greatly tempted by the religion of the Canaanite to turn from Jehovah. It was, therefore, a religious crisis that made it essential that the Hebrews unite and in the name of Jehovah over throw the Philistines and establish a nation that would rightly represent to all nations Jehovah as the God of their race. (5) The nations around them such as Egypt and Assyria with their seats of royalty had excited their pride and they were moved with a desire to be like their heathen neighbors-a desire which involved disrespect for their divine king and want of faith in him.

The Principle of the Kingdom. The folly of the people did not lie in their asking for a king to rule over them, but in the spirit of forgetfulness of God with which they made the request. Indeed Moses had provided for a kingdom and given the law upon which the king was to rule (Dt 17:14-20). He was to be unlike other kings. He was not to rule according to his own will or that of the people but according to the will of Jehovah. He was to be subject to God as was the humblest Israelite, and, under his immediate direction, was to rule for the good of the people. This was a new principle that showed it self in all the future history of Israel. Saul attempted to be like others-to assert his own will-and disobeyed God and was deposed while David identified himself with God and his purposes and was successful. One represent the ideal of the people, the other that of the Scripture.

Saul the First King. He began his career under the most auspicious circumstances. His tribe and its location as well as his fine physical appearance gave him great advantage. He was enthusiastic and brave, and yet in the early days he charms us with his modesty. After he was anointed by Samuel and had been made to see the great career opening to him he returned to his regular toil until the people were called together at Mizpah and proclaimed him king. Samuel supported him with his influence and the people gave him allegiance. He was for a while subservient to the will of God and greatly prospered. But later he became self-willed and failed to see that the nation was God's and not his. He developed a spirit of disobedience, perverseness and evil conduct that mark him as insane.

Saul's Great Achievements. The oppression of Israel's enemies which in part at least made necessary their king had to be dealt with at once. In his contest with them Saul had a very successful military career. He was successful in the following campaigns: (I) Against the Ammonites (I Sam. 11) in which he delivered from ruin the inhabitants of Jabesh-Gilead on the east Of Jordan and won the love of all the Hebrew people. (2) Against the Philistines (I Sam. 13-14) in which Jonathan was the hero. Before the battle he disobeyed the will of God by performing the duties of a priest and was told he should lose his kingdom on account of it. At the close of the campaign he lost his temper and proposed to kill Jonathan, his son, the hero of the day because he had unwittingly disobeyed a foolish command. (3) Against Moab, Ammon, Edom and Zobah (I Sam. 14:47) of which there are no particulars given. (4) Against the Amalekites (I Sam. 15) in which, though he defeated Amalek, he disobeyed God in not wholly destroying all Amalek and his possessions and thereby lost for the time being Samuel's help and finally his kingdom. It was after this battle that David was anointed to become king in Saul's stead.

Saul's Decline. From Chapter 16 on the story tells of the rapid decline of Saul and of the rise of David to the kingdom. (1) There is given the story of the madness of Saul and the introduction of David to the court as the king's musician. (2) The campaign against the Philistines in which David kills Goliath, the giant that was defying Israel, and won great honor from the king. (3) His effort to destroy David. During many years he, with bitter jealousy and an insane hatred, tried to destroy David who was as constantly delivered by a divine providence. Whether on account of sickness or other reason, he seems to have had fits of insanity during this period. (4) His last battle and death. The Philistines arrayed themselves against Saul. With a sense of defeat he tried to get in touch with Samuel, but finally met a death in harmony with his life and thus ended one of the most melancholy careers of all history. All because of his disobedience to God (I Chron. 10:1.1-14).

Lessons of the Period. (1) God adapts his methods to the needs and conditions of the people from tribal government to kingdom. (2) A man out of harmony with God will certainly fail-Saul. (3) A man in harmony with God's plan will succeed no matter how much opposed by others-David. (4) God never forgets to punish those who oppress his people-Amalekites.

(5) The success of God's work does not depend upon our attitude toward his will, but our condition when it has succeeded does. (6) A righteous man can succeed without doing wrong to do it. (7) God's anointed will suffer if they sin. (8) Kindness to enemies-David to Saul. (9) The strength of true friendship-Jonathan and David.

For Study and Discussion. (1) The condition that led to the establishment of the kingdom. (3) Four statements Samuel made to Saul and four ways by which he tried to impress him with the responsibility to which he was called I Sam. 9:19-10-8. (3) The prophet bands or school of prophets. (4) The story of Jonathan's exploits against Michmash by Saul and his escape, I Sam. 14. (5) The story of David's choice and anointing, I Sam. 16:1-13. (6) The killing of Goliath and defeat of the Philistines. I Sam. Ch. 17. (7) Story of Jonathan and David, I Sam. 18:1-4; 19:1-7; 20:1-4, 12-17, 41-42; 23:16-18. (8) David's wanderings, 21:10-22-5. (9) Compare Saul and David at the time of the anointing of each as to their chances of success. (10) David's sojourn in Philistia with the experience of embarrassment and advantage, I Sam. Chs. 27-28. (11) Saul's last battle and death, (a) the appeal to Samuel through the witch, I Sam. Ch. 28, (b) the battle, his and his son's death, I Sam. Ch.31.

11
THE REIGN OF DAVID.

2 Sam.; 1 Chron. Chs. 11-29; 1 K 1:1-2:11.

His Reign over Judah. The reign of David is divided into two parts. The first part was over Judah, with the capitol at Hebron, and lasted seven and one-half years. During this period Ishbosheth, son of Saul, reigned over Israel in the North. It is probable that both of these kings were regarded as vassals of the Philistines and paid tribute. On account of rival leaders, there was constant warfare between these two rival kings. The kingdom of Judah, however, gradually gained the ascendancy. This is beautifully described in the Scripture "David waxed stronger and stronger, but the house of Saul waxed weaker and weaker" (2 Sam. 3:1). Seeing this, Abner undertook negotiations looking to the onion of the two kingdoms, but was treacherously killed by Joab. The act of Abner in coming to David was in reality one of secession. It was soon followed by the murder of Ishbosheth and the utter failure of Saul's kingdom.

His Reign Over All Israel. Saul's kingdom having fallen, Israel assembled in great numbers at Hebron and asked David to become king over all the nation. Upon his ascendancy to the throne of the united nations the Philistines sent an army into the Hebrew country. The brief record of these wars shows that they were very bitter and that at one time David was forced to take refuge in the Cave of Adullam and carry on a sort of guerrilla warfare. But finally in the valley of Rephaim he was enabled to strike such a crushing blow to the Philistines as to compel a lasting peace and leave him free to develop his kingdom. This reign of David, lasting thirty-three years after he became king of all, was the ideal reign of all the history of the Hebrews.

The element of success and chief acts of his reign may be summed up somewhat as follows: (1) **His capture of Jerusalem** (formerly called Jesub,) a Canaanitish stronghold that had resisted all attacks from the days of Joshua, and making it his capitol. This choice showed great wisdom. (2) **His foreign relations**. David's foreign policy was one of conquest. He not only defended Israel but subdued other nations. Besides the subduing of the Philistines and capture of Jebus, already mentioned, he conquered the Moabites. the Syrians, the Edomites and the Ammonites. He also made an alliance with Hiram, the king of the Phoenicians, who became his lifelong friend. (3) **His home relations and policies**. His policy at home may be said to be one of centralization. One of his first acts was to bring up the ark and place it on Mount Zion and to center all worship there. This would tend to unite the people and to make more powerful his authority over all the people. In line with this plan he conceived the idea of building the temple and during the years he gathered materials and stored riches with which to build it. He acted with a wise consideration for the rights of his subjects and in every way sought to promote their happiness. As a ruler, he differed very widely from the kings of other countries. He possessed none of their selfish aims. He did not oppress his subjects with heavy taxes, nor spoil them of their possessions, nor seize them for soldiers against their will. He recognized that the king was for the people and not the people for the king.

His Great Sin and Its Bitter Consequences. David's high ideals and noble chivalry could not withstand the enervating influence of his growing harem. The degrading influence of polygamy with its luxury, pleasure seeking and jealousies was soon to undermine his character. His sins and weak indulgencies were destined to work family and national disaster. These sins reached a climax in his trespass with Bathsheba, the wife of Uriah. In this crime he fell from his exalted position to the level of an unprincipled eastern monarch. It stands out as one of the darkest crimes of all history and "shows what terrible remnants of sin there are in the hearts even of converted men". Primitive society followed the course of nature in condemning adultery as worthy of more severe punishment than murder itself. And "no crime today involves more sudden and terrible consequences in the individual; no crime is capable of exerting as malign an influence upon the innocent family and later descendants of the culprit; no crime leaves in its wake as many physical and moral ills."

The Bitter consequences of this sin soon became apparent. Nathan brought to him a worthy rebuke and he showed himself different from other kings of his time by the bitter repentance with which he bewails his iniquity in the fifty-first Psalm. God forgave his sin but its evil consequences in his family and nation could not be removed. The nature of his chastisement is suggested in the following incidents: (1) The death of his child born to Bath-sheba. (2) Ammon, his oldest son, one of the pitiable products of his oriental harem, shamefully treated his sister, Tamar, in the gratification of his brutal lusts. (3) Absalom treacherously murdered Ammon as a matter of revenge for the outrage upon his sister, Tamar. (4) The rebellion of Absalom, his son, which almost cost David the throne and led to the destruction of Absalom. (5) The rebellion of Shebna and following events, which almost destroyed the empire. (6) Many incidents in the family and kingdom of Solomon, his son.

While David must always be judged by the social standards of his age it must be remembered that his own generation did not hesitate to condemn his act and we must not excuse in the least this awful sin. The message it has for us is supremely applicable to our present age in which social evil threatens to undermine our boasted Christian civilization.

The Inspiring Career of David. The life of David is so varied and beautiful that one finds difficulty in outlining any study of him in the space allowed here. There are several ways of studying his career. Sometimes it may be profitable to consider him from two viewpoints, (1) His character, (2) His life after he became king. For our purpose, however, it would be better to look at him somewhat as follows: (1) **As a shepherd lad**, where he laid the foundations of his great career. (2) **As a servant at the court of Saul**, where he became the object of a bitter jealousy and suffered great indignities. (3) **As a refugee from Saul**, during which time he exhibited his unwillingness to do wrong even against one who was doing him great injustice. (4) **As a friend**, especially shown in his relation to Jonathan. By it he was influenced throughout his whole career and was caused after becoming king to extend kindness to the house of Saul, his enemy. 2 Sam. ch. 9. (5) **As a musician**. His accomplishments in this field are witnessed both by his ability in the use of the harp and in the great body of psalms which he left us. (6) **As a loyal subject**. In no other place, perhaps, did he show more fine qualities than in this. To him Saul was God's anointed, and, though wronged by Saul and though himself already anointed to be king in Saul's stead, he remained perfectly loyal to Saul as king. (7) **As a ruler**. He knew how to govern both his own people and those whom he had subdued. He also succeeded in forming friendly alliances with other kings and changed the enfeebled and divided tribes into a mighty empire. (8) **As a military leader**. Through his skill he organized a most successful army (1 Chron. 27:1-5; 2 Sam. 23:8-9), and defeated at least five surrounding nations and so impressed the great world powers beyond that they did not oppose the growth of his kingdom. (9) **As a servant of God**. Though making his mistakes, he was a "man after God's own heart." He made Jerusalem the great center of religion and organized the priests and Levites so that their work could be done effectively and with order. The key-note of his life seems to have been expressed to Goliath (I Sam. 17:45). (10) **As a type of Christ**. Of all the human types of Jesus in the Old Testament David is probably the most eminent. This fact makes the study of his life and experiences of great interest and profit to the Christian.

His Last Days. The last days of David are made sad because of his own weakness. The memory of his guilt and disgrace had led him to withdraw more and more from the public life and, therefore, to neglect the duties of judge and ruler. His court became the scene of plotting concerning his successor, whose name he had apparently not announced. It was only by the valuable help of Nathan that he succeeded in having his wish in the matter.

The dying words of David have in them much that is prophetic of the Messiah and points out to Solomon, his beloved son, who was to reign in his stead, the way of all success and blessing. It, however, contains what has been designated as "the greatest blot on David's character"-His charge to Solomon to put to death Shimei and Joab. Such vindictiveness does not seem to comport with his spirit manifested in the sparing of Saul in the days of his jealous hatred and in his kindness to the house of Saul (2 Sam. Ch. 9). Nor does it comport with this patience formerly shown to Shimei (2 Sam. 16:5-13). We can not explain these charges of hatred upon any other grounds than that of an old man in his dotage. He is "no longer his manful self."

Psalms. While the time covered by the collection of the Psalms is more than a thousand years, reaching from the time of Moses to the period of the exile, it is probably best to study them in this period. The majority of them are ascribed to David and the whole collection early became known as the Psalms of David. Reference should be made to *The Bible Book By Book* for an introduction to their study.

The Lessons of the Period. (1) Divine appointment to a great task does not guarantee one against falling into evil. (2) Luxury and the indulgence of the appetites tend to degradation. (3) The personal forgiveness of sin does not remove its evil consequences. (4) Our sins are often as harmful to others and even more so than to ourselves. (5) Righteousness exalteth a nation. (6) God controls the issues of wars.

For Study and Discussion. (1) The location of the several nations conquered by David and how the victories were won, especially the capture of Jebus. (2) David's plan to build the Temple and God's message to him II Sam. Ch. 11. Point out the different elements in it. (3) Absolom's conspiracy and final defeat, II Sam. Chs. 15 and 18. (4) The death of the child of Uriah's wife, II Sam. Ch. 12. (5) The different times David showed kindness to his enemies, II Sam. 9, 10, 16, and 19. Learn the details of each case. (6) The organization of his kingdom, II Sam. 8:16-18, 15:37, 16:16, 20:23-26; I Chron. 27:33. (7) Tie rebellion of Sheba, II Sam. 20:1-22. (8) The story of Adonijah, I K. Ch. 1. (9) List David's last commands to Solomon, I K. 2:1-9. (10) Nathan's parable to David, II Sam. 12:1-9, 13-15. (11) The greatest fault of Absalom, of Joab. (12) Joab, the avenger, II Sam. 2:17-32, 3:22-30, 18:9-15, 20:4-10.

12

SOLOMON'S REIGN.

I K. Chs. 1-12; II Chron. Chs.1-9.

The Riddle of Solomon's Character. Few Biblical characters manifested such contradictory elements of character. Early in life he manifested an earnest, conscientious and religious spirit. He was prayerful and sought above all else wisdom and that for the good reason that he might be able to rule well. He built the temple and thereby magnified the worship of Jehovah.

His prayer at the dedication of this temple were not only humble and fervent but were expressive of the very highest loyalty to Jehovah as the one supreme God and to all the high purposes of the divine will in Israel. But in spite of all this he put upon the people such heavy burdens of taxation as to crush them. He trampled under foot the democratic ideals of the nation and adopted the policy of oriental despots which tended to make free-born citizens mere slaves of the king. He lived a life of the basest sort of self-indulgence. He depended upon foreign alliances rather than upon Jehovah to save his nation. He married many strange wives and through them was led to establish in Israel the worship of strange Gods. I K. 11:1-8. On the whole his reign was such as to undo what had been accomplished by David and proved disastrous. Although counted the wisest he proved to be in many ways the most foolish king that ever ruled over Israel.

His Policies. As a ruler it is easy to think of his policies under three heads, (1) **His home policy**. This was one of absolution. He became a despot and robbed the people of their freedom and put them under a yoke of oppression by imposing upon them heavy burdens of tax that he might carry out his unholy plans for selfish indulgence. (2) **His foreign policy**. This was a policy of diplomacy. By means of intermarriage, by the establishment of commercial relations and by the adoption of the customs and religions of other nations he bound them in friendly alliance. (3) **His religious policy**. This was a policy of concentration. He built die temple and, through the splendor of its worship, tried to concentrate all worship upon Mount Moriah. This desire may also have contributed to his erection of altars to foreign deities.

Solomon's Building Enterprise. The greatest of all his building accomplishments was the temple. It is almost impossible to conceive of its magnificence. According to the most modern computation the precious materials, such as gold with which it was embellished, amounted to something like six hundred million dollars. Next in importance was his palace, which in size and time of construction surpassed that of the temple. This palace consisted of several halls, the chief of which were: The Forest of Lebanon, the Hall of Pillars, and the Hall of Judgment. Near the palace was the residence of the king himself and his Egyptian Queen-a house that would compare well with the royal palaces of her native land. Indeed all Moriah and the ground about its base were covered with immense structures.

Besides the temple, palace and other great buildings at the capitol, Solomon undertook various other great building enterprises. He built many great cities not only in the territory of ancient Palestine but in his now extended empire. The most famous of these were Tadmor or Palmyra and Baalath, or Baalbic. The former built at an oasis of the Syrian desert seems to have been a sort of trade emporium for the traders of Syria and the Euphrates to exchange wares with the merchants of Egypt. The latter was near Lebanon and was chiefly notable for its temple of the sun which was one of the finest edifices of Syria.

It would be difficult to put too high a value upon the influence wrought by these vast building enterprises. It can hardly be doubted that the building of the temple was the most important single event of the period of the United Kingdom. From this time on Israel ceased to look back to Sinai and regard Jerusalem as the dwelling place of Jehovah. Its priesthood and services became the support of all the coming kings. The prophets proclaimed their immortal messages from its sacred precincts and through it was nurtured the pure religion of Jehovah.

Solomon's Writings. During this period as in the previous one literary culture made a great advance. Solomon, like David his father, possessed extraordinary literary gifts and as a writer had large influence. Three books of the Scripture are ascribed to him. (1) **The Book of Proverbs**. There is no reason to believe, however, that he wrote all of them. It is a collection of proverbs or rather several collections. Some were written by Solomon, collected by him from the wise sayings of others and still others were added collections of later times. (2) **Ecclesiastes**. The purpose of this book seems to be to show the result of successful worldliness and self-gratification compared with a life of godliness. It is intended to show that the realization of all one's aim and hopes and aspirations in the matters of wealth, pleasure and honor will not bring satisfaction to the heart. (3) **The Song of Solomon**. To the Jews of that time this book set forth the whole of the history of Israel; to the Christian it sets forth the fullness of love that unites the believer and his Savior as bride and bridegroom; to all the world it is a call to cast out those unworthy ideals and monstrous practices that threaten to undermine society and the home.

Nations Surrounding Israel. The life of any people is always influenced by the nations around them. During this period Israel had intercourse with many other nations. (1) **Phoenicia**. This commercial people, through Hiram of Tyre, one of its kings, supplied the cedar wood and the skilled laborers who made possible the building of the temple. (2) **Egypt**. Solomon married a daughter of Pharoah and carried on with Egypt an extensive commerce and for his wife's sake no doubt introduced the worship of Egyptian gods. (3) **Assyria**. This country as well as Egypt had lost much of her former power and was not in a position to antagonize Solomon. (4) Among the other nations with which Solomon had dealings may be mentioned **Sheba**, thought to be in the most southern part of Arabia, **Ophir** and **Tarshish**, and from the nature of articles purchased and the three years required for the voyage he is thought to have sent trading vessels to **India**.

Evidences of National Decay. From the brief history of this period given us by the biblical writers it is evident that the nation began to disintegrate before the death of Solomon. Among the more apparent signs of decay were several revolts: (1) that of Hadad the Edomite, who threw off the Hebrew part of Edom independently: (2) that of Adad, the Midianite, who defiled the authority of Solomon; (3) that of Rezon, the Aramean, who revolted and became master of Damascus around which grew up an important kingdom; (4) that of Jeroboam, an Ephraimite, who was an officer of Solomon at Jerusalem and while unsuccessful showed the existence of a deep-seated discontent in Jerusalem itself. It is significant that the prophet Ahijah of Shiloh encouraged Jeroboam by telling him that, on account of the idolatry fostered by Solomon, ten tribes would be removed from Solomon's son and committed to him. This indicates that the prophets saw that disunion alone would preserve the liberties and pure religion of Israel.

Lessons of the Period. (1) All national methods bring disaster if God is left out of account. (2) Material progress is absolutely of no value without a spiritual life. (3) National prosperity always endangers the nation. (4) The wisest and best of men may go wrong, if they subject themselves to evil influences. (5) Temples or houses of worship are of value in giving dignity to faith and in preserving the spirit of worship. (6) If the common people feel that they are unjustly treated nothing will prevent the disintegration of the nation. (7) Religion that does not issue in proper ethics will suffer at the hands of true ethics. (8) The security of society depends upon simple justice.

For Study and Discussion. (1) The several incidents attending Solomon's accession to the throne, I K. Chs. 1-2. (2) David's last charge to Solomon, I K. Ch. 3; 4:29:34. (4) [sic] Solomon's temple: (a) Its size and plan; (b) Its equipment; (c) Its dedication. (5) Solomon's prayer at the dedication of the temple, I K. Ch. 8: II Chron. Ch. 6. Look for a revelation of his character, religious spirit and conception of God. (6) Solomon's sins, I K. Ch. 11. (7) Solomon's treatment of his foes I K, 2:19-46. (8). What Solomon did to stimulate trade, I K. 9:26-10:13; 10:22-29. (9) Statements in Ecclesiastes that point to Solomon as author or to experiences he had. (10) Statements in Song of Solomon that throw light upon the times or seem to refer to Solomon and his experiences.

13
THE DIVIDED KINGDOM.

1 King, 12-2 K. 17. 2 Chron. 10-38.

The Division of the Kingdom. Several things must be set down as contributory causes of the division of the nation. (1) There was an old jealousy between the tribes of the north and south reaching as far back as the time of the Judges. The very difference in the northern and southern territories and their products tended to keep alive a rivalry between the tribes occupying them. (2) During the time of Solomon the people had turned away from Jehovah and engaged in the idolatrous worship of other gods, especially those of the Zidonians, Moabites and Ahijah, the prophet, had foretold the division (1 K. 11:29-39). This weakening of the people's faithfulness to God gave place for the manifestations of their former jealousy. (3) Solomon had put upon the people heavy burdens of taxation and of forced labor, which were fast taking away the people's liberties and reducing them to serfdom. This policy inflamed the jealousy of the northern tribes into a bitter discontent. They would rebel rather than submit to the loss of their liberty which to them meant also disloyalty to God. (4) The ambition of Jeroboam, of the tribe of Ephraim, a valiant officer of Solomon, no doubt led him to stir up the ten tribes to revolt. Ahijah, the prophet, had made known to him that, upon the death of Solomon, he should become the head of these tribes. (5) The final and immediate cause was the foolish course of Rehoboam. He went to Shechem to be accepted as king by the northern tribes. They demanded that he should relieve them of the heavy burdens laid on them by Solomon. The older and more experienced men counseled him to grant their request, but he heeded the advice of the young men, who were ignorant of conditions, and answered them with a threat of even severer burdens. Incensed by this foolish threat, the ten tribes revolted and enthroned Jeroboam as their king and the division of the empire was accomplished. This was the turning point of the nation. It was the undoing of all that had been accomplished by the three kings that had proceeded.

Comparison of the Two Kingdoms. Each kingdom had its advantages and its disadvantages. (1) The northern kingdom, from the material point of view, was far superior to the southern. It had a larger and more fertile country. It had three times as many people and a much better military equipment. Ramah, Bether and Gilgal with their sites of their schools of the prophets were all in their borders. Their country was also the scene of greatest prophetic activity and their cause was just. But the kings were inferior and wicked. Not a single one of the nineteen kings were godly. They established idolatrous and abominable worship as a religion of the king. This idolatry counterbalanced all the material advantages. (2) The Southern Kingdom was far superior from a spiritual point of view. It possessed the religious capital of the nation with the temple as a center of Jehovah worship. True it had only one third as many people, one half as much territory and that less fertile, and an inferior military equipment, but its superior spiritual power and its superior line of kings made it last 135 years longer than the northern kingdom.

The Kings of the Northern Kingdom.

1. Jeroboam, 1 K. 12:20-14:20. Reigned 22 years and died.
2. Nadab, 1 K. 15:25-27. Reigned 2 years and was slain.
3. Baasha, 1 K. 15;27-16:6. Reigned 24 years and died.
4. Elah, 1 K. 16;6-10. Reigned 2 years and was slain.
5. Zimri, 1 K. 18:11-20. Reigned 7 days and suicided.
6. Omri, 1 K. 16:31-28. Reigned 12 years and died.
7. Ahab, 1 K. 16:29-22:40. Reigned 22 years and was slain in battle.
8. Ahaziah, 1 K. 22:51-2 K. 1:18. Reigned 2 years and died from an accident.
9. Jehoram, 2 K. 3:1-9:24. Reigned 12 years and was slain.
10. Jehu, 2 K. 9:1-10:36. Reigned 28 years and died.

11. Jehoahaz, 2 K. 13:1-9. Reigned 17 years and died.
12. Jehoash, 2 K. 13:10-14:16. Reigned 16 years and died.
13. Jeroboam II, 2 K. 14:23-29. Reigned 41 years and died.
14. Zechariah, 2 K. 15:8-10. Reigned 6 months and was slain.
15. Shallum, 2 K. 15:13-14. Reigned 1 month and was slain.
16. Menahem, 2 K. 15:14-22. Reigned 10 years and died.
17. Pekahian, 2 K. 15:23-26. Reigned 2 years and was slain.
18. Pekah, 2 K. 15:27-16:9. Reigned 20 years and was slain.
19. Hoshea, 2 K. 17:1-6. Reigned 9 years and put in prison.

The Kings of Judah.

1. Rehoboam, 1 K. 12:21-24; 14:21-31; 2 Chron. 11:1-12:16. Reigned 17 years and died.
2. Abijah, 1 K. 15:1-8; 2 Chron. 13:1-22. Reigned 3 years and died.
3. Asa, 1 K. 15:9-24; 2 Chron. 14:1-16:14. Reigned 41 years and died.
4. Jehoshaphat, 1 K. 13:24; 23:41-50; 2 K. 3:1-27; 2 Chron. 17:1-21:1 Reigned 25 years and died.
5. Jeboram, 2 K. 8:16-24; 2 Chron. 21:1-20. Reigned 8. years and died.
6. Ahaziah, 2 K. 8:25-29; 9:27-29; 2 Chron.

22:1-9. Reigned 1 year and was killed by order of Jehu.
7. Athaliah, 2 K. 11:1-21:2; 2 Chron, 22;10-23:6. Reigned 6 years and was slain when Joash became king.
8. Joash, 2 K. 11:3-12:21; 2 Chron. 24:1-27. Reigned 40 years and was slain.
9. Amaziah, 2 K. 14:1-20; 2 Chron. 25:1-28. Reigned 29 years and was slain.
10. Uzziah or Azariah, 2 K. 14:21-25; 2 Chron. 28:1-23. Reigned 52 years and died.
11. Jotham, 2 K. 15:32-36; 2 Chron. 27:1-9. Reigned IB years and died.
12. Ahaz, 2 K. 16:1-30: 2 Chron. 28:1-27. Reigned IS years and died.

Important Events in the History of Israel. The following are perhaps the most important events in the history of tie northern kingdom during this period. (1) The establishment of idol worship at Dan and Bethel. (2) The removal of the Capital, by Omri, from Tirzah to the hill site of Samaria. (3) The wicked reign of Ahab, who introduced Baal worship into Israel. (4) The reformations of Jehu, who swept Baal worship from the land and overthrew the hated dynasty of Omri. (5) The successful reign of Jeroboam II, who brought the nation back to a state of prosperity that resembled the time of David and Solomon. (6) The activity of the prophets during the entire period. This activity is seen in the important place given (1 K. 17-2 K. 13) to the work of Elijah and Elisha; in the prophecy of Jonah, Amos and Hosea, who prophesied in the time of the reign of Jereboam II, and in part in the reign of Micah who preached during the reign of Hoshea. (7) The conquest of Israel by the Assyrians which came as the result of forty years of constant decline following the death of Jeroboam II. After this Israel disappears from history. She had sinned away her opportunity.

Principal Events In the History of Judah. The following are the principal events of the history of Judah from the division of the kingdom until the captivity of Israel. (1) The foolish answer of Rehoboam to the ten tribes which led to their revolt and the continual enmity of the northern and southern kingdoms that followed. (2) The invasion of Judah by Shishak of Egypt, who greatly weakened the nation. (3) The reign of Jehoshaphat whose judicial, military and educational or religious reforms introduce a new and good day in Judah and whose unhappy alliance with Ahab, led his son, who followed him as king to introduce idolatry into Judah, with all the evil of the reign of Jehoram, Ahaziah and Athaliah. (4) The prosperous reign of Uzziah, who was contemporary with Jeroboam II of Israel. (5) The Apostasy under Ahaz, who encouraged Baal worship and practiced great cruelty even on the members of his own family. The prophet Isaiah (chs. 7-9) appeals to Ahaz and to the people to return to Jehovah.

The Relation between the Two Kingdoms. The bearing of the two kingdoms toward each other during this period was constantly changing. (1) There was almost constant war for about sixty years. During this time the kings of Judah cherished the hope that they would regain their control over the ten tribes. (2) There was a period of close alliance. This alliance was sealed by an intermarriage between the families of Ahab, king of Israel and Jehoshaphat, king of Judah. The purpose seems to have been that they might better resist the encroaching power of Assyria. (3) There was a fresh manifestation of hatred. Jehu is enthroned in Israel and destroys the house of Ahab. This shatters the alliance between the two nations and causes a breach that is never healed. The northern kingdom becomes more and more idolatrous, suffers at the hands of the Syrians and is finally carried captive by the Assyrians in 722 B. C.

The Messages of the Prophets of this Period. It is not within the purpose of this study to raise any of the questions of criticism concerning these books. Nor is there time to summarize the contents or teachings of nay or all of them. The prophets of this period are Jonah, Amos and Hosea, and the prophecy of each should be read following the outline given in the author's *The Bible Book by Book*.

Lessons of the Period. (1) Jehovah rules not only in Israel but over all peoples. (2) Each nation is responsible to God according to its opportunity and enlightenment. (3) God judges people according to their acts, not according to religious creeds or ceremonies. (4) Though a merciful God, Jehovah will and must finally punish willful and continuous evil doers. (5) Sin is infidelity to God and brings pain to his heart. (6) All punishment is administered to the end that the sinful may repent and be forgiven. (7) Jehovah loves men and demands that they love him in return. (8) Repentance is the only way of escape from doom. (9) God seeks to save men and nations from the sins that are to destroy them.

For Study and Discussion. (1) The events leading to the division of the kingdom. (2) The story of each king in each nation, (a) How he came to the throne, (b) The chief acts of his reign, (c) The character of the king himself, (d) The length of his reign, (e) His enemies and his friends, (f) How his reign ended. (3) The story of Ahab. (4) The story of Elijah. (5) The story of Elisha. (6) The miracles of the period. (7) The different enemies with which the tribes were surrounded and the trouble they had with each. (8) Jonah and his service. (9) The evidence of wealth and luxury of the time. (10) The sins of cruelty and injustice in society and government.

14
THE KINGDOM OF JUDAH.

II K. 18-25; II Chron. 28-36.

Note: This period covers the time from the fail of Israel to the fall of Judah. It begins in the sixth year of the reign of Hezekiah, whose name is given as the first king of the period since most of his reign was in this instead of the former period.

The Kings of this Period.

13. Hezekiah, 2 K. 18:1-20-21; 2 Chron. 29:1-32:33. Reigned 29 years and died.
14. Manasseh, 2 K. 21:1-18; 2 Chron. 33:1-20. Reigned 55 year and died.
15. Amon, 2 K. 21:19-26; 2 Chron. 33:20-25. Reigned 2 years and was slain by a conspiracy of his servants.
16. Josiah, 2 K. 22:1-23; 2 Chron. 34:1-33:27. Reigned 31 years and was killed in battle.
17. Jehoahaz. 2 K. 23:30-34; 2 Chron. 36:1-4.

Reigned 3 months and was dethroned and carried into Egypt where he died.
18. Jehoiakim, 2 K. 23:34-24:6; 2 Chron. 36:4-8. Reigned 11 years and died.
19. Jehoiachin. 2 K. 24:6-16; 2 Chron. 36:9-10. Reigned 3 months and was carried captive to Egypt.
20. Zedekiah. 2 K. 24:17-25; 2 Chron. 36:11-21. Reigned 11 years and carried captive into Egypt.

The Principal Events of the Period. Among the more important events of this period the following should be noticed. (1) The reforms of Hezekiah who attempted to restore the whole Mosaic order. (2) The invasion of Judah by Sennacherib, king of Assyria who at first humiliated Hezekiah, but later, was destroyed by divine intervention and Jerusalem saved. (3) The wicked reign of Manasseh, who sought to destroy all true worship and established idolatrous worship in its stead. (4) His captivity in Babylon and release and attempted reform. (5) The good reign of Josiah, who destroyed the altars of idolatry, repaired the temple and caused the book of the law to be read-all of which resulted in a very thorough-going revival of true worship. (6) The conflicts with their enemies which finally resulted in the downfall of Jerusalem and the captivity of the people. This captivity was completely accomplished through three invasions of the hosts of Nebuchadnezzar, (a) In the reign of Jehoiakim at which time he carried away captive Daniel and his friends; (b) In the reign of Jehoiachin or Jeconiah, when he carried to Babylon the treasures of Jerusalem and the skilled workmen as well as the officers of the court; (c) In the reign of

Zedekiah, when the city and temple and walls and principal houses were destroyed and large numbers carried into captivity.

The Prophets of the Period and Their Messages. Of all the periods this is signalized by the greatest prophetic activity. There was constant need both on the part of the king and on the part of the people for the warnings and rebukes of the people. Some prophets delivered part of their message in one period and the rest in another. No doubt Isaiah and Micah did part of their service during the former period and Jeremiah performed a part of his in the next. But they are all put down here because this is the period of their greatest activity. The other prophets of the period are Joel, Nahum, Zephaniah, Habakkuk and Obadiah. The messages of these prophets should be carefully read following outlines given in *The Bible Book by Book*.

The Teachings of the Prophets. It is difficult to put down in brief form the various teachings announced and implied in the writings of the prophets. Their sermons covered a wide range of subjects, religious, political, commercial and social. They touch upon matters that are national and also those that are personal. The following may be regarded as among their most important teachings. (1) That Jehovah is a moral being-holy, just, wise and good. (2) That Jehovah was the God not only of Judah and of Israel but off all nations. (3) That no man, no set of men and no nation can thwart the plans of God. (4) That God's judgments were certain to overtake the sinful. (5) That religion was not separate from life, but the very central factor of it-that religion and ethics are so blended that "to act justly, to love mercy and to walk humbly before his God" is shown to be man's whole duty. (6) That religion is a personal spiritual relation between God and man. This is especially the contribution of Jeremiah and lays the foundation for all true faith and is a basal principle of our Christianity.

The False Prophets, Through all the history of Israel false prophets were a source of great trouble. Among those of earlier times may be noted: (1) An old prophet of Bethel, 1 K. 13:11. (2) 400 prophets with a lying spirit, 1 K. 22:6-8. 22-23. (3) 450 prophets of Baal, 1 K. 18:19, 22, 40. (4) 400 prophets of Asherah. 1 K. 18:19. A study of these will show that some are idolatrous prophets and others are perverted worshipers of Jehovah, who did not really prophesy at all. Some were no doubt deliberate deceivers of the people while others were perhaps self-deceived.

During the years immediately preceding the Babylonian captivity false prophets played a prominent role and their pernicious influence upon Judah's history can hardly be overestimated. They lured the people to their ruin and undermined the influence of the true prophets. Isaiah talks about the prophet that teaches lies (Is. 9:15). Jeremiah talks of prophets of lies, who prophesy, not having been sent of Jehovah (Jer. 14:13-15; 23:21-22). Micah tells of the prophets who make the people err (Mi. 3:5). Jeremiah was openly opposed by Hananiah (Jer. Ch. 28). These prophets destroyed confidence in the message of true prophets and brought about a time when the voice of these messengers of God ceased to be heard in Israel.

The Great Religious Revivals of this Period. The whole history of the kingdom of Judah is marked by periods of religious decline and revival. The most striking of these are indicated by the following outline. (1) A decline under the reign of Rehoboam. (2)

A revival begun under Asa and made complete under the reign of Jehoshaphat; (3) A decline begun in the reign of Jehoram and continued until the reign of Ahaz where the lowest spiritual state was reached. (4) A new revival under Hezekiah, who introduced sweeping social and religious changes. (5) A decline under Manasseh who reared images to Baal, defiled the temple and overthrew the good work of his father Hezekiah. (6) A revival under Josiah, grandson of Manasseh, whose piety began to manifest itself at the age of sixteen. He began his reforms at the age of twenty and spent six years in hewing down the altars and images of idolatry. The temple was repaired, the law found and enjoined upon the people and the Passover celebrated. (7) A final decline that carried Judah on downward until her glory was destroyed and she was led away into Babylon as captive.

The study of these successive efforts at returning to the true worship of Jehovah and their quick collapse indicate that the kindlings of spiritual life which they seem to manifest were not real spiritual revivals. Many people did no doubt turn in truth to God. but the rapidity with which each effort was followed by a return to deeper depths of immorality, such as those indicated by Amos 5:16, 7:17, 8:6; Is. 1:23, 10:1; and Hos. 9:15 give evidence of the abounding wickedness of the period.

The Wealth and Luxury. There is much in the discourses to indicate that wealth abounded and that kings and other influential men lived in luxury. The upper classes indulged in all the follies of the idle rich and showed the usual heartlessness toward the poor. The following list of scriptures will indicate some of the things which they possessed and which they did: Amos 5:11, 3:15, 6:4; Jer. 22:14; Is. 5:11-12, 3:18-23,

21:7. To this list the student by comparison and reference can add many others.

Contemporary Nations. No study of this period would be complete without a knowledge of the other nations that influenced this time. Egypt, Assyria, Babylon, Media, Phoenicia, Carthage, Greece and Rome all influenced Judah. From the Bible narratives and from secular history the student should become acquainted with the leading events in the history of this period of each of these nations.

Lessons of the Period. It is most difficult to put down the permanent lessons or teachings of this period. To the teachings of the prophets given above the following are well worth preserving as lessons for our day as well as theirs. (1) All reformation must begin at the house of God and in connection with his worship-witness the reform work of Asa, Jehoshaphat, Joash, Hezekiah and Josiah. (2) Religion must set the standards for the conduct of national affairs. (3) Sin is infidelity to love, or spiritual adultery. It not only breaks law but cruelly wounds love. (4) Sin blinds men to their best interests, turns them against their best friends and issues in their ruin. (5) The political sentiment or the politician that neglects or attacks God, or the national recognition of him is perilous to the nation. (6) The loss of the sense or vision of God leads to "degraded ideals, deadened consciences and defeated purposes." (7) True love: (a) is not blind to the sins of the one loved; (b) does not try to cover up the faults but tries to turn one from them; (c) does not desert one when calamity comes because of persistence in sin. See the attitude of Jeremiah to Judah before and after the captivity.

For Study and Discussion. (1) Study each of the teachings of the prophets given above: (a) Try to find scripture basis for it; (b) Discuss it as a universal principle. (2) Study each of the scriptures referred to in the discussion above on false prophets: (a) From references collect other passages on the subject; (b) Make a list of their prophecies and tell how to determine whether a prophet is false. (3) From the scriptures given above on wealth and luxury and from others to be pointed out: (a) List the evidences of wealth; (b) Compare the conditions then and now. (4) Following the instructions for study in the paragraph above on contemporaneous nations prepare a list of facts concerning each, especially of matters that affected Judah. (5) Name the kings of this period. Tell (a) how each came into office, (b) how long he reigned, (c) how his career ended, (d) what prophet preached to each and the nature of the prophecy. (6) Hezekiah's sickness, 2 King 20:1-11; 2 Chron. 32;24-26; (7) His song of thanksgiving, Is. 38:10-20. Carefully analyze it. (8) Sennacherib's invasion, 2 K. 18:14-19 end; Is. 14:24-27; 36:1-37:10; 2 Chron. 32:1-23. (a) The object of the expedition; (b) The conference with Hezekiah; (c) The outcome. (9) Josiah's reformations. (10) The three invasions of Nebuchadnezzar.

15
THE CAPTIVITY OF JUDAH.

Eze., Dan., Lam.

The Ten Tribes Lost. After the fall of Samaria we hear but little of the ten tribes. They were carried off into the regions of Ninevah by the Assyrians. All effort to locate them has failed and no doubt will fail. Sargon, in an inscription found at Ninevah, said that he carried away into captivity 27,290. These were perhaps leaders of Israel whom he thought might lead a revolt. He sent others back to take their place and the Israelites seemed to have mingled with the races about them and to have lost their identity. No doubt some of them as individuals were faithful to the worship of Jehovah and may have found their way back to Palestine under the leadership of Ezra and Nehemiah. But it was different with Judah who all the time kept true to her ideals and looked for the return that had been prophesied. This hope was realized through the work of Ezra and Nehemiah following the decree of Cyrus.

Judah Led into Captivity. The captivity of Judah was accomplished by three distinct invasions of the Babylonians and covered a period of twenty years. (1) ***The first invasion and captivity***. This was in 607 B.C., at which time Daniel and his friends along with others were carried into captivity, 2 K. 24:1, Jer. 25:1, Dan. 1:1-7. (2) ***The second invasion and captivity***. This was 597 B.C., at which time king Jehoiakim and 10.000 of the people were carried into captivity. Among these were Ezekiel and one of the ancestors of Mordicai, the cousin of Esther, 2 K. 24:10-16; Eze. 1:1-2; Est. 2:5-6. (3) ***The third invasion and captivity***. In 587 B.C. Jerusalem was conquered and its walls and palaces as well as the temple were destroyed and the inhabitants carried away into exile, 2 K. 24:18; 24:1-27; 2 Chron. 36:11-21; Jer. 52:1-11. This is the end of the southern kingdom.

The Period of the Captivity. Jeremiah predicts that the captivity will last seventy years (Jer. 25:12; 29:10; see 2 Chron. 36:21; Dan. 9:2: Zech. 7:6). There are two ways of adjusting the dates to fulfill this prediction, (1) From the first invasion and the carrying into captivity of Daniel and others, 607 B. C. to 537 B. C., when the first company returned under Zerubbabel. (2) From the final fall of Jerusalem. 587 B. C. to the completion of the renewed temple and its dedication, 517 B. C. Either satisfies the scripture. In history it is customary to speak of this exile as covering only the fifty years from 587 B. C. when Jerusalem was destroyed and the last company carried away to 537 B. C. when the first company returned under Zerubbabel.

The Fugitives in Egypt. When Jerusalem fell the king of Babylon allowed many of the poorer people to remain in Palestine and Jedediah, a grandson of

Josiah, was appointed to rule over them. 2 K. 25:22. His career was a very useful one, but through jealousy he was soon murdered, 2 K. 25:25. This led the people to fear lest Nebuchadnezzar would avenge his death, whereupon they fled into Egypt 2 K. 25:26. Jeremiah attempted to keep them from going to Egypt (Jer. 42:9-22.) but, when he failed, he went along with them and shared their destiny, Jer. 43:6-7. They settled at Tahpanhee (Jer. 44:1), a frontier town where many foreigners lived under the protection of Egypt. They seem to have built a temple there and did much to retain their racial ideals. Jeremiah seems to have continued his faithful prophecies and the people seem to have continued as faithfully to reject his counsel. We do not know how he ended his career but Jewish tradition says he was put to death by his own people.

The Exiles in Babylon. The state of the exiles in Babylon may not be fully known but from the contemporary writers very much may be known. (1) **Their home**. They were settled in a rich and fertile plain, intersected by many canals. It was on the river, or canal, Chebar (Ez. 1:1.3; 3:15, etc.) which ran southeast from Babylon to Nippur. It was a land of traffic and merchants and fruitful fields (Ez. 17:4-5). They were rather colonists than slaves and enjoyed great freedom and prosperity. (2) **Their occupation**. By reason of their intellectual and moral superiority the Jews, as they are called from this time forward, would secure rapid advancement. Some of them such as Daniel obtained high position. Others became skilled workmen. Following the advice of Jeremiah (Jer. 29:5), many of them no doubt gave themselves to agriculture and gardening. Probably most of them yielded to the opportunities of the "land of traffic and merchants" mentioned above and engaged in commercial instead of agricultural pursuits. (3) **Their government**. For a long time they were allowed to control their own affairs as their own laws provided. The elders of the families acted as judges and directed affairs in general. For a while they probably held the power of life and death over their own people, but the capital cases were punished later by authority of Babylon (Jer. 29:22.) (4) **Their religion**. Here also the information is meager and must be gathered from statements and inferences found in several books. Several things are certain: (a) For the most part they preserved their genealogies, thus making possible the identity of the Messiah as well as their proper place in worship when they were restored; (b) They gave up all idolatry and were never again led into its evil practices as they had been wont to do before. Indeed, there are, even to the present day, no idolatrous Jews; (c) They gave up the elaborate ceremonials and the public and private sacrifices and the great festivals. In their stead prayer and fasting and Sabbath observances constituted the main part of their religious life. The observance of the Sabbath became a ceremony and was robbed of its simple divine purpose; (d) They assembled the people together on the Sabbath for the purpose of prayer and the reading of the scripture. This custom probably formed the basis for synagogue worship so influential later; (e) All this private devotion and prayer such as was seen in the thrice-a-day worship of Daniel was opening the way for a purer and more spiritual religion; (f) The Canon was greatly enlarged and new spiritual teachings were announced or new light thrown on old teachings. The prophesies of Daniel and Ezekiel with many psalms were added. The book of Lamentations and chapters 40-44 of Jeremiah were also the products of this date but refer especially to the conditions of those in Egypt.

The Prophets of the Exile. This period is calculated to bring great discouragement to the Jews. They so far failed of their expectations that there is danger that they will give up their proper regard for Jehovah. They have great need that some one tell them the significance of their suffering and point out for them some word of hope for the future. This service was rendered by the prophets. There was great activity on the part of false prophets (Jer. 39:4-8, 21-23; Ez. 13:1-7, 14:8-10), but they were blessed by the following true prophets: (1) **Ezekiel**. These prophecies began by recounting the incidents of the prophet's call and the incidents between the first and the second captivities; they then denounce those nations that had part in the destruction of Jerusalem and those that had been bitter and oppressive in their dealings with Israel and Judah; they close with messages of comfort and cheer for the exiled people; (2) **Daniel**. (3) **Lamentations**. Besides a portion of the book of Jeremiah and probably of Isaiah which, as suggested above, belongs to this period, the book of Lamentations, written while in exile in Egypt, should be placed here. All three of these books should be read by following the outline given in *The Bible Book by Book*.

The Benefits of the Captivity, Dr. Burroughs gives as benefits that the Jews derived from the captivity the following four things: (1) the destruction of idolatry; (2) the rise of the synagogue; (3) a deepened respect for the law of Moses; (4) a longing for the Messiah. To these might be added or emphasized as being included in them: (1) a vital sense of repentance was created; (2) the change from the national, festal and ceremonial worship to a spiritual and individual religion; (3) a belief that Israel had been chosen and trained in order that through her Jehovah might bless the whole world.

Lessons of the Period. The experiences of Judah as recorded in this period bring us several important truths. (1) That sin will tear down both men and nations. (2) Men are responsible and suffer for their own sins but not for the sins of others, Ez. 18:2-3; 33:10-11. (3) God controls all circumstances toward the ultimate accomplishment of his purposes. (4) He makes free use of all "world rulers as his tools to execute his will" (5) God sets up and destroys nations. (6) God cares for his people and overrules all for their good. See Dan., etc. (7) One can live right in spite of one's surroundings (see Daniel) and such living will lead men to know God. (8) Evil grows more and more determined while good grows more and more distinct and hence the question "Is the world growing better?" (9) God rejoices in the opportunity to forgive his erring people and in restoring them again into his partnership.

For Study and Discussion, (1) When, to whom and by whom the exile was predicted: (a) 2 K. 20:17-18; (b) 2 K. 21:10-16; (c) 2 K. 22:16-17, Dt. 28:25, 52-68; (d) Jer. 25:9-11; (e) Jer. 34:2-3; (f) Mic. 3:12; (g) Zeph. 1:2-6. (2) The different classes of exiles: (a) Those in favor with the court, Dan. 1:19-21, 2:45-49; (b) Common laborers-lower classes, Jer. ch. 29, Eze. ch. 13; (c) Pretentious prophets, Eze. ch. 13, Jer. ch. 29. (3) The social condition of the exiles, 2 K. 25:27; Dan. 1:19-21; Is. 60:1; Jer. 29:4-7, Esth., and passages in Eze. (4) The details of each of the three invasions and the captivities as outlined above. See scriptures. (5) The exiles in Egypt: (a) Who they were, (b) How they fared. (6) The activity and influence of false prophets of this age. (7) The story of Nebuchadnezzar's dreams and their interpretation: (a) the image dream, (b) the tree dream. (8) The stories of (a) The fiery furnace; (b) of the lion's den. (9) The feast of Belshazzar. (10) The visions of Daniel 7:1-14, 8:1-12, 10:4-6. (11) The four beasts of Daniel and their significance. (12) The oracles against foreign nations, Eze. chs. 25-32. (13) The benefits mentioned above. (14) The lessons mentioned above. Find scripture basis for them.

16

THE RESTORATION.

Ezra, Neh., Esth., Hag., Zech.

Scripture Analysis. The books of Ezra and Nehemiah furnish the outline of the period and its achievements. The two books were formerly counted one book and a continuous outline of the two is best suited to the proper emphasis of the various events of the period. The following outline will appear simple and yet sufficient for our purpose. (1) The rebuilding of the temple (Ezra, chs. 1-6). (2) The reforms of Ezra (Ezra, chs. 7-10). (3) The rebuilding of the walls (Neh. chs. 1-7). (4) The covenant to keep the law (Neh. chs. 8-10). (5) The inhabitants of Jerusalem (Neh. 11:1-12:26). (6) The dedication of the wall and the reform of Nehemiah (Neh. 12:27-13-end).

Predictions of the Return. The return from captivity had been prophesied long before the fall of Jerusalem. Several prophets had foretold the captivity and in connection with it had told of the destruction of Babylon and Judah's restoration. Even the length of their stay in exile was announced. While they were in exile they were constantly encouraged by the promised return foretold to them by Ezekiel, Jeremiah and others. (1) Restoration at the end of seventy years is predicted. (Jer. 25:12; 29:10; Dan. 9:2). (2) Other Scriptures that foretell the overthrow of Babylon or the return to Jerusalem or both may be found in Is. chs. 13, 14, 21, 44-47; Jer. 28:4-11; chs. 50-52; Ez. ch. 27, etc.

The Rise of Persian Power. This was a period of world change. Great empires in rapid succession fell under the power of new and rising kingdoms. (1) The Assyrian Empire, which superseded the Chaldean Empire about 1500 B. C., and now loomed so large in the eyes of the world, fell, when the combined forces of the Medes and Babylonians captured Ninevah her capital (B. C. 607) and was numbered among the dead nations. (2) The Babylonian Empire rose to supremacy and was the dominating power when Judah went into captivity. She was the most splendid kingdom the world had ever seen. (3) The Persian power conquered Media and the greater part of Assyria and the Medo-Persian Empire under Cyrus conquered Babylon and held almost universal sway at the time of the restoration.

The Decree of Cyrus. It is now about 150 years since Isaiah in his prophesies called Cyrus by name and predicted that he should restore God's captive people to their own land and now in fulfillment of that prophecy God stirred up the spirit of Cyrus and caused him to issue a proclamation for the return of the Jews and the rebuilding of the temple. He gave orders that his people should give the Jews silver, gold and beasts. He also restored to them the vessels of the house of the Lord (Ezra. 1:1-3) and instructed the governors along the way to assist him.

Three Expeditions to Jerusalem. The return from Babylon covered a long period of time and consisted of three separate detachments under as many different leaders. There were important intervening events and contributory causes. (1) The first colony to return was **under Zerubhabel** (536 B. C.) and consisted of about fifty thousand. Ezra chs. 1-6. We have given us the records of activities of this colony for a period of about twenty-one years, during which time the temple was rebuilt and dedicated. Much opposition was encountered in the matter of rebuilding the temple and the work was finally stopped. It is here that Haggai and Zechariah delivered their stirring prophesies which together with the influence of Jerubbabel and Jeshua, the priest, stimulated the people to renew their building operations and complete the temple (B. C. 515). In the course of history, Haggai and Zechariah would come in between the fourth and fifth chapters of Ezra. (2) The second colony returned to Jerusalem **under the leadership of Ezra** (Ezra chs. 7-10) and consisted of about 1800 males with their families. There is here a lapse of about fifty-seven years from the completion and dedication of the temple to the time of Ezra's going to Jerusalem-the last thirty years of the reign of Darius, the twenty years of the reign of Xerxes and seven years of the reign of Artaxerses. Ezra obtained permission from Artaxerxes to return and also letters of instruction to the rulers to give him assistance. He was a scribe of the law of Moses and his mission was primarily a religious one. He was a descendant from the house of Aaron and as such he assumed the office of priest when he reached Jerusalem. Upon his arrival he found that the first colony had fallen into gross immoralities and into unsound religious practices. He rebuke He rebuke all these sins and brought about a great reform. It is not certain that he remained in Jerusalem. His leave from the king may have been only temporary and he may have gone back to Babylon and returned again to Jerusalem in the time of Nehemiah. (3) The third colony was **led to Jerusalem by Nehemiah** (the book of Nehemiah). The number returning is not given. Nehemiah was the cupbearer to the Persian king and upon hearing of the distress of his people at Jerusalem secured permission from him to go to Jerusalem as the governor. In spite of very determined opposition he was enabled to repair the wall of the city and dedicate it with great ceremony (Neh. chs. 6 and 12). Nehemiah is counted as one of the greatest reformers. He corrected many abuses such as those of usury and restored the national life of the Jews based upon the written law. Together with Ezra he restored the priests to their positions and renewed the temple worship. He went back to the Persian court where he remained several years and then returned to Jerusalem and continued his reforms. This ends the Old Testament history.

The Prophecy of Hagai and Zechariah. The task of these prophets was the same and was by no means an easy one. The work of rebuilding the temple, which had been begun when Jerubbabel and his colony came to Jerusalem, had been stopped by the opposition which they met. Along with this laxity of effort to build the temple the Jews were busy building houses for themselves (1:4) and had become very negligent of all duty. They had begun to despair of seeing their people and the beloved city and temple restored to the glory pictured by the prophets and were rapidly becoming reconciled to the situation. These two prophets succeeded in arousing interest and confidence in the people and through their appeals secured the finishing of the temple.

The Prophecy of Malachi. This prophecy condemns the same sins as those mentioned in the last chapters of Ezra and Nehemiah. He denounced their impure marriages, their lack of personal godliness, their failure to pay tithes and their skepticism. The special occasion for the discourses was the discontent which arose because their expectation of the glorious Messianic Kingdom had not been realized. They had also had unfavorable harvests. It is thought by many that the time of the prophecy is between the first and second visit of Nehemiah to Jerusalem. The purpose seems to be: (1) to rebuke them for departing from the law; (2) to call them back to Jehovah; (3) to revive the national spirit.

The Story of Esther. King Ahasuerus of the book of Esther is thought to be Xerxes the Great. On this view the events narrated occurred some time before the second colony came to Jerusalem and the story would fall between chapters 6 and 7 of the book of Ezra. The book throws much light on the condition of the Jews in captivity and also upon the social and political conditions existing in the Persian Empire at this period. While the name of God does not occur in the book, his providential care over his people is everywhere manifested. The deliverance of the Jews from death by the intercessions of Esther became the occasion of the establishment of the feast of Purim which ever after commemorated it in Jewish history. These four books should be read following the outline given in *The Bible Book by Book*.

Synagogues and Synagogue Worship. The emphasis which Ezra gave to the study of the Book of the Law no doubt did much to destroy idolatry and led to a new devotion to the word of God, at least to the letter of the law. This led to the institution or the re-establishment of the Synagogue. There had no doubt been from the early times local gatherings for worship, but the Synagogue worship does not seem to have been in use before the captivity, After the captivity, however, they built many of them, in every direction. They were places of worship where they engaged in reading the law, in exhortation and in prayer. The reading and expounding of the law became a profession, those following this calling being designated "lawyers."

The Significance of the Period, In all the annals of national life there is probably not a more significant sweep of history than that of the Jews during the restoration which covers a little more than ninety years. With the captivity their national life had ceased and now that they are back in their own land they do not seem to make any attempt to reestablish the nation. Stress is now put upon the true worship of God and it is beginning to dawn upon them that the glory of God will be manifested in some higher spiritual sense than had been expected. They had seen the decay of the mightiest material kingdoms, while spiritual Israel lived on, and were seeing how God and his cause and those whom he saves can not die. The Old Testament, therefore, closes with the Jews back at their old home, with the temple restored, with the sacred writings gathered together, with the word of God being taught and with the voice of the living prophet still in the land. After this followed a somewhat varied history of about 400 years through all of which the light of the hope of the coming Messiah never died out.

Lessons of the Period. The discussions of the previous sections have brought out some of the significant teachings of this period, but the following statement of lessons will probably serve to stimulate thought. (1) God will use as his instruments others than his own people. See Cyrus and Artaxerxes. (2) God's work is both (a) constructive, as when he builds up, inspires, edicts and qualifies workers, and (b) destructive, as when he overcomes opposition. (3) A consecrated man is courageous and uncompromising, but none the less cautious. See Nehemiah. (4) There is a wise providence of God that includes all nations and displays perfect righteousness, perfect knowledge and perfect power. See the book of Esther, also the others. (5) Contentment may be false and harmful. See Hag. and Zech. (6) The comparative strength of the friends and enemies of a proposition does not determine the results. God must also be considered. (7) It pays to serve God. the Moral Governor of the world. See Mal. (8) The safety of a people demands that the marriage relation shall be sacredly regarded. (9) A rigid observance of the Sabbath is vital to the growth and well-being of a nation. (10) Mere forms of religion are displeasing to God unless accompanied by ethical lives. (11) Rules that oppress the poor court the Divine disfavor.

For Study and Discussion. (1) The lessons given in the last paragraph. (2) The decree of Cyrus. (3) The adversaries of Judah (Ezr. ch. 4; Neh. ch. 4), who they were and what they did. (4) The reforms of Ezra. (5) The reforms of Nehemiah. Compare them one by one with those of Ezra. (6) The traits of character of Ezra and Nehemiah. (7) Nehemiah's plan of work in rebuilding the temple. (8) The traits of character displayed by Vashti, Mordecai, Esther and Haman. (9) The Spirit of the return. Compare with the story of Ezra. Is. ch. 40, 48:20-21; Dan. 9:20; Ps. 137. Point out (a) the religious impulse, (b) the national pride, (c) the local attractions. (10) The rebuilding of the temple and of the wall. (11) The different sins rebuked by Malachi. (12) The kings of Babylon since Nebuchadnezzar, (b) [sic] The feast of Belshazzar, Dan. ch. 5, (c) The conquering of Babylon, (d) Organization of the kingdom under Darius, Dan. ch. 6, and of Ahasuerus, Esth.

17

FROM MALACHI TO THE BIRTH OF CHRIST.

No Scripture.

The Close of the Old Testament History. We now come to the close of Old Testament history and prophecy. Ezra and Nehemiah were at Jerusalem, one the governor and the other the priest of the people. Jerusalem and the temple had been restored and the worship of Jehovah re-established. This was about 445 B. C. and Judea was still under Persian rule. From this date to the opening of New Testament history, a period of about four hundred years, there are no inspired records. Neither prophet nor inspired historian is found among the Jews and there is no further development of revealed religion. It was, however, a period of vast importance and the history of the chosen people may be traced from secular sources. For convenience the history of the period may be divided into four sections: (1) The Persian Period. (2) The Greek Period. (3) The Period of Independence. (4) The Roman Period.

The Persian Period. The Persians continued their rule over Judea a little more than one hundred years after the close of Old Testament history. But in 332 B. C. Alexander the Great was enthroned over the monarchy, then under Darius, and inaugurated the era of Grecian supremacy. During this period, however, little happened in Palestine that was of much interest.

Under the Rule of the Greek Kings. Alexander the Great seemed to have formed a good opinion of the Jews and granted them many special favors. He regarded them as good citizens and gave them privileges as first class citizens of Alexandria and encouraged them to settle throughout his empire. Upon his death his kingdom was broken up into four kingdoms (Macedonia, Thrace. Syria and Egypt) and Judea was alternately under the rule of Syria and Egypt. All Palestine was permeated with the influence of the Greek language and philosophy. It was while Judea was under the rule of Ptolemy of Egypt that the Septuagint version of the Old Testament was made. This made possible the reading of the Hebrew Scriptures in the Greek language and was one of the greatest missionary works of all times.

The Period of Independence. In 170 B.C. Antiochus Epiphiones began to oppress the Jews in an attempt to force them into idolatry and about 167 B.C. Judas Maccabeus began to lead a revolt which two years later was successful in throwing off the foreign yoke and establishing the independence of the Jews. They were now governed by a succession of rulers from the Maccabean family for a period of one hundred years. These rulers performed the double function of both civil and ecclesiastical head of the people. They were descendants of David and under their leadership Edom, Samaria and Galilee were added to their territory and much of the splendor and wealth of the golden days of the kingdom was restored.

The Roman Period. This period may be said to have begun in B.C. 63 and to have extended to A.D. 70. In B.C. 63 Pompey overran Palestine, destroyed Jerusalem and brought the Jews under Roman rule. By this conquest Jewish independence was forever lost. In B.C. 37 Herod the Great was appointed by the Roman emperor to the position of ruler of Palestine. In B.C. 20-18 he rebuilt the temple at Jerusalem, though it (all the buildings and walls) was not finished until many years after his death. He also built the temple of Samaria and continued to reign until Christ came and much longer.

The Entire Period. This entire period spans the time from the history of Nehemiah and the prophecy of Malachi to the coming of the Messiah. It opens with the Persian empire supreme and closes with Augustus Caesar as the head of Rome, the mistress of the world. When Jesus came Herod the Great governed Palestine and all the world was at peace.

The End of the Period. There are many points of view from which to study the conditions existing at the close of this period. But for our purpose it will probably suffice to consider (1) some signs of decadence or defects; (2) some hopeful signs. The facts touching these matters are to be gathered not only from secular history but from the life and work of Jesus as they are seen at work either for or against the progress of his work. (1) Unpropitious conditions. Among the signs of decadence or errors that needed correction should be noted: (a) There was a defective view of God. They regarded God as too far away; (b) They laid too much stress upon outward obedience and, thereby, left no place for motive in their service; (c) This led them to rest salvation upon a system of works and to multiply rules of obedience; (d) This led to too great demand for respect for the learned and of subordination to them; (e) The Jews thought that they had a special place in the salvation of God and as children of Abraham only felt the need of national deliverance. (2) Hopeful signs. Several conditions that bespeak good should be noted: (a) The Jews did have the truest conception of religion to be found anywhere in the world; (b) Their religion was a matter of deep concern to them and they showed an undying devotion to their religious institutions; (c) There was a keen sense of the worth of the individual; (d) There were many synagogues which led to a zeal to proselyte foreigners and opened the way for Gentile evangelism; (e) There was a widespread expectation of the Messiah whom the whole world could receive as its spiritual king; (f) The home life of the Jews was strongly religious and children were held in high esteem.

For Study and Discussion. (1) The career of Alexander the Great. (2) The reign of Ptolemy Soter and Ptolemy Philadelphus in Egypt. (3) The acts of Antiochus Epiphanes. (4) The story of Judas Maccabeus. (5) The story of the subjection of Judea to Rome. (6) The persecution of the Jews under the several rulers of the different countries to which they were subject during this period. (7) The religious parties of the period, especially the Pharisees and Sadducees.

Literature. The information necessary to understand these topics may be found in any one of the better Bible dictionaries, in Josephus and more or less in text books on Biblical history such as Blakie.

18
FROM THE BIRTH TO THE ASCENSION OF JESUS.

The Four Gospels.

The Story of this Period. It is common to designate this period as the "Life of Christ," meaning the time he spent on earth. There is, however, no scripture life of Jesus. The gospels do not claim to present such a life. They do, however, give us a vast amount of material and though different in purpose and consequently in content, they do present the same general picture of Jesus. The matter of arranging the material in an orderly way presents much difficulty. If a topographical outline is attempted it can only be approximately correct because at some points the gospels leave us in uncertainty or in ignorance. If a chronological outline is attempted there is no less of uncertainty.

The following outline, however, may be accepted as a scheme of study for the period. (1) The childhood and youth of Jesus. From the birth of Jesus, B.C. 4 to the beginning of the ministry of John the

Baptist, A.D. 26. (2) The beginning of Christ's ministry. From the beginning of John's ministry to Christ's first public appearance in Jerusalem, A.D. 27. (3) The early Judean ministry. From his first public appearance in Jerusalem to his return to Galilee, A.D. 27. (4) The Galilean ministry. From the return to Galilee to the final departure for Jerusalem, A.D., 29. (5) The Perean Ministry. From the departure from Galilee to the final arrival in Jerusalem, A.D. 30. (6) From the final arrival in Jerusalem to the resurrection, April, A.D. 30. (7) The forty days. From the resurrection to the ascension. May, A.D. 30.

The Childhood and Youth of Jesus. (1) **The long preparation for his coming**. The prophets had most emphatically proclaimed his coming and all things had from the beginning been divinely directed so that preparation might be made for his advent. His human ancestry had been selected and prepared. When the time drew near for him to appear, the coming of John the Baptist his forerunner, was announced to Zacharias his father (Lu. 1:5-25). This was quickly followed by the announcement of the birth of Jesus to Mary his mother (Lu. 1:26-38) and soon thereafter to Joseph, the espoused husband of Mary (Matt. 1:18-25). The beautiful story of his birth is told in the second chapter of Luke.

(2) **The infancy**. Of Jesus infancy we have several facts and incidents, (a) The appearance of the angels to the shepherds and the shepherds' visit to the babe, Lu. 2:8-20. (b) The circumcision at eight days old, Lu. 2:21. (c) The presentation in the temple where he was recognized by Simeon, Lu. 2:22-32. (d) The visit of the wise men (Matt. 2:1-12) and (e) The flight into Egypt, Matt. 2:13-23.

(3) **His boyhood and youth**. This is commonly

called the years of silence: (a) We have the record of his parents' settlement in the city of Nazareth, Matt. 2:23; (b) We know that he had a normal growth, Lu. 2:40; (c) At twelve years old he was remarkably developed and from his reply to his mother we may infer that he was conscious of his mission, Lu. 2:41-50; (d) From Luke 2:50 we may infer something of the spirit which possessed him during the rest of his private life; (e) We also know his occupation (Mk.6:3).

The Beginning of Christ's Ministry. Here are several matters of importance. (1) **The ministry of John the Baptist** (Matt 3:1-12; Mk. 1:2-8; Lu. 3:1-18; John 1:6-33) who announced Christ's coming and prepared a people for him. This he did by preaching repentance and by baptising them as a profession of repentance and as a sign that they were forgiven. (2) **The Baptism of Jesus**. (Mt. 3:13-17; Mk. 1:9-11; Lu. 3:21-23; John 1:29-34.) At this time he put off the life of seclusion and entered upon his public career. He also received the Father's attestation to his sonship and the special equipment of the Holy Spirit for his work by which also John knew him to be the Messiah, John 1:33. By this act he also set the stamp of approval on John's work and showed that he was not in competition with John. (3) **The temptation of Jesus** (Mt. 4:1-11; Mk, 1:12-13; Lu. 4:1-13). We are given the place and length of time of this temptation, also three of the temptations and how they were met. In Heb. 2:18 and 5:18 we have some light on the purpose of this trial. It is probable, however, that all the import of it cannot be fully understood. (4) **The work of Jesus begun**. Here it is necessary to study two things: (a) The winning of his first six disciples (John 1:35-51); (b) **His first miracle** (John 2:1-11). At this point it will also be of help to call to mind that the method of Jesus was to preach, teach and heal (Mt. 4:23). At the close of the marriage feast, which usually lasted six or seven days, Jesus went down to Capernaum (John 2:12).

The Early Judean Ministry. The records of this period are very brief and may be studied under three heads, (1) **The incidents at Jerusalem during the first Passover of Christ's public ministry**. The two principal incidents were the cleansing of the temple (John 2:13-22) and the conversation with Nicodemus, Jno. 3:1-31. (2) **The work out in Judea**, where he won and baptized many disciples, whereupon John was led to make testimony to Jesus at Aenon, John 3:22-36. (3) **His successful work in Samaria**, concerning which there is given the story of his message to the woman at the well and of his two days' stay at Sychar. The period is made notable by two of the greatest discourses of all his ministry: (a) that to Nicodemus; (b) that to the woman at Jacob's well.

The Gallilean Ministry. This is by far the longest and most important period of Christ's work. It is not wholly confined to Galilee. For during this time he certainly attends the feast at Jerusalem and also makes some excursions into the north country. If the study of the last period was embarrassed because of the scarcity of material, this one is all the more so because of the amount and variety of it. The following outline will, however, simplify the study. (1) **The beginning of his work in Galilee**. (Matt 4:12-25; 8:2-4, 14-17; 14:3-5. Mk. 1:14-45; 6:17-18; Lu. 4:14-3; 16; John 4:43-54). In this section we have the account of (a) John's imprisonment and of Christ's arrival in Galilee; (b) of the healing of the nobleman's son, and his settlement at Capernaum; (c) of the call of four fishermen and many miracles wrought at Capernaum; (d) of his first brief tour of Galilee.

(2) **The antagonism of the scribes and Pharisees**. (Matt 9:1-17, 12:1-14; Mk. 2:1-3:6; Lu. 5:17-6:11; John ch. 5). The more important matters of this record are: (a) The healing of the paralytic; (b) Matthew's call and feast; (c) the healing of the man at the pool of Bethsaida; (d) the story of the disciples in the grain fields and (e) the healing of the withered hand. In all these there is indicated the rising hostility to Jesus and his method, especially as regards his claim of power to forgive sins and in his attitude toward the despised classes and toward the Sabbath.

(3) **The organization of his kingdom**. (Matt. 12:15-21, 10:2-4; chs. 5-7; Mk. 3:7-19; Lu. 6:2-49.) The fame of Jesus began to spread and it became necessary for him to create an organization to carry forward his work. This was done by calling out his twelve apostles and outlining to them the principles of his kingdom. This he did in the sermon on the mount.

(4) **The second tour of Galilee**. (Matt. 8:5-13; 11:2-30; Lu. 7:1-8:3.) The narration here gives the stories (a) of the Centurion's servant and the widow's son of Nain, (b) of John's last message and (c) of Jesus anointed by the sinful woman.

(5) **His teachings and miracles by the Sea of Galilee**. (Matt. 12:22-13:53, 8:23-34, 9:18-34; Mk. 3:19-5:43; Lu. 8:4-56.) In this section we have a large group of parables with their varied teachings and four very interesting miracles: (a) The stilling of the tempest; (b) The healing of the Gadarene demoniacs; (c) The story of Jainus' daughter; (d) Two dumb and a blind man.

(6) **The third tour of Galilee**. (Matt. 13:34-

15:20, 9:35-11:1; Mk. 6:1-7:23; Lu. 9:1-17; John ch. 6.) Leaving Capernaum Jesus again came to his own city, Nazareth, where the people acknowledged the marvel of his wisdom and of his power but again rejected him-this time because of their knowledge of his lowly birth and unpretentious youth. Upon this rejection, Jesus and his disciples made another circuit amongst the cities and towns of Galilee. This tour is made notable by several incidents: (a) We have the sending out of the twelve on a tour of preaching, healing and raising the dead; (b) The story of the death of John the Baptist, who was the first New Testament person to suffer martyrdom for his conviction; (c) Two great miracles, that of feeding the five thousand and of walking on the sea; (d) Two great discourses of Jesus, that on "The Bread of Life" and on "Eating with unwashed hands."

(7) **His first retirement into the north and return to the sea of Galilee**. (Matt. 15:21-16:12; Mk. 7:24-8:26). Jesus went up into the coast of Tyre and Sidon where he healed the daughter of the Syrophoenician woman. On the return trip he passed through Decapolis where he healed a deaf and dumb man and performed many other miracles. After his return we have the record of the feeding of the four thousand, of his encountering the Pharisees about his authority and the story of the blind man of Bethsaida.

(8) **The second retirement to the north and return to Capernaum**. (Matt. 16:13-18 end; Mk. 8:27-9 end; Lu. 9:18-50). Jesus again journeys into the north and came into the parts of Caesarea Philippi where he drew from Peter the great confession, predicted his coming death, was transfigured before the favored three and healed the lunatic boy. On his re-

turn, as he neared Capernaum, he again foretold his death and resurrection and after he arrived at Capernaum, we have recorded the story of the coin in the fish's mouth and his discourse on humility, offenses and forgiveness.

(9) ***Jesus at the Feast of Tabernacles***. (John chs. 7-8). By this time the joyous season of the Feast of Tabernacles drew near and his brothers, who though they did not believe in his deity, seemed to have some pride in him and urged him to go up among the people and make a display of his power. This he refused to do but went up secretly, probably with the hope of escaping the antagonism that was now being manifested toward him. There was, however, great excitement at Jerusalem concerning him and he found it necessary to go into the temple and boldly proclaim the teachings of his kingdom. These teachings may be studied under four heads: (a) The teaching of the first day and the division of the Jews concerning him; (b) The story of the adulterous woman; (c) His teaching concerning himself as the "Light of the World." He probably looked upon the great light over the treasury of the Lord's house which burned each night in commemoration of the cloud of fire that always guided and lighted Israel in the wilderness and was reminded of his own service for humanity and was prompted to this discourse; (d) His discourse on spiritual freedom and true children of Abraham.

The Perean Ministry. At the close of the Feast of Tabernacles Jesus returned to Galilee where he seems to have gathered around him a little company of loyal followers and made ready for his final departure to Jerusalem where he was to meat the death already foretold. The incidents of this period occurred during the journey. The material easily falls into three parts marking distinct sections of time. (1) **From the departure from Jerusalem to the close of the Feast of Dedication**. (Matt. 19:1-2, 8:18-22; Mk. 10:1; Lu. ch. 10; John ch.s 9-10). This is one of the most interesting sections of all and records several incidents of far-reaching importance: (a) The story of the healing of the man born blind and the investigation of it by the Sanhedrin; (b) The story of the sending out of the seventy and their return is told. As the Lord's work drew near its close, he felt hat others should be sent out to do a like work to his own; (c) The story of the Good Samaritan and of his visit to Martha and Mary; (d) The allegory of the Good Shepherd; (e) The report of his visit to the Feast of Dedication.

(2) **From the Feast of Dedication to the withdrawal to Ephraim**. (Lu. 11:1-17:10; John 11:1-54). This section of the period is even more crowded with activity than was the former one. It is very difficult, therefore, to refer here to anything like all that is recorded of the period. Among The subjects discussed the following are the most important: (a) The true nature of prayer and the follies and hypocrisies of the Pharisees, Lu. ch. 11; (b) The danger of hypocrisy, of denying Christ, of covetousness and of the judgments of Christ, Lu. ch. 12; (c) The need and nature of repentance, the proper use of the Sabbath, the number that shall be saved and the fate of Jerusalem, Lu. ch. 13; (d) The law of conduct in the matter of feasts and counting the cost of discipleship, Lu. ch. 14; (e) Three parables of grace and two parables of warning, Lu. chs. 15-16; (f) Forgiveness and faith, Lu. 7:1-10; (g) The raising of Lazarus and withdrawal to Ephraim, John ch. 11.

(3) ***From the withdrawal to Ephraim to the final arrival at Jerusalem***. (Matt. chs. 13-20; 26:8-13; Mk. ch. 10; 14:3-9; Lu. 17:11-19:28; John 11:55-12:11). This section is notable for the preponderance of teaching over the miracles reported. There are two miracles, that of healing ten lepers and the blind man of Jericho. The following show how large a place is given to teaching: (a) Concerning the coming of the kingdom; (b) concerning prayer, illustrated by the importunate widow and the Pharisee and publican; (c) Concerning divorce; (d) the blessing of little children; (e) the ambitions of James and John; (g) the visit to Zachaeus; (h) the parable of the pounds and the anointing of Jesus for burial.

The Final Ministry in Jerusalem. Of all the periods of the life of Christ this is the most significant. The gospels put most stress upon it and particularly upon his trial and death. The disciples soon learned to triumph in the cross, the seeming defeat out of which Jesus, through his resurrection, snatched victory. Everything recorded of this period has a ring of the tragical and seemed a preparation for the coming doom he was soon to meet. The material readily divides itself into three sections or periods. (1) ***From the final arrival in Jerusalem to the last hours of private intercourse with his disciples***. (Matt. 21:11-26:16; Mk. chs. 11-13; 14: 1, 2, 10, 11; Lu. 19:29-22:6; John 12:12 end). Like every other section of his active ministry among the people this has in it some teachings and some miracles. The greatest act of all was, perhaps, the triumphal entry of Jesus into Jerusalem as king of the Jews. In this act he openly accepted the position of Messiah.

There is one important miracle, that of cursing and withering the fig tree. Some consider that a miraculous power was also used in the cleansing of the temple. The teachings may be grouped as follows: (a) The question about Christ's authority and his reply by question and the three parables of warning; (b) Three questions by the Jews and Christ's unanswerable question; (c) Seven woes against the scribes and Pharisees and the widow's mite; (d) The Gentiles seeking and the Jews rejecting Jesus; (e) a discourse on the destruction of Jerusalem and the end of the world; (f) the last prediction of his death and the conspiracy of Judas and the chief priests.

(2) Christ's last hours with his disciples. (Matt. 26:17-35; Mk. 14:12-31; Lu. 22:7 end; John chs. 13-17). Jesus has now withdrawn from the crowd and is alone with his disciples giving to them his final words of instruction and comfort. The whole of the material of this section seems to be surrounded by an atmosphere of sacredness that almost forbids our looking in upon its little company. This last evening that Jesus and the little group of disciples were together, is, however, so important that it is reported by the apostles. All the incidents of the evening seem to center around the institution of the last or Paschal Supper. But for the sake of study and as an aid to memory the events may be divided into three groups, (A) The supper. The order of events in connection with it seem to be: (1) the strife of the disciples for the place of honor; (2) the beginning of the Passover meal; (3) the washing of the disciples' feet; (4) the pointing out of the betrayer; (5) the departure of Jesus from the table; (6) the institution of the Lord's upper.

(B) The final instructions to the disciples. It is difficult to analyze these discourses. There are running through them one thread of teaching and one of comfort. In some sections one element seems to predominate and in other the other, To illustrate; chapters 13 and 15 of John seem to be more largely taken up with teaching, while chapters 14 and 16 have a larger element of words intended to comfort them. The effort seems to be to convince them that it is better for them for him to go away, that their spiritual fellowship with him would be more complete and their understanding and power more perfect because of the Comforter whom he would send.

(C) The final or intercessory prayer for them. With the close of this prayer, in which he prayed for their preservation, their preparation for service and their final union with him in his glory, and which he prayed that they might have fullness of joy (John 17:13) his ministry with them ended till after his death.

(3) **Christ's suffering for the sins of the world**. (Matt. 26:36-27 end: Mk. 14:32-15 end; Lu. 22:39-23 end; John chs. 18-19). From some good text on the Life of Christ or from the critical commentaries, the pupils can find a discussion of this section. The following outline will, however, be sufficient for our purpose here: (A) The agony in the garden and the betrayal and arrest. This picture of the suffering of soul experienced by the Savior in which he also yielded himself to the will of the Father stands out in blessed contrast against the weakness of his sleeping friends and the unspeakable criminality of the betrayer. Even in his arrest Jesus once more finds opportunity to show himself merciful in healing the ear of Malchus thereby, counteracting the injury caused by the folly or rashness of one of his friends.

(B) The Jewish trial. The order of this trial seems to have been somewhat as follows: (1) A preliminary trial before Annus; (2) A trial before day with only part of the Sanhedrin present; (3) A trial before the whole Sanhedrin at daybreak. Knowing his rights Jesus several times refused to act. (1) He refused to bear testimony because no legal charge had been made against him. (2) He refused to testify against himself which was within his right. (3) He demanded that they bring witnesses because that was just according to law. These last three points at which Jesus claimed and acted upon his rights instead of upon their request shows the tendencies of the trial to be unfair and illegal. If one understands the Jewish law of trial it will be easy to see how glaringly out of harmony with the law this trial was. There are at least ten illegalities in it.

(C) The Roman trial. This whole story abounds in evidences of the prejudice and moral degeneracy of the Jewish leaders. They hated Roman rule past all words to tell and yet would pretend loyalty to Caesar to carry out their wicked purpose. By this means they put Pilate in a position that to release Jesus would make him appear to be untrue to Caesar in releasing one announced to be Caesar's enemy. The trial may be studied in the light of the different ones before whom he was tried. (1) The public and private examination before Pilate. (2) The examination before Herod. (3) The second examination before Pilate. This also was partly private and partly public. Again, following he outline of John, we may consider the events as they happened alternately outside and inside of the praetorium.

(D) The crucifixion. It would be difficult to exaggerate the cruelty and torture of crucifixion. "It was the most cruel and shameful of all punishments." The disciples, however, dwell most of all upon the shame of it. Such a death in the eyes of a Jew was the sign of the curse of God. Several things are of importance and should be remembered. (1) The throng that saw it. A few were friends, some were bitter enemies and many were curious on-lookers. Altogether there was a great crowd and Jesus was derided and mocked in his death. (2) The story of the two thieves who were crucified with Jesus and especially the conversion of the one who repented. (3) The seven sayings of Jesus while he is on the cross reveal his spirit and planning while undergoing this human outrage. They are worthy of careful study. (4) The miraculous occurrences of the day. There are three outstanding events that should be thought of as divine manifestations. They are: the darkness that covered the earth for three hours; the rending of the veil of the temple and the earthquake. The people were deeply moved by these marvelous signs. (5) The element of grace seen in it all. This is seen in the punishment of the innocent Jesus, while the guilty Barabbas went free; the saving of the guilty but penitent thief and several of the sayings of the cross.

(E) The burial and tomb. The burial was very hurried, lest they should break a Jewish law. Joseph of Arimathea and Nicodemus together took him from the cross and buried him and the officers made his grave as secure as possible and placed a guard over it. All this they did because of his saying that he would rise again in three days.

The Forty Days. (Matt. ch. 28; Mk. ch. 16; Lu. 23:56-24 end; John chs. 20-21; Acts 1:3-12; 1 Cor. 15:5-7.) It is hard to divide this period into sections in such a way as not to present many difficulties. The several events may, however, be grouped under the following heads. (1) The early morning. (2) The walk to Emmaus and appearance to Peter. (3) The appearance to the ten when Thomas is absent. (4) The appearance to the eleven, Thomas being present. (5) The appearance to seven disciples by the sea of Galilee. (6) Several other appearances mentioned by Paul. (7) The last appearance, when the commission was given and he ascended. The order of events as outlined cannot be assured with any certainty. Then, too, there are differences of detail as to the occurrences here outlined. Each of them, therefore, presents its own difficulties. The most perplexing of all these problems is the arrangement of the events of the resurrection morning and especially the movements of the various women mentioned.

Touching the whole resurrection problem all of the gospels agree upon several important matters: (1) In giving no description of the resurrection itself; (2) that the evidence of it began with the women's visit to the sepulcher in the early morning; (3) that the first sign was the removal of the stone; (4) that they saw angels before they saw the Lord; (5) that manifestations were granted to none but disciples; (6) that the disciples were not expecting such manifestations; (7) that at first they received these manifestations with hesitancy and doubt; (8) that these appearances were made to all kinds of witnesses, male and female, individuals and companies; (9) that they were so convinced of his resurrection and appearance to them that nothing could cause them to doubt it.

The resurrection was necessary to show that we had not a dead and suffering Christ but a living and triumphant one. "The ascension is the necessary completion of the resurrection" and is presupposed in all New Testament teaching. Jesus is everywhere thought of as having all power and is expected to return again from the presence of the Father with great glory.

Teachings of the Period. The most of the emphasis is put on the final teachings in connection with his death and resurrection. It may be well, however, to gather together a few truths touching his whole career. (1) **Those concerning his humanity**: (a) He grew and developed as any normal child; (b) His education and work was that of any normal person; (c) But the whole of his childhood was set in divine manifestations; (d) In life he showed all the effects of hunger, sorrow, etc., found in any normal man. (2) **Those concerning his super-human power**. He exercised power over: (a) Physical nature; (b) sickness and physiological defects; (c) life and death; (d) demons and all spiritual powers; (e) over sin to forgive it. (3) **Those found In his general teachings**. There are many of these but the following are important to remember: (a) The truthfulness of the Old Testament scriptures; (b) The holiness and goodness and love of God; (c) The sinfulness of man and his need of salvation; (d) The value of repentance and faith as a means of bringing men into the favor of God; (e) His own duty and oneness with the Father; (f) The work and power of the Holy Spirit; (g) The purpose and work of his kingdom and church; (h) The power and nature of prayer; (i) The value of spiritual and the worthlessness of formal worship; (j) The true way to greatness through service.

(4) **The teachings growing out of the crucifixion**: (a) It proves that God will forgive; (b) It shows the great evil of sin; (c) It shows the need of cleansing before we can enter heaven; (d) It shows God's value of the soul; (e) It shows the value of salvation and the worth of eternal life; (f) It furnishes a motive to turn

from sin that so offends God and endangers us; (g) It brings hope of forgiveness and cleansing.

(5) ***The teaching of the resurrection and ascension***: (a) that Jesus is in truth God's son; (b) that there is another life; (c) that we shall also be resurrected; (d) that we shall know in the next life our loved ones of this life; (e) that our lives here have an influence and meaning beyond the grave.

For Study and Discussion. (1) Master all the material as given in this chapter, looking carefully into scripture references. (2) Study the geography of the country. (3) List all the divine manifestations in connection with the birth and childhood of Jesus. (4) Outline the entire career of John the Baptist, beginning with the vision to Zachariah before his birth. (5) Study in outline the sermon on the mount. (6) Find examples showing Christ's power exerted in each of the five directions suggested in "2" of "the teachings of the period" given above. (7) Discuss any outstanding events in the life of Jesus and his disciples that seem to members of the class to be epoch making in their influence. (8) Read and discuss Jesus' farewell addresses to his disciples. (9) Study carefully the scriptures covering the trial and crucifixion of Jesus. (10) Study the scriptures covering the period and outline further the events and teachings.

19
FROM THE ASCENSION TO THE CHURCH AT ANTIOCH.

Acts Chs. 1-12.

The Book of Acts. The book of Acts is the only purely historical book of the New Testament. It is as a continuation of the gospel of Luke. It follows the fortunes of the infant church and gives us all the light we have in regard to its further organization and development, but it does not claim to be a complete history of the work of the early church. As a history it is as remarkable for what it omits as for what it narrates. The central theme is the triumph and progress of the gospel in spite of all the opposition and persecution which its advocates met. The chief purpose seems to be to show the progress of Christianity among the Gentiles and only so much of the work among the Jews is given as will authenticate the other. The whole book falls into three sections: (1) The church at work in Jerusalem, chs. 1-7. (2) The church at work in Palestine, chs, 8-12. (3) The church at work among the Gentiles, chs. 13-28.

The material of the period which we are now to study includes the first two points and should be read in connection with the following outline:

I. The church at work in Jerusalem, chs. 1-7.

1. Preparation for witnessing, 1:1-2:4. Under this there is given: (1) Christ's last instructions and ascension and (2) The church in the upper room including the election of Matthias and the coming of the Holy Spirit.
2. The first witnessing. Here are given 2:5-47: (1) The first witnessing, (2) the first message, (3) the first fruit of the witnessing.
3. The first persecution 3:1-4:31. Here we have the first persecution and the occasion for it.
4. The Blessed state of the church, 4:32-5 end There is great love and unity and God indorses their work by the destruction of Ananias and his wife and by the release of apostles from prison.
5. The first deacons, 6:1-7.
6. The first martyr 6:8-7 end.

II. The church at work in Palestine, chs. 8-12.

1. Witnesses scattered, 8:1-4.
2. Philip witnesses in Samaria and Judea, 8:5-40.
3. The Lord wins new witnesses, 9:1-11:18. (1) Saul. (2) Aeneas, etc. (3) Dorcas, Mary, etc. (4) Cornelius.
4. Center of labor changed to Antioch, 11:19 end.

5. The witnesses triumph over Herod's persecution, ch. 12.

The Principle Events of this Period. Many things which on the surface seem to be of little importance, contributed much toward shaping the destiny of the early church. The following, however, should be remembered as the great outstanding events of the time. (1) The ascension with the incidents connected with it. (2) The Baptism of the Holy Ghost with the consequent sermon of Peter and its results. (3) The first persecution of the Apostles, with Peter's sermon and the measures taken by the Sanhedrin to stop the movement. (4) The punishment of Ananias and his wife. (5) The appointment of the first deacons. (6) The martyrdom of Steven. (7) The work of Philip in Samaria and the conversion of the Eunuch. (8) The conversion of Saul of Tarshish. (9) The conversion of Cornelius with connected events. (10) The church's acknowledgement of the validity of this work among the Gentiles, Acts 11:18. (11) The great work at Antioch. (12) The martyrdom of James and the death of Herod.

The Organization and Control of the Early Church. Jesus had set up his church and left it his final commission. Its organization was a matter of growth and was increased only as new conditions arose that made it necessary to the success and efficiency of their work. They elected, at the suggestion of Peter, Matthias to take the place of Judas as one of their witnesses. When conditions arose that threatened the success of their work, they elected deacons to assist the apostles in caring for the more temporal work of the church. In it all it is clear that the church as a whole transacted the business. The Apostles no doubt had a very good influence but did not assume to dictate to the church what did not "please the whole multitude" (Acts 6:5). All responsibility was put upon the church as a democratic and self-governing body.

The Persecutions of the Church. In the persecutions which Jesus suffered the Pharisees took the lead, but the opposition met by the early disciples was led by the Sadducees. This was because of the doctrine of the resurrection, preached by the apostles. The persecutions deepened and widened very rapidly. (1) They were given public hearing, commanded not to teach in Jesus' name and after threatening were let go. (2) They were released without punishment only by the appeal of Gamaliel, a doctor of the law. (3) On account of the universal aspect of Christianity, preached by Steven, the Pharisees joined the Sadducees in opposing the Christians and their joint persecution led to the death of Steven and the scattering of the disciples from Jerusalem, 6:8-8:3. (4) The Romans who for the most part had been indifferent to the movement also joined the Sanhedrin in the attempt to suppress the brethren. Accordingly Herod Agrippa, hoping to gain the good will of the Jews, seized the apostle James and put him to death and seeing that this made him popular seized Peter and would have destroyed him but for divine intervention.

In spite of all this persecution these early Christians made wonderful progress. They were unmoved in their purpose to establish their faith. They went everywhere preaching the gospel of the kingdom. They openly declared that they would not refrain from preaching what they conceived to be their duty to God. They boldly threw their doctrine into the teeth of their antagonists. Such courage was something new in the history of the Jews. They even "rejoiced that they were counted worthy to suffer dishonor for his name."

Their Growth and Influence. The courage already mentioned could not fail to bear fruit. The second chapter tells of three thousand, added to them in one day and then of others day by day. In chapter five it is said a multitude of believers both men and women added to them. Chapter six says that "the disciples multiplied in Jerusalem exceedingly; and a great company of the priests were obedient to the faith." The priests were for the moat part Sadducees and the fact that many of these who had been active in arresting the disciples now came to accept their teaching is highly significant touching the matters of their success.

Extension of the Gospel to the Gentiles. One of the most interesting topics for study found in the records of this period is the way in which Christians gradually extended into the borders of the Gentiles. Many questions were raised that had to be solved-questions that had not been before raised among the followers of Jesus. (1) Philip went into Samaria and many of these half-bred Jews believed. Here he was following the steps of Jesus who had also met with success and introduced his teachings before going outside to those in no wise akin to the Jews. (2) Peter and John were sent to Samaria and not only approved the work of Philip but bestowed upon these Samaritans the Holy Spirit and themselves preached to many Samaritan villages. (3) Peter made a tour of certain Judean villages and came down to Joppa where he lodged with a tanner and would, according to Jewish law, have been unclean. This tends to show that he was coming to see that the ceremonial distinctions of the Levites were not so binding. (4) Peter preached to Cornelius a Gentile and he and his household received the Holy Ghost and baptism and spake with tongues. (5) Having heard Peter's explanation of his course the church glorified God and acknowledged that God had granted repentance and life to the Gentiles. (6) Paul the chosen vessel to bear the Gospel to the Gentiles was saved. (7) The work spread to Antioch of Syria and Barnabas was sent to investigate it and soon went to Cilicia and brought Paul to Antioch and the two labored there a year, then made a visit to Jerusalem to carry gifts to the poor and returned to Antioch bringing John Mark. This period closes with them still at Antioch.

The Teachings of this Period. (1) Men can succeed in any right cause in spite of opposition. (2) Popularity is not required to give one success as a Christian work. (3) Small numbers are not a sign of weakness and do not foretoken defeat. (4) The gospel truth, courageously preached, can win its way into the hardest hearts. (3) Consciousness of duty, divinely imposed is the most powerful stimulus to action.

For Study and Discussion. (1) The Great Commission, ch. 1. (2) Peter's sermon on the day of Pentecost. (3) Stephen's address of defense. (4) The liberality of these Christians or their provision for the poor. (5) The place of prayer in the work of these disciples. (6) The references to the Holy Spirit and his work. (7) The teachings of the period concerning Jesus. (8) Concerning the resurrection. (9) All the events, persecutions, teachings, etc., mentioned above.

20
FROM ANTIOCH TO THE DESTRUCTION OF JERUSALEM.

Acts 13-28 and all the rest of the New Testament except the epistles of John and Revelation.

The Changed Situation. We have now come to a turning point in the whole situation. The center of work has shifted from Jerusalem to Antioch, the capital of the Greek province of Syria, the residence of the Roman governor of the province. We change from the study of the struggles of Christianity in the Jewish world to those it made among heathen people. We no longer study many and various persons and their labors but center our study upon the life and labors of Paul.

The Divine Call. Certain prophets of the church at Antioch were engaged in solemn prayer and worship when the Holy Spirit instructed them to send Paul and Barnabas to do the work to which they were called. Here, then, the Holy Spirit takes charge of the movement. He inaugurates, directs and promotes this work. When the call came it is probable that Paul had but little idea of the magnitude of the work which he was to do. He was not aware that his work and teaching would change the religion and philosophy of the whole world.

The Time and Extent of Paul's Journeys. The most of his work was accomplished during three great missionary journeys. The time occupied for these great journeys with the distance traveled has been estimated as follows: the first journey 1400 miles and three years; the second journey 3200 miles and three years; the third journey 3500 miles and four years; or a total of 8100 miles representing ten years of labor. To this must be added his journey to Rome which required a whole winter and was about 2300 miles and many side trips of which we have no record. It is also commonly thought that he was released at the end of two years at Rome and again entered upon mission work that probably lasted four years and carried him again into Macedonia, Asia Minor, Crete and Spain.

The First Missionary Journey. (Acts, chs. 13-14). The company consisted of Saul and Barnabas and John Mark. They went by way of the isle of Cyprus and at Paphos the capital of the island the governor was converted and Saul was afterward called Paul. They reached Pamphylia and Pisidia in Asia. John Mark left them in Pamphylia and returned home. In the cities of Pisidia Paul was persecuted and opposed. At Antioch he made a complete break with the Jews and at Lystra they stoned him until they thought he was dead. From Derbe the missionaries retraced their steps except that they did not go through Cyprus on the return to Antioch. Their stay at Antioch was marked by an important church council at Jerusalem, Acts 15:1-35. At this council it was decided that Gentile Christians were not bound by the requirement of the Jewish law. This decision was instrumental in determining that Christianity was not simply a new branch of Judaism but was a new religion.

Second Missionary Journey. (Acts. 15:36-18:22). Paul proposed that he and Barnabas visit the brethren in every city "where he had already preached," but he declined to yield to the wish of Barnabas to take Mark with them and in consequence separated from Barnabas. He took Silas and went overland through Syria and Cilicia to the scene of his former labors. At Lystra he was joined by Timothy. He was restrained by the Holy Spirit from further work in Asia and called into Europe by the "Macedonian call" while at Troas. While in Europe he labored at several places, the most conspicuous service being rendered at Philippi, Thessalonica and Corinth. Strong churches grew up at each of these places to which he later wrote letters. He returned to Antioch by way of Ephesus where he spent a little time, and Caesarea, from whence he probably visited Jerusalem.

While on this Journey during his long stay at Corinth Paul wrote First and Second Thessalonians and probably the book of Galatians also. If the time to be devoted to this course will allow, these epistles should be read at this point. The author's *The Bible Book by Book* will furnish an outline guide for such reading.

Third Missionary Journey. (Acts. 18:33-21:17). How long Paul remained at Antioch at the close of the second journey is not known. But when he had finished his visit he set out again to revisit some of the places formerly touched and to cultivate some new fields. The outline and work of this journey may be put down as follows: (1) He passes through Galatia and Phrygia strengthening the disciples. (2) His work of nearly three years at Ephesus. (3) The trip through Macedonia and Greece. (4) The return trip through Macedonia to Jerusalem. Luke seems to desire to narrate only what is new and most important. He, therefore, goes fully into the work at Ephesus. (1) There was the incident of the work of Apollos and the baptism of some of John's disciples. (2) Three months work among the Jews. (3) Two years of teaching in the school of Tyrannus. (4) A "season" after he sent Timotheus and Etastus into Macedonia. The success of this work is seen especially in two incidents. (1) The burning of the books of the Jewish exorcists which were valued at over $31,000. (2) The checking of the sale of images of the idol, Diana, which resulted in a great tumult.

After this tumult at Ephesus Paul departed into Macedonia and seems to have visited the principal cities and finally arrived at Corinth where a plot to kill him was formed. Upon discovering this plot he set out on his return trip to Jerusalem, going back through Macedonia. This trip is notable for several things. (1) The seven days stay at Troas which was significant because of an all night service and the accident to Eutychus. (2) The conference at Miletus with the Elders of Ephesus in which he reviewed his work among them and indicated to them that they would see him no more. (3) A week's stay at Tyre where he was persuaded not to go to Jerusalem. (4) Many days spent at Caesarea during which Agabus, who had formerly told them of the coming drouth, predicted that the Jews of Jerusalem would bind Paul and deliver him to the Gentiles. (5) The arrival at Jerusalem where he was kindly received by James and the elders.

This journey also was marked by the writing of some of Paul's most notable epistles. (1) The First Letter to the Corinthians. He wrote this letter while at Ephesus just before leaving for Macedonia. (2) The Second Letter to the Corinthians. After Paul came into Macedonia he met Titus with tidings from the Corinthians whereupon he wrote them this second letter, probably from Philippi. (3) The Letter to the Romans. From Macedonia Paul went into Achaia where he stayed three months and while staying with Gaius in Corinth (Rom. 16:23; 1 Cor. 1:14) he wrote this great epistle. The occasion, purpose, outline and other information concerning these epistles may be found in *The Bible Book by Book.*

At Jerusalem. Although Paul was received kindly by the brethren and although he took a certain precaution that he might not offend the many thousands of Jews that were in Jerusalem at the feast, some Asiatic Jews saw him and raised a great tumult. (1) They began to beat him and he would no doubt have been killed had he not been rescued by Roman soldiers. (2) As a prisoner he was being borne to the Tower of Antonia, but on the stairway asked and obtained permission to speak to the angry Jews. (3) When they would no longer hear him he was removed to the castle and ordered scourged. He saves himself from this by claiming his Roman citizenship. (4) He was brought before the Jewish Sanhedrin which he threw into confusion by expressing his belief in the resurrection and afterwards was put in prison. (5) On account of the plot to kill him which was discovered by Paul's nephew he was sent away under heavy guard to Caesarea.

Paul at, Caesarea. When Paul reached Caesarea he was under Roman jurisdiction. He was allowed some privileges. The most important incidents of this two years' imprisonment may be put down somewhat as follows. (1) His trial before Felix during which he was prosecuted by Tertullus and he himself made a speech of defense. (2) His second hearing before Felix, no doubt in private, with his wife Drusilla after which he held him in the hope that he would bribe Felix. (3) His trial before Festus during which he claimed his right as a Roman citizen and appealed to Caesar. (4) He had a hearing before Festus and King Agrippa II during which Paul spoke.

Paul's Six Last Addresses. In connection with the story of Paul in Jerusalem and Caesarea we have preserved for us six of his last addresses. In the light of his imprisonment and eminent danger they show his great faith and courage and are given here for study. (1) His Speech before the Jewish Mob, Acts 21:1-29. (2) His speech before the Jewish council. Acts 22: 30-23:10. (3) His speech before Felix. Acts 24:10-22. (4) His speech before Felix and his wife Drusilla, Acts 24:24-27. (5) His speech before Festus, Acts 25:7-11. (6) His speech before Festus and King Aggrippa II, Acts 26:1-32.

Paul's Journey to Rome. Paul now takes up his long journey to Rome. The voyage consumes most of the winter and three ships are used to convey him. (1) From Caesarea to Myra, a city of Lycia. Their ship touched at Sidon where Paul was allowed to visit his friends. (2) From Myra to the Island of Malta. On this voyage they touched at Fair Havens, tried to reach Phenice and had fourteen days of storm. (3) They were cast the island of Malta, where they spent three months. (4) The journey completed to Rome, going by way of Syracuse, Rhegium, Puteoli, Apii Forum and Three Taverns.

Paul at Rome. The Roman Christians came out to meet him at Apii Forum, forty-three miles from Rome. Several things should be noticed. (1) Paul after three days explained his situation to the Jews and planned another day when he would further address them. (2) Next he turned to the Gentiles and taught them. (3) He hired (rented) a house and for two years had liberty of speech and taught whoever would come to him. The story of Acts closes here, but it is commonly believed that Paul was released and visited Spain and Asia and later was rearrested and brought to Rome again where he was put to death.

The Epistles of this Period. The epistles written during this period may be divided into two groups: (1) Those written by Paul; (2) Those written by others. Those written by Paul are the following: (1) Philippians, Ephesians, Colossians and Philemon. All of these were written from Rome during Paul's first imprisonment at Rome and would come in the years 62 and 63 A.D. (2) First Timothy and Titus. These were probably written in Macedonia about A.D. 66. This is on the supposition that Paul was released from the imprisonment at Rome and made other preaching tours. (3) Second Timothy. This was written from the Roman prison just before his death about A.D. 67 or 68. This would have been a second imprisonment and we know nothing of this except by tradition. (4) Hebrews. There are many eminent scholars who think some other than Paul wrote this book, but it is put down here because it was so long and so unanimously considered his and because the point against his authorship does not seem fully established. It was written some time before A.D. 70, as the temple and its worship were still in force.

There are four other letters of the period. (1) The

Epistle of James. This epistle was probably written about A.D. 50 but some think it was written as late as A.D. 62 and it is put in for consideration here because of the uncertainty. (2) The First Epistle of Peter, which was written about A.D. 66. (3) The Second Epistle of Peter, written about A.D. 67 and certainly before the fall of Jerusalem. (4) The Epistle of Jude, written about A.D. 66. *The Bible Book by Book* will furnish the student with a statement concerning the occasion, purpose, outline of contents and other introductory discussions.

Lessons of the Period. (1) One man with proper consecration can be a blessing to all the world. (2) The same teaching sometimes wins one and repels another. (3) The fact that one is divinely led does not guarantee that one may not be wrongly treated by men. (4) Persecution can not destroy one's happiness if one is conscious of doing the will of God. (5) Strategic centers are the most fruitful fields of mission work. (6) False religious beliefs are less tolerant than the true. (7) God may save a whole company for the sake of one man. (8) No matter what calamity comes to us we may in the midst of it be a source of blessing to others.

For Study and Discussion. (1) The countries visited by Paul. Draw maps and indicate his journeys. (2) The history and importance of the principal cities visited by him (make a list of them and consult the Bible dictionaries). (3) Paul's companions in the work (make a list of them and consult the Bible dictionaries). (4) The Apostle Paul himself: (a) His birth and childhood; (b) his education; (c) his conversion. (5) The persecutions of Paul. (6) The miraculous or superhuman element seen in this section. (7) The value of the Roman citizenship to Paul. (8) Paul's letters: (a)

Name them and tell where in these journeys each comes in; (b) learn something of the occasion, purpose and outline of each. (9) The other epistles of this period. (10) The time and extent of Paul's journeys. (11) The church council at Jerusalem. (12) The Roman officers met in this narrative-what sort of men, etc. (13) Paul's speeches as given here.

21
DESTRUCTION OF THE TEMPLE TO THE DEATH OF THE APOSTLE JOHN.

Epistles of John and Revelation.

The Period of History. This period begins with the fall of the city of Jerusalem, A.D. 70, and ends with the death of John, the last of the apostles. We have but little scripture touching the conditions of this period. Indeed, all of it is inferential so far as the scripture is concerned. We may, however, learn much from secular history and tradition.

The Destruction of Jerusalem. Jesus had predicted the fall of this beloved city. Many frightful massacres of Jews had occurred in Judea before the end of the last period, but it was in A.D. 70, about two years after Paul's death, that Titus destroyed Jerusalem and the temple and Judaism had its downfall. After this the marks of separation between Christianity and Judaism became more and more distinct. From that time the Jewish religion has never gained ascendancy in any country.

From A.D. 70 to A.D. 100. The general history of

this period has in it little of interest. At the end of the very creditable reign of emperor Vespasian, who was on the throne of Rome when Jerusalem fell, Titus, called "The delight of the human race," reigned in his stead. During his reign occurred that awful eruption of Vesuvius that buried Pompeii. Titus was succeeded by his brother Domitian, who was one of the greatest tyrants that ever ruled in any country. It is generally supposed that John was banished to the Isle of Patmos during the reign of Domitian. After Domitian reigned Nerva and Trojan, the last of which showed great talent and brought back much of the early vigor to the empire. The cyclopedias and histories of Rome will give information about the period.

The Literature of the Period. The history of the Christians in this period is very obscure because of the scanty literature produced in it. What literature we have of these years may be divided into two classes: (1) Scripture books. These are the three epistles of John, which were written at Ephesus a while before his banishment, probably about 80 or 85 A. D., and the Revelation, which was composed while in exile on Patmos about 95 or 96 A. D. (2) Some early Christian writings not included in the canon of the New Testament. Of this class of writings is the Epistle of Clement of Rome to the Corinthians, written about 96-98 A.D., and the Epistle of Barnabas and the Teaching of the Twelve Apostles, probably written sometime before A.D. 100. This then is a period of transition from the Canonical to the Patristic literature.

Death of John and End of Scripture History. John was on the Isle of Patmos as an exile because of his testimony for Jesus. He seems to have lived until the end of the first century and is said to have met death in a cauldron of boiling oil. The last of the apostles being now dead the canon of the scripture is closed and the power of miracles removed and Christianity left to win its own way by means of the efforts and the prayers of the disciples and the grace which God ordinarily grants to them. Thus ends the scripture history-with a completed revelation and the Christian churches set up as a witness for Christ.

Lessons of the Period. It is difficult to draw, from a period of which we know so little, any certain conclusions. We are perhaps safe in making some observations. (1) Christianity must always make its way against opposition. (2) The Christian faith gives courage and joy in the most trying circumstances. (3) Christianity will finally triumph over its enemies.

For Study and Discussion. (1) From the Bible dictionaries, cyclopedias, etc., study the reigns of the different Roman emperors of this period. (2) Learn something of the nature and contents of the Patristic literature mentioned in this discussion. (3) The four New Testament books of this period.

Copyright © 2022 by SSEL
Scribere Semper Et Legere
Cover design and layout : SSEL
Ebook ISBN 9791029913976
Paperback ISBN 9791029913983
Hardcover ISBN 9791029913990
All rights reserved.

www.ingramcontent.com/pod-product-compliance
Lightning Source LLC
LaVergne TN
LVHW031604060526
838201LV00063B/4728